Secrets of the Norman Invasion

Nick Austin

OGMIUM PRESS

Landscape Studios, Crowhurst,
East Sussex TN33 9BX
Originated in Great Britain

ISBN 978-0-9544801-4-1

Printed and bound by CPI Group (UK) Ltd, Croydon, CR0 4YY

1

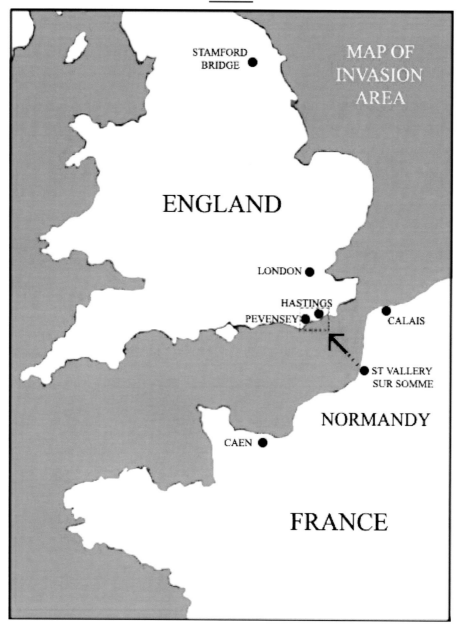

SUSSEX COAST MAPS

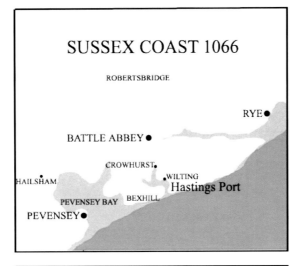

SUSSEX COAST 1066

ROBERTSBRIDGE

RYE ●

BATTLE ABBEY ●

CROWHURST ●

HAILSHAM ●

●WILTING

Hastings Port

PEVENSEY BAY BEXHILL

PEVENSEY ●

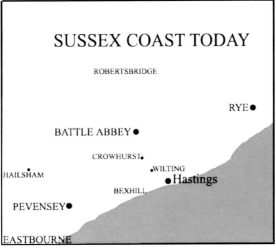

SUSSEX COAST TODAY

ROBERTSBRIDGE

RYE ●

BATTLE ABBEY ●

CROWHURST ●

HAILSHAM ●

●WILTING

●Hastings

BEXHILL

PEVENSEY ●

EASTBOURNE

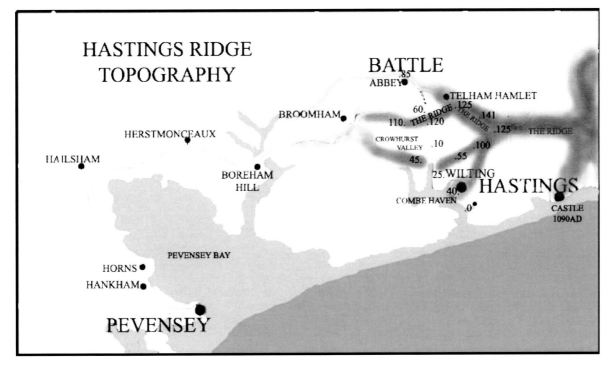

HASTINGS RIDGE TOPOGRAPHY

BATTLE

ABBEY● .85

TELHAM HAMLET

BROOMHAM ● .125
.141

60. THE RIDGE .125
110. .120 THE RIDGE

HERSTMONCEAUX ●

CROWHURST VALLEY .10 .100

HAILSHAM ● 45. .55

BOREHAM HILL ● 25.WILTING
40. HASTINGS

COMBE HAVEN

.0 CASTLE 1090AD

PEVENSEY BAY

HORNS ●

HANKHAM ●

PEVENSEY ●

INTRODUCTION

This book contains new evidence obtained from the study of the Domesday Book data of the values of manors in East Sussex in 1066. The evidence confirms that the Norman landings took place at Upper Wilting Farm in the Domesday parish of Crowhurst on the outskirts of Hastings, where evidence of the first camp of William the Conqueror still exists. The story you have read in history books detailing the Norman Invasion having taken place at the town of Pevensey is a Victorian myth, perpetrated through false assumptions published at that time. This book also contains evidence that confirms that the Battle of Hastings took place in the Crowhurst Valley, in the same Domesday parish as Wilting Farm, immediately adjacent to Hastings, where a new road is planned. Contrary to traditional belief the Battle of Hastings did not take place at the site claimed by English Heritage at Battle Abbey. The information supporting this new site of the Battle of Hastings comes from a number of different sources including the Bayeux Tapestry, the Carmen of Hastingae, Wace, the Chronicle of Battle Abbey and others written within 150 years of the Invasion. The Battle Abbey battlefield story is revealed as having been built around a fraud perpetrated by the monks of Battle Abbey. The evidence published in this book confirms there is no contradiction in any of those documents studied, once the correct sites of both the Invasion and the Battle of Hastings are known. The place where the Battle of Hastings was really fought must be protected and this book publishes the first pictures of the correct battle site. There can only be one site for the Battle of Hastings. The historical evidence in this book shows exactly where that was.

Nick Austin

14th October 2010

PREFACE

This book was written over a 24 year period documenting the work I was carrying out, often as it happened. My reason for doing this was not explained at the time and I believe it is justified by the results.

This story started in 1986 when I moved to the Crowhurst valley, just three miles from Hastings. I had moved there to set up a music business. I was the founder of the Beggars Banquet record label, famous for artists like Gary Numan. I wanted to create a recording studio in the country and was living an idyllic dream, when events took an unexpected turn.

I decided to investigate whether it was true that the Normans arrived in 1066 at Pevensey and marched down the coast to Hastings. I lived at Hye House in Crowhurst. This property looked over a vast expanse of water in the winter, called the Combe Haven valley. That valley was on the western boundary of Hastings and it was clear to me that what ever the history books said it was not possible, in the past or even the present, to have marched from Pevensey, on the south coast, to Hastings returning along the coast eastwards, without crossing this expanse of water in the winter. I knew enough about logistics to know that no invading army could cross the Combe Haven marsh at any time of the year. Like many others who have come before me I started on the quest to get to the bottom of this mystery.

This book solves that mystery by providing answers that can only be explained by the application of common sense. In the past, the documents written near the time of the Invasion have not been understood. They always produced unexplained anomalies. No such anomalies exist when you know the correct site of the Battle of Hastings and the Norman Invasion. The errors that have crept into history over nine centuries are removed by the evidence in this book. In order to understand how this has happened all that you need is a clear head and the ability to understand the evidence put in front of you. In order not to confuse you I shall therefore try to present my evidence to you in the language of the ordinary man.

It would have been of no interest to anyone, what I was doing in the fields around Crowhurst in 1994, if it were not for the fact that out of the blue an announcement was made that a major trunk road was to be built through the site that I was investigating. Indeed I had started that investigation in 1986 and was well advanced in reaching a conclusion. I therefore decided that I had to defend the site, which I had by then identified as the probable Norman landing site and camp of William the Conqueror. It seemed to me incredible that a road would be built through open countryside, if it was an important heritage site. I considered it my duty to produce a report that the inspector of the public inquiry could read and then take the appropriate action. That report formed the start of this book, for presentation to the public inquiry into the proposed Hastings and Bexhill Bypass in 1996. I also decided that I should create a web site to host the documents and evidence, which I was in the process of collecting. It started as a place where people could get new information and comment.

That web site is still active today and subsequently became the most read site on the Norman Invasion, according to the Google search engine. The reason so many visitors found my website was in my view surprising simple. It was because the material I posted there was not just another rehash of previous old tired and unproven theories of what might or might not have happened in 1066. This book, like my web site, details actual analysis of source documents, including data from the Domesday Book, which simply cannot be interpreted any other way. It takes you on the journey that I have travelled over the last twenty four years, often up to my eyes in the mud of the Combe Haven valley in winter, or mosquitoes the size of a ten pence piece in summer. You must also remember that I was a lot younger when I started this path. Now I am older and hopefully wiser. I would therefore beg your indulgence of a younger man who found himself at that time full of enthusiasm, but with little experience, when faced with such fierce opposition to the thesis that the Normans did not land at Pevensey. It was a heresy, since there wasn't a man on the planet who believed this could possibly be true.

Now the position is much clearer twenty four years on. Often I feel like the mastermind expert who sits in the chair on television with his specialist subject '28th September to 14th October 1066 – The Norman Invasion', having read every document known to exist on the subject. I am pleased to report that the road, which put the site under threat in 1996, was not built. Now, another road is planned, deviously called a 'link road' by politicians, and so this evidence needs to become public again. This book is about historical truth coming out, even if no-one in the world knows it exists. Join me now in understanding why that historical truth is important.

The manuscript element which follows now was first published 23rd December 1994. It provides valuable research information, which answers many of the questions as to why the Normans chose the site at Hastings to land, and why contrary to popular belief, they could not have landed at the town of Pevensey. It should be noted that some minor editing has taken place since 1994, in order to make the text more readable. Certain more challenging chapters requiring an understanding of archaeological techniques, such as those required to understand the resistivity surveys and aerial photographs have been edited to more manageable elements. Those who are interested in those specific subjects can still find the information posted upon the original web site. There are no substantive changes to the over all text and it should be remembered that the record from Chapter 1 through to Chapter 63 was written at that time and is still valid today – providing vital background information to the main section of this book, which starts at Chapter 64.

It is important to understand that observations made at the time those web pages were written were made when the site of the Battle of Hastings was suspected, but not included in the evidence presented to the Highways Agency inspector. That evidence was directed solely towards the threatened Norman landing site at Wilting. Now with the benefit of hindsight we can see that both sites, the Norman Invasion site and the site of the Battle of Hastings, support each other through the whole of the available historical record. Part One and Part Two of this book are therefore essential and integrated information, which are required reading, in order to reach the conclusions that are I believe unavoidable.

TABLE OF CONTENTS

PART ONE

In order to evaluate the hypothesis contained in this document it is necessary to follow the logic of the documents in chronological order.

INTRODUCTION

The following work arose out of my insatiable desire to know exactly where the Normans landed prior to the Battle of Hastings. This interest was awakened shortly after moving to the village of Crowhurst (one of Harold's personal manors) where I was able to hear at first hand some of the local accounts of the Norman landing and search for Norman remains in the village.

Over the last six years I have tried to read everything important associated with Norman landings and the battle. I have spent many months carrying out detailed searches of the documents contemporary with the battle. I have become increasingly alarmed at the discrepancies between the texts and the lay of the land where the landings were supposed to have taken place. In this work I attempt to explain how all these discrepancies can be reconciled only if the contextual references are applied to a landing site different from Pevensey.

The text that follows is divided into two parts. The first part deals with the clues to the landing site contained in the contemporary source documents, whilst the second part looks at the physical evidence thrown up by surveys, aerial photographs, field walking and archaeological work.

THE LANDING SITE

And Camp of William the Conqueror

It is the intention of this document together with the one currently under research to bring to the attention of the reader new evidence concerning the events of the Norman Invasion. The evidence in this text relates purely to establishing the correct site of the Invasion and Norman camp from the examination of authentic manuscript documents of the time, in conjunction with geographical and archaeological evidence that has never before been available. I shall show that where descriptions in one manuscript might be considered contradictory to statements in another, the actual events of the time can be explained in a rational and logical way once the correct site is known. It is the intention to show the reader, in a detailed manner, evidence that rewrites our previous understanding of history concerning what is considered by many to be the most important singular event in English history - the Norman Invasion.

This document relates solely to those matters relevant to the landing of the Norman Invasion fleet and the circumstances concerning the period up until the Norman army left to fight the Battle of Hastings. Having established the authentic landing and camp site, where the Norman army was based, many more questions are raised concerning the events of the day of the Battle of Hastings. These too have remained a mystery to those who have studied the fine details and I propose to be the first to answer all of the outstanding questions leaving no matter unresolved. Due to the recent decision by the Department of Transport to build a major trunk road through the centre of the landing site, I have no alternative but to publish my initial findings now. The alternative could be the loss of a site of national historical and archaeological importance, which would be wholly unacceptable. In consequence and in the interests of all concerned I propose to deal with these further matters in a second volume, titled THE BATTLE OF HASTINGS, at a later date.

Chapter 1: MANUSCRIPT EVIDENCE

It is necessary to look initially at what the written historical record tells us about the events of the time. I have therefore only taken into account those manuscripts that are believed to originate within 150 years of the date of the battle that can throw light on the events of the landing. It is not my intention to prove or disprove the authenticity of the writings contained in the texts examined. It is my belief that all of them reported the events of the time, in an honest manner, to the best of their ability. The discrepancies that occur in consequence of seeking to apply the substance of these texts to the wrong landing site are studied in detail and instead of supporting the argument that any of the documents are unreliable, effectively endorses their accuracy when applied to the correct site. Thus all the manuscripts examined have a thorough consistency valid to only one landing site.

Chapter 2: WILLIAM OF JUMIEGES (Gesta Normannorum Ducum 1070 app.)

This manuscript is taken from the seventh book of theGesta Normannorum[1] and is considered to be important in representing Norman sentiment at that time. It has very little detailed information, translating into just under two A4 pages of text, covering the complete period from Edward the Confessor's death[2] to William's coronation[3]. In consequence it bears no serious comparison with the far more detailed account of other manuscripts which follow. It was probably written very close to the events, in the region of 1070, and has therefore assumed an importance that might otherwise be difficult to justify.

Jumieges does state the size of the fleet, giving little other useful information upon which to base a judgement for the search for the landing site. He writes:

'He therefore hastily built a fleet of three thousand ships. . .' and continues *'. . . and crossing the sea he landed at Pevensey where he immediately built a castle with a strong rampart. He left this in charge of some troops, and with others he hurried to Hastings where he erected another similar fortress'*

The reference to 3,000 ships is accepted by most historians to be romantic rhetoric of the day. Major General J. F. C. Fuller goes into great detail concerning the logistics of such an operation in his book The Decisive Battles of the Western World 480BC - 1757[4] No-one knows for certain how many ships were involved, because until now no evidence has been found. I propose that 3,000 ships is far too many to be a correct figure, this is endorsed by Fuller's own conclusions in which he states that William's army could not have exceeded 5,000 men, because the time taken from departure at St Valery to the landing was only twelve hours. Fuller explains from a military perspective that it is impossible, from a logistics point of view, for any more than this to have been involved. The claim that 3,000 ships were involved therefore undermines the authority of the narrative in at least one major respect that can be proven to be incorrect on logistics alone. It appears from the most recent observations on the matter, albeit earlier this century, that no less than 5,000 and probably no more than 10,000 men accompanied William on his conquest[5]. To provide 3,000 ships would not be viable bearing in mind the logistics of the day[6].

The authority of the Jumieges account is further eroded by the claim that William built a castle at Pevensey, with a strong rampart, at the time of the Invasion. It has been assumed that this defence must have been at Pevensey castle, since no other site in the area has any archaeological profile which could fit this description and the text appears quite specific in the claim. Pevensey castle was in fact built by the Romans at least 600 years before the Norman Invasion in the 4th century [7]. In consequence the towering walls of that fortress, known as Andereida, already existed, stretching to a height of over forty feet and occupying a site of at least ten acres. Since Pevensey castle was constructed of stone the claim that the Normans built it in a day is clearly an error, or the text needs to be interpreted differently. As a result of taking Jumieges text and looking at it in conjunction with another manuscript called The Carmen of Hastingae Proelio[8], the anomaly can be explained.

Jumieges statement was believed upon the basis that William must have used the existing walls of the Roman fortress upon, or within which, to build the first defence. This disregards the fact that any wooden structure would not have been needed, when the massive structure of the walls were already in place. It contradicts the Bayeux Tapestry evidence, which clearly details a wooden fort on top of a mound and flies in the face of any logic when neither Jumieges nor any other contemporary writer details such a massive building at the site of the landing. Only the Carmen version provides the weakest possible conjecture that could be interpreted to mean that the camp was built upon the site of a ruin[9] at Pevensey. That ruin is however stated by the Carmen to be at Hastings, by virtue of the fact that it states that the Norman camp, which was built there, was at Hastings. This interpretation of the texts provides an ingenious, if not convoluted explanation of why no evidence or remains of the Invasion have ever been found at Pevensey, because the evidence was effectively destroyed by the Norman building work after the Invasion was complete.

No other alternative offers a realistic explanation of what amounts to a fundamental flaw in Jumieges naming Pevensey as the landing site. It is my view that there has been no realistic evaluation of these issues in recent history, mainly as a result of the growth of the tourist industry in the area and the consequent need to match this very thin hypothesis to the commercial benefits to the local community. Using one line out of context, from the Carmen, in order to justify Jumieges statement, which on its own does not stand scrutiny, is in my view an error of judgement. The two statements when read in the context of both manuscripts clearly refer to different places[10] and in these circumstances one cannot be used to justify the other. Jumieges makes the point that the defence was built quickly and therefore taken in conjunction with other reported eye-witness accounts could not have been anything other than the normal type of wooden structure expected at an invasion bridge head. I propose therefore that upon the evidence rendered by Jumieges that the landing could not have taken place at Pevensey castle. If that is the case, given the unreliable number of boats and the error relating to the fortifications, it is more than likely that naming Pevensey, as the landing site, may also be an error.

There is a small item of information to be found in the text that may have important implications for identifying the correct site of William's camp and in consequence the landing site. It is my belief that Jumieges is being quite specific in differentiating between a castle in the case of Pevensey and a fortress in the case of Hastings, if the translation we have studied is correct. If it was intended to identify a castle at each site then I believe different terminology would have been used. Jumieges appears to describe two different defences and if he had personal knowledge of events would have known that there was a castle at Pevensey. He certainly appeared to believe that William built it, but we know this to be incorrect[11].

Jumieges states that Pevensey was left with some troops in charge and:

'*with others he hurried to Hastings where he erected another similar fortress*'.

This may, upon first examination, appear to endorse current historical thinking and at the same time provide a reason why the camp was at Hastings, whilst the landing was at Pevensey. There are however a number of further flaws in both the logic and ability of the Invasion force to act in this way.

Firstly the Invasion was a unique adventure for the Norman knights who accompanied William. They were following in their Viking ancestors footprints by taking to water in boats for the first time. These were men accustomed to fighting on horseback, who had probably never before been to sea. Sailing across open sea in the 11th century was a high risk enterprise even by standards of the day. In fact the risk was considered so great that the wives of those involved are reported in Orderic Vitalis[12] to have written begging letters to their husbands to ask them to return from England on account that they themselves would not come to England, because the sea journey was new to them. William was not only a good commander, but he knew the value of man's weakness for wealth, offering those who came great riches should the enterprise be successful.

Taken in this context, with the absence of any statement that the troops re-embarked to sail back to Hastings along the coast, it must be assumed that the Norman troops were on foot and horse. Given the successful unopposed landing it is highly unlikely that William would risk his troops in open sea unnecessarily. The question must also be asked why they would return, to sail or march back down a coast they sailed past the previous day, having come from St Valery in northern France. Sailing would allow the possibility of having to fight at a second landing and give the enemy an unnecessary opportunity to form a defensive bridgehead. The Bayeux Tapestry makes the point clearly, that the troops landed and no further sailing was involved. There is no attempt by any other writer of the time to suggest that the Normans re-entered their boats to move to Hastings. I must therefore conclude that if the Normans did land at Pevensey, as Jumieges claims, they must have moved to Hastings by land.

The problem with this alternative hypothesis is that this too does not stand scrutiny on account of the manorial value evidence provided in the Domesday Book. This is examined in detail in a later chapter dedicated to the Sussex edition. It is further undermined by the geography of the coastline, as it was known to be at that time. This shows that two major obstacles stood between Pevensey and Hastings, which cannot be satisfactorily explained. The first of these was Pevensey Bay, requiring a 30 mile detour in order to cross from the west to the east. If Hastings was the ultimate destination, sailing to Pevensey, on the west side of what was then a vast expanse of water, was totally counterproductive. In order to find Hastings the army would need to firstly move en mass, in order to be prepared to meet Harold's army. Secondly they would need to move through open countryside, to avoid ambush, and thirdly they would need to follow the coast to avoid getting lost. This last point is the most obvious, but in fact the least likely. This is because the sea inlet to the west of Hastings, known as the Combe Haven, would cut any invading army off and leave it stranded on the peninsula where Bexhill now stands. This point appears to have been overlooked by many historians, most probably because Bulverhythe and the lower part of the Combe Haven Valley to the east of Hastings are no longer flooded, as they were in 1066[13]. Hence marching along the coast from Pevensey to Hastings was also impossible. The probability that they came that way, or in fact any other after landing at Pevensey first, without leaving an identifiable record, is a theory that in my view is untenable when the known facts are examined.

It could be argued that I am reading too much into little more than a paragraph. It should be remembered that this particular paragraph has immense implications in underwriting what we currently are led to believe is the Norman Invasion story. At this point we have only looked at one of a number of different manuscripts, each of which tells the same story from a different perspective. If it is to be believed that Jumieges account should stand sway over much longer and detailed texts,, it is necessary to take on board each element of these manuscripts, both in isolation, and in conjunction with what other writers tell us. In consequence given the lack of credible individual evidence in this case, I must ask the reader to keep an open mind and weigh what has been written here with those others that follow.

In conclusion it would seem that Jumieges story is unreliable and probably suspect, even though written very close to the events. The size of the fleet is certainly inflated, possibly for political reasons or to flatter his readers of the day. The claim relating to Pevensey Castle is more than likely to have been made for the same reason, whilst the journey from Pevensey to Hastings is unsubstantiated and given the circumstances impossible if taken along the coast. He confirms that William embarked on a massive operation, involving a large number of ships and accompanying men. He also confirms in this manuscript that Hastings and Pevensey featured in the events of the landing, although the references to who built the castle or forts, and when, does not stand up to scrutiny.

Current historical thinking appears to place particular emphasis on the authenticity of William of Poitiers[14] version of events, as detailed in his manuscript[15]. As a result, we are taught at school that William landed at Pevensey and moved down the coast to Hastings, where he camped to wait for Harold to arrive. Poitiers states:

'Thus, with a favourable wind, they all reached Pevensey, and there without opposition they freely disembarked '

Here we have the first of many contentious issues, since Poitiers makes the point that the landing was unopposed. In the following paragraph the point is pushed home by the statement:

'Rejoicing greatly at having secured a safe landing, the Normans seized and fortified Pevensey and then Hastings...'

However Pevensey had a large fortified castle, which was known to be garrisoned throughout that summer by the local militia[16], who had been called out by Harold in anticipation of the coming invasion. There is no mention by any chronicler of resistance and Poitiers makes the point that none was encountered. This flies in the face of what should have happened if the Invasion force had landed at the place where the towns of Pevensey and Hastings stand. The Bayeux Tapestry seems to endorse this, suggesting landing in an agricultural area, rather than a town. The question has therefore to be asked whether Poitiers evidence is really that reliable, or are we seeking to match the text to the current site of Pevensey and Hastings towns, with their established castles, when the correct site may have been somewhere else in the vicinity. I therefore propose that in the interests of prudence and in the absence of any physical remains, we can only conclude that Poitiers believed the landing site to be Pevensey, but it may not be Pevensey as we know it today. There is, as far as I am aware, no actual hard archaeological evidence to substantiate the claim that Pevensey was the landing site, and if the rules of trial were to be applied, the evidence, as presented, would be thrown out of court. It is my view that Poitiers and Jumieges both make the same mistake of naming Pevensey, since they were innocently copying down what they had been told. The real error lies with those who accept these written statements in the absence of any scientific verifying data, in an age when the ingenuity of man can send a robot to the remote parts of the solar system. If the Normans had occupied Pevensey and then Hastings, in the manner described, scientific proof would have by now been found. Until now no such scientific evidence has been found and in its absence it beholds the scientist and sceptic to reserve judgement, rather than accept one version of events over another, which may be equally valid.

More information is gained by reading Poitiers text, since he relates the story of William reconnoitring the area with 25 knights. He writes:

'Because of the roughness of the ground he [William] had to return on foot.'

The consequence of this observation is that having established their beach head, the site where the Normans had built their camp was of sufficient ruggedness to require the riders to dismount. Having just made the immediate area secure, a knight on foot was particularly vulnerable. I must therefore conclude that there must have been no alternative, suggesting very difficult ground. The point of the statement is to advise the reader that whilst it was too difficult for horses, it was still able to be negotiated on foot. I interpret this to include the probability of waterlogged ground, given the nature of the clay subsoil in the area and the fact that most texts note that weather for the previous months had been too poor for William to depart from France.

Further clues concerning the location of the camp and the landing site can be gleaned from the text confirming that the events in question were adjacent to water. Poitiers writes:

'One day then the Duke was visiting the guards of his fleet, and was walking about near the ships, he was told that a monk had arrived, sent by Harold.'

Later further confirmation about the location is made by specific reference to the sea, at the pre-battle pep talk from William to his men, in which he refers to their predicament:

'. . behind you, there is the sea where an enemy fleet bars your flight.'

Then in the same paragraph Poitiers claims:

'They said in jest that he who had guarded the coast [Harold] with such insensate zeal should be buried by the seashore.'

Quite a remarkable claim, since this would not be what you would expect to happen to a vanquished King. A King at this time would be expected to be given the honour of a Christian burial in a holy place. Poitiers text infers that no such honour was granted. Instead he reports the burial to be by the sea shore.

Lastly Poitiers provides us with yet another small clue to the place where these events happened. At the point where Harold commits to take up the fight Poitiers reports:

'The King [Harold] was the more furious because he had heard that the Normans had laid waste the neighbourhood of their camp. ...'

A clear statement by a chronicler of the day that the surrounding area was in his words '*laid waste.*'

In conclusion, Poitiers tells us quite a lot, including the fact that like Jumieges, Pevensey and Hastings were both possible sites of the Invasion, but this is tempered by the fact that Poitiers may have heard or seen Jumieges slightly earlier account. The reasons for believing that Poitiers may have repeated Jumieges mistake in naming Pevensey are for the same logistical and tactical reasons that I outlined in the Jumieges text. The questions raised by these issues cannot be simply dismissed. I am not however suggesting that Poitiers invented what amounts to a remarkable account of events.

He adds some valuable information including the fact that the ground in this locality was rough or impassable on horseback. He tells us that the fleet were nearby and the '*camp was close to the sea.*' In particular the statement that the surrounding area was '*laid waste*' by the invading army, has further implications when examined in conjunction with the Domesday Book, examined later. In consequence the Poitiers evidence adds considerably to our knowledge of the landing site. The fact that this does not fit with what we believe to be the Pevensey Castle site does not undermine the authority of the account. It simply reinforces the probability that Pevensey Castle was probably not where the landing actually took place. In any event, to be fair to Poitiers, it can be argued that so little detail is given in relation to Pevensey that Poitiers reported the matter in a way that suggested little conviction. Taken over all, it appears that Poitiers claims Hastings as the centre of activity, yet still accounts for Pevensey in his opening lines, leaving out all the detail which meticulously accompanies the following text. This clever device avoids conflict with the earlier Jumieges text, whilst studiously avoiding any further detail, which might not stand up to scrutiny.

Chapter 4: THE CARMEN OF HASTINGAE PROELIO (Bishop Guy of Amiens app. 1067)

This manuscript[17], known as 'The Carmen', is believed to have been written by Guy Bishop of Amiens (1058 - 1075) and takes on new significance, as a result of recent work[18] by Elisabeth M. C. van Houts, of Nunham College Cambridge. This supports the view that contrary to recent belief, the Carmen was written as early as the autumn of 1067. It is suggested that the Bishop dedicated his poem to Lanfranc, in the hope that he would mediate between himself and Pope Alexander II. The conclusion is that the Carmen is the first known Latin poem to have been written for the Anglo-Norman court, containing 835 lines of Latin text and liable to contain information that is of great value in authenticating any possible site for the Invasion.

The Carmen provides us with a series of new clues to the actual site of the landings. After describing the departure from Saint-Valery and a mid Channel rest prior to dawn, there is a flowery report concerning the first hours of that day.

'But after rosy dawn brightened the lands and sun cast beams over the world, you [William] gave command to set course and make sail, ordering that the vessels should weigh anchor. When you reached safe landing-places, leaving the sea astern, the third hour of day was rising over the earth.'

I believe this is an interesting observation, since the writer is being very precise in text that could easily be overlooked. It does not say that a bay was entered, nor does it say the fleet entered a river. Terminology is used that describes leaving the sea behind them at the third hour and landing places is in the plural. The third hour would be 9am, being three hours after dawn[19]. Even now the fleet has not landed, yet somehow it has left the sea behind.

In the following paragraph the mystery deepens by the next description:

'Robbed of her terrified inhabitants, the land destined for you joyfully received you and yours in a calm bay.'

What we appear to be told is that a calm bay has now materialised, at which point the landing happened. This confirms the Poitiers reference of the area being *'Robbed of her terrified inhabitants'* endorsing the landing as unopposed and further undermines Pevensey, since Pevensey is not named, nor is the castle that stood there. Given that Pevensey was dominated by the castle structure of the time, in an otherwise unnamed landscape, the omission is, I believe, significant. How could a chronicler of the day describe the Invasion yet omit the key point of describing where it took place? This question is of course answered later in the same text when the site is named.

If the text was referring to Pevensey Bay, as has been accepted to date, it is worrying that the description does not fit that of Pevensey Bay, which was mainly open to the sea and would appear to any invasion force as little more than a coastal feature. In anything other than fine weather the far side of the bay would not always be visible, due to the distance across the estuary entrance. In order for the water to be calm it had to be confined in a much smaller area. The reference to the *'calm bay'* is in direct conflict with the fact that they had sailed the previous night, because sailing conditions were good[20]. Good sailing conditions would mean an onshore wind, which would leave no area in Pevensey calm. Given the time of year[21], the claim that Pevensey Bay was a calm bay, either during or within 24 hours of an onshore wind, on such a large relatively unprotected expanse of water, cannot be realistically sustained. The only conclusion must be that the bay was protected in some way from the sea. The most likely solution being that the bay was either in a protected estuary, capable of landing several hundred boats, with a relatively narrow entrance, or more likely a harbour. This latter proposal is supported by the description of William's camp, whilst stating these events took place at a port, later in this same manuscript[22].

Having landed, a number of further mysteries unfold, all within the confines of a single paragraph:

'Fearing to lose the ships, you surrounded them with earthworks and guarded the shores. You restored the dismantled forts which had stood there formerly and set custodians to hold them. Having gained control, though over no great space, your people attacked the region, laid it to waste, and burnt it with fire.'

The Carmen claims William ordered that the ships that had brought them to England be earthed up(23) in some way. The implication being that should the army decide to desert, the way home was barred because the earthing up process would cause them to be permanently beached. The text refers to '*surrounded them with earthworks*' – an inexplicable expression, which can only be explained with reference to the correct Norman Invasion site. The logic tells us this was the move of a wise commander and if correct it is highly likely that remains of the Invasion fleet still exist even today. It should also be noted that the guards stood over the '*shores*' in the plural. This confirms the presence of a number of shores that would be found in a small bay rather than a single sea shore such as that at Pevensey.

Next there is a reference to restoring '*dismantled forts*' at the site of the landing. This is most interesting, since the scribe puts the forts in the plural. This has been used by scholars in the past to seek to justify Hastings as the Invasion site, since it has been suggested that a series of mounds at Hastings adjacent to the castle stretch back to before the Romans(24). The Carmen is phrased quite specifically and says that the forts were '*dismantled*' - suggesting dereliction and that William restored them as part of the landing arrangements. This does not fit Pevensey or Hastings and is yet another mystery that we shall seek to resolve. Charles Dawson, who wrote the definitive history of Hastings Castle in 1909(25) was one of the first contemporary writers to notice the possibility that something could be wrong with the reporting of Hastings Castle in the Invasion story, when he wrote:

'That the raising of such mounds was a common Norman system of defence is well established; on the other hand, the supposition that they were raised by the Anglo-Saxons at any period rests upon no known facts.'

The Bayeux Tapestry does not set all doubts at rest respecting the date of the mound at Hastings. What we see is something taking place at Hastings Ceastra. Assuming that Hastings Ceastra is identical with the site at Hastings Castle (which is a reasonable presumption) the question remains as to whether there was already a mound and castle before the date of the Invasion, which latter may have been dismantled on Harold's departure for the North in the autumn of 1066. The Latin words annexed to the view of the Tapestry are somewhat unusual, if not exceptional. Does the word '*foderetur*' (third-person singular imperfect passive subjunctive of fodio – to dig) mean that the digging was with the intention of entrenching an already-existing mound and '*Castellum*' at Hastings Ceastra, or does it mean that it was done for the purpose of raising the mound upon which the '*Castellum*' (castle) was erected? There are figures in the foreground digging(26), but no figures are shown in perspective building the '*Castellum*'. The '*Castellum*' is shown already there, whilst the digging is going on, and might equally well represent a castle that had been dismantled, as one in the course of erection. The words of the Carmen de Hastingae Proelio, one of the oldest authorities referring to the landing of William says:

'You rebuild the castles that were lately destroyed [durita] *and place custodians in them to guard them'*

It is difficult to adapt these words to the erection of the ready made forts, which William is said to have brought with him(27).

In consequence a big question mark rests over any valid claim that Hastings Castle was in existence at the time of the Invasion. The castle's leading authority expresses doubts when trying to reconcile the authority of the Bayeux Tapestry, against what he believes to be the position of the mound at the time, if any mound existed. The basis for the belief that Hastings Castle must have been in existence prior to the Invasion rests upon the presumption that the pictures shown in the Bayeux Tapestry are those of

Hastings castle. That castle was built after the Invasion in stone, but might have existed in wood before the Invasion. No evidence however exists for such a castle pre 1066.

Lastly, in relation to the strange paragraph referring to dismantled forts and earthworks in the Carmen there is a clear indication from the text that the Normans gained control of an area that was relatively small; otherwise there was no need to state: *'Having gained control, though over no great space. . . '*

There then follows the story of how the English heard of the Invasion.

'One of the English, lying hidden close to a sea-rock, perceived how the countless ranks spread far and wide and saw the fields glittering, full of glancing arms. He saw the people, their homes ravaged by flames for their perfidy[breach of faith], perish by the raging sword, and what tears the children shed for their fathers' slaughter. He ran to mount a horse and sped to tell the king. '

Whilst it has little relevance to the establishment of the landing site, I believe it indicates the likelihood that these events did take place as written. My reason for believing this is the recounting of the same story in another text, which I shall deal with when analysing the Wace manuscript[28].

Much later in the text the Carmen tells the same story as the Poitiers pre-battle pep talk, but this time given by William during the famous rout by the English on the battlefield, which nearly cost the Normans the battle. As a rallying call to his men he raises his helmet to turn the tide:

'To the Normans he showed a furious countenance. . . . . . You fly from sheep, not men, and fear without cause; what you are doing is most shameful! The sea lies behind you: the sea-voyage back is formidable, wind and weather against you. It is hard to return home, hard and long the voyage; here no way of escape remains for you.'

The reference to the sea lying behind them is certainly something that was of great relevance to most of the men, who had probably never before been on a major sea voyage. Whether these events took place on the battlefield or at the Norman camp, cannot be established and could certainly have been both.

In common with Poitiers, the Carmen confirms that Harold's body is returned to the Norman camp for the necessary rites. This is a remarkable confirmation of events that runs contrary to what would be expected from a Christian invader. It also runs contrary to the popular belief that Harold was buried at Waltham Abbey.

'The corpses of the English, strewn upon the ground, he left to be devoured by worms and wolves, by birds and dogs. Harold's dismembered body gathered together, and wrapped what he had gathered in fine purple linen; and returning to his camp by the sea, he bore it with him, that he might carry out the customary funeral rites[29].'

Harold's mother then offers to purchase the body with his weight in gold:

'But the Duke, infuriated, utterly rejected both petitions, swearing that he would sooner entrust the shores of that very port to him - under a heap of stones. Therefore, even as he had sworn, he commanded the body to be buried in the earth on the high summit of a cliff. '

This tale is further expanded with the description of the marker stone embossed with the words:

'By the Duke's commands, O Harold, you rest here a King, that you may still be guardian of the shore and sea'.

What is remarkable is the proposal by the Carmen that Harold was effectively given a Viking funeral[30] on a headland nearby.

The why's and wherefores at this time are not for me to consider, but given the failure in the past to find certifiable confirmation of Harold's grave[31] I have as yet no reason to disbelieve this version of events. What interests me is that the camp is clearly identified as being by the sea and is stated as being at a port. This is the first time this expression is used is and one of great importance.

As if to endorse this point, the Carmen rounds off the events at Hastings by naming the site of the camp:

'*For a fortnight William remained in the camp at the port of Hastings and from there he directed his march towards Dover[22a].*'

At no point in the previous text has this scribe named any place in England. Only after the battle is won is Hastings named and it is described as being at the camp from which all these events occurred. There is no room for doubt that the camp that the text describes is at '*the port of Hastings.*' If this is correct, as I believe I can show, along with all the other unresolved matters, the question must be asked why no certain archaeological remains have ever been found at this port, when the town of Hastings was being developed. I believe that this question can be best answered when we look at the castle and port site.

In conclusion, the Carmen states that the landing places were probably inland away from the coast, since the sea was left behind at nine in the morning and the turn of the tide on that day was believed to be between 11am and 12 noon[32]. Given the fact that the Invasion fleet was a considerable size[33] it is more than probable that William, being an excellent commander and organiser, would have directed the landing to take place in unison at the turn of the tide. If this theory is correct, several hours elapsed between William's entrance to the port (as the text later describes the site) and the actual landing. This leads to the inevitable conclusion that the landing site was in a bay, that was off of the immediate coast line, capable of holding several hundred ships, especially if more than one shore needed defending. It could be argued that although Pevensey Bay is very large and did not fit the comments in the text exactly, the rhetoric was sufficiently flowery to allow artistic interpretation to take over. Whilst this could account for yet another inconsistency it appears questionable, to a sceptical reader, that the writer would be so specific if it was intended to leave room for doubt.

Any reasonable person describing such a landing would have named the site as Pevensey Bay if they had landed at Pevensey and known the name of the place. The omission of this information and an alternative detailed description being supplied of a name of the port, which leaves out the name of the bay, makes it far more probable that the name of the bay was either the same name as the port (later named as Hastings) or alternatively, but far less likely, unknown.

As the story unfolds, further information is revealed, suggesting that the fleet, or at least part of it, may still be where it was left. If they had earthed up their ships, upon William's orders, then some timbers would inevitably remain, even after what was visible above the water had been removed by the local inhabitants for housing or other use. The fact that the main army left the site, two weeks after the battle and never returned, makes a strong case that the invasion fleet remains to be found somewhere in the vicinity of the proposed camp.

The Carmen tells us that William secured a small area of land at the time of the Invasion and later tells us quite directly, in the same narrative, that their camp was geographically located at the port of Hastings. I do not believe it necessary to place the complete text in front of the reader, since this is available to those who wish to verify the matter. The complete text indicates to me that the events of the landing, the building of the first wooden fort and the location of the Norman camp, were all at the same place. If this is correct, as I believe it is, then finding the port is the first element that is required to find the site of the landing. The problem is that to date no-one has been able to do this. I believe that I can provide the necessary archaeological and geographical proof that backs up each of these manuscript claims.

There is one last observation that I would make in relation to the Carmen that should be aired. This is the fact that throughout history, until the end of the Victorian era, the Carmen was always considered a wholly authentic document. As recently as 1944 its authenticity was attacked by G. H. White(34), contributing to its virtual removal from bookshelves and from current thinking, in relation to the events of that time. It is my view that all the objections raised by White have now been studiously discredited, as a result of the detailed work(35) by Catherine Morton and Hope Muntz, thus reinstating its legitimate standing as one of the most thorough accounts available of the Norman Conquest.

Chapter 5: THE CHRONICLE OF BATTLE ABBEY (Anon. app. 1180 AD.)

This manuscript(36) is an account of the affairs of the famous Abbey, said to be built upon William's personal instructions, on the actual site of the Battle of Hastings. It is written in two different sections featuring over 100 pages of invaluable detail of events of the time. The first 22 folios, written in one hand, covers the period of the Invasion and lays out the background to the story of the founding of the Abbey, whilst the remaining text continues in a new hand relating to the events of the day. Although the holy scribe devoted less than a page to the actual landing, in so doing he made a significant statement, which now has new and great importance.

In this instance we are told:

'*At length he* [William] *landed safely near the town called Pevensey. . . the army extensively along an area of shore. . . . .* '

The text of this manuscript has been copied in the past and a number of key words are missing. It continues in the next paragraph:

'*So with things going as he wished, the Duke spent no long time there, but made his way with his men to a near-by port called Hastings. There he found a suitable place, and with foresight he quickly built a wooden fort.*'

Upon first inspection we appear to be given the same story as that in the Poitiers and Jumieges manuscripts. Like those that we have previously examined, there is no claim that William landed at Pevensey. The manuscript states that it was specifically near Pevensey. This is further enlarged upon by confirming that they moved to the port of Hastings and built a wooden fort there. It should be noted as a '*wooden fort*' rather than a castle. No time scale is mentioned and since all these events are drawn in the same sentence, it is reasonable to assume, although by no means certain, that these matters probably occurred simultaneously.

The same paragraph in the Chronicle of Battle Abbey continues:

'*Arriving at the hill called Hedgeland, which lies towards Hastings, while they were hurriedly getting one another into armour, a hauberk(37) was held up to the Duke to get into, and unaccountably it was offered the wrong way round.*'

This was taken to be a bad omen by those in attendance, but William makes the point that he does not believe in omens, otherwise he would not go into battle that day.

The implications of this paragraph are not obvious unless taken in conjunction with the text of Robert Wace in his work entitled Roman de Rou(38). This ancient manuscript was until the mid 19th century accepted by most historians as the authoritative detailed account of the landing and events of the battle. By way of example it is the only English or French text that I know of from the period to suggest Harold was hit with an arrow in the eye, yet colloquial history still accepts this version of events today. It was discredited(39) in the United Kingdom, for reasons which now appear to be unsound, yet is still held as the leading authority by scholars in France[40]. The consequence of this literary attack was the virtual removal from the library and British academic scene.

In Wace's version we have exactly the same story about the hauberk, but this time it recounts the event taking place in William's camp, prior to leaving for the battle, in an ordered chronological sequence. In the Chronicle of Battle Abbey the text infers that the hauberk was offered the wrong way round whilst on the way to the battle site. The evidence of two independent texts, detailing the same events, indicates the high probability that these matters actually occurred, but only one of them is correct as to the location. Since the Battle Abbey Chronicle was written in an ambiguous way I conclude that Wace probably presents the authentic story, because it was not logical for William to put his battle dress on after leaving his camp to engage in battle. In consequence William's camp was according to the Chronicle at a place called Hedgeland.

This in itself may not appear to have any great implication, except for the fact that the Battle Abbey monks named the Hedgeland site on the road between the Abbey and the far hill. It has always been assumed that this was where Hedgeland was located, so no-one to my knowledge has ever looked anywhere else for such a place name. I believe that like the charters that the same monks forged in the 1150's[41], to attempt to prove their claim to the site, Hedgeland was a convenient invention. The ridge road, leading from the Abbey to Hastings, was the only place that could have been Hedgeland, if the Battle Chronicle version is correct in stating that William put on his armour on the way to the battle site. The monks had no choice but to identify the site on the ridge as Hedgeland, or else take the risk of undermining the authority of the Abbey. That authority was based upon the report in this Chronicle that William made a battlefield oath to build an Abbey on the spot where Harold fell. Since no other manuscript made this claim the absence of Hedgeland from the vicinity of the Abbey would have totally undermined that authority.

It is only in this Chronicle that we have the events of William's camp and those of the battlefield mixed. The same paragraph continues:

'*And to strengthen the hands and hearts of you who are about to fight for me, I make a vow that on this very battlefield I shall found a monastery for the salvation of all, and especially for those who fall here.*'

The whole paragraph is highly suspect and open to interpretation, since it appears to have been written long after the actual events[42], and is the only one to mention the battlefield vow. It continues:

'*..Harold, the usurper of the realm, speedily collected an army, and fearlessly, but rashly, hurried to the place which is now called Battle.*'

The text starts in Hastings, continues through to the camp at Hedgeland and ends with the battlefield oath naming Battle in one long confused paragraph which leaves too much open to interpretation.

This would probably have suited the monks of the day, who did not require justification for their privileges, in days when the written word was not required. As time passed and the written word gained in importance, every piece of collaboratory evidence took on new significance, no matter how slight. By the time this manuscript was written, Battle was well developed as an historical site, making it even more necessary for documentary evidence to justify the claim for the Abbey and leading to the invention of the forged documents.

In conclusion little new emerges from the Battle Chronicle text, except further confirmation that William camped at the port of Hastings. He built a wooden fort there and this was near the town of Pevensey, with the army along a large area of shore. A significant new factor is added, as a result of new examination of the Wace chronicle. This establishes that the events with the hauberk were at William's camp and we have there the only example where the site is named - Hedgeland. If such a site was not where the monks of the day marked it, half way between the ridge at Telham and the battle site, then another record of Hedgeland somewhere else, would provide an alternative argument for the correct site. But no other reference can be found and only in the Chronicle is the site named. It is called a hill, something that the monks seemed to have overlooked in their attempt to identify a suitable place within sight of the Abbey.

It must be remembered that we know that the monks who wrote this document had access to Wace's manuscript in their library. They would have known that a key element of that document tells us that there was a line of sight connection between the Norman and Saxon camps on the night of the Battle. It was therefore necessary for Hedgeland to be located within that line of sight location as viewed from where they sat writing the new documents. The only place they could choose was on the ridge opposite.

The ridge site cannot be satisfactorily described as a hill unless approached from the east or west - something that was probably impossible, because of the wooded nature of the terrain. As far as I can establish there are no written descriptions of Hedgeland near Battle as a hill or otherwise, apart from the Battle Chronicle. It is not surprising this place was chosen, as it is an integral part of the ridge between Hastings and Battle. However the fact that the ridge rises from north to south does not justify the monk's claim that Hedgeland on that ridge was a hill. Looking at the issue from a critical perspective, rather than seeking proof of the site, there are strong grounds for doubt when a visual inspection finds no hill and no recognisable summit. This inconvenience adds to the inconsistencies we have referred to earlier, but would only be noticeable if the authenticity of that site were challenged. How many historians from the past have actually been to examine the Hedgeland site? Why should they? The matter had no relevance unless the authenticity of that site were to be challenged.

The fact that the authorities at Battle Abbey, at the time that the Chronicle was written, were prepared to forge documents to authenticate their claims and privileges does not bode well for the reliability of any of the historical background in this document. However it must be pointed out that nothing was to be gained by naming the site Hedgeland 100years after the battle and then falsely inventing its position, only for the truth to materialise to undermine the story at a later date. The name appears to have passed into the record correctly, most probably from the first scribe who wrote down the name very near the date of the original document was made, whilst the location was not recorded. The solution, when 100years later it was necessary to support the forged document, was to create Hedgeland where logic dictated it should be. The correct identification of the Duke's camp at Hedgeland, as a hill and the name of the same camp at the port of Hastings, is crucial new evidence that has been misinterpreted in the past to mean different places, even though the manuscripts themselves refer to one Norman camp at Hastings.

When the texts are taken as a whole, rather than on a paragraph by paragraph basis there is only one conclusion: the camp at Hedgeland and the camp at the port of Hastings are one and the same? Only with this conclusion are both Wace and the Chronicle of Battle Abbey in agreement. Only in this context does the chronology of the paragraph in the Chronicle of Battle Abbey make full sense. The words 'arriving at a hill called Hedgeland' refers to the previous sentence *'He found a suitable place'* (to camp). Seeking to match the text to the ridge site, which had been invented out of necessity, is an error that has passed from generation to generation until now. Those who drew up the Chronicle could not know the error, but like generations before them interpreted the text to mean that Hedgeland was within sight of the Abbey. It appeared to readers of the Chronicle that this must be the case, as the reference to Hedgeland appears in the same paragraph as the battlefield oath (which unknown to later generations was an invention).

Hedgeland could only be situated on the ridge if these events took place within sight of the Abbey. That was why they invented it, in order to protect the interests of the Abbey by substantiating the written evidence of the Chronicle. (Author's note: As we shall see later in the second half of this book this is a fatal flaw).

If this interpretation of the Chronicle of Battle Abbey is correct then the Normans built their first camp and fort at a place called Hedgeland. This was not upon the ridge, within the possible boundary of the Abbey battlefield, but at a hill called Hedgeland, somewhere near at the port of Hastings. A place they knew nothing about, because it was not populated and long since absorbed into Wilting Manor once the Normans took over. Even today few know the names of woods or hills over three miles away. It comes as no surprise that the name therefore passed into the record, but it's location was recorded incorrectly in order to justify the privileges of the Abbey.

Chapter 6: MASTER WACE (Roman de Rou 1160 app.)

This manuscript(43) is believed to have been written around the year 1160. The author tells us that Wace was born in Jersey and educated at Caen. The account appears to name his father as the authority from which the information comes. Yet at one point in the text, when speaking about the comet preceding the Conquest, he refers to the report of eye-witnesses, as his personal authority(44). The manuscript has additional verification as an authentic document of the time by its inscription naming it as a copy from the library of Saint Martin at Battle Abbey, dating from about 1200. In consequence the story that it contains was likely to be in the possession of those monks who drew up the Chronicle of Battle Abbey. It is by far the most detailed manuscript of the era(45), accepted as a definitive version of events until the middle of the nineteenth century in the UK and still considered such in France.

The story starts with how William became Duke and the Barons revolted against him. It goes into great detail concerning the battle at Val des Dunes, how William foiled the King of France and how Harold came to Normandy and swore allegiance on the bones of the saints. In many ways the text acts as an accompaniment to the same story told in the Bayeux Tapestry and it could be more than coincidence that Wace was given a prebend(157) at the cathedral of Bayeux. What is of great interest is that great amounts of additional detail have been added by Wace and he is not afraid to tell what he believes to be the truth, even if this runs contrary to earlier versions of events.

The first interesting example of this is regarding the circumstances where William secures Harold's oath of allegiance - a central issue concerning the reason for the Invasion.

In Wace's version the text runs:

'To receive the oath, he caused a parliament to be called. It is commonly said that it was at Bayeux. . . . He sent for all the holy bodies thither, and put so many of them together as to fill a whole chest, and then covered them with a pall; but Harold neither saw them, nor knew of their being there; for nought was shewn or told to him about it. . . . . . When Harold placed his hand upon it, the hand trembled, and the flesh quivered; but he swore, and promised upon his oath, to take Ele to wife, and to deliver up England to the Duke. . . . after the death of Edward, if he should live, so help him God and the holy relics there! Many cried 'God grant it' and when Harold had kissed the Saints, and had risen upon his feet, the Duke led him up to the chest, and made him stand near it; and took off the chest pall that had covered it, and shewed Harold upon what holy relics he had sworn; and he was sorely alarmed at the sight.'

It is clear that Harold has been tricked, by hiding relics at the site of the oath and producing them after the event, to secure bondage to them. These matters could only be incorporated into the story once sufficient time had passed(46) and would only have been included if it was believed to be true by the readers of the day. Such a matter would be verging upon an insult to the crown, if incorrect, and that is not the type of mistake that a scribe of the day would make more than once. Wace had no reason to invent such a plot and would only have included it if he felt secure in its truth. The fact that he relates the story of the hidden relics in such detail indicates a willingness to relate the whole story, as he knew it, without pandering to political niceties.

It continues covering the period between Harold being crowned and the preparations for war, how William persuades the Barons to support his claim to the English throne and how William engages the support of the Pope. Chapter 11 starts the period that we are interested in, concerning the preparations for the Invasion. In it he says:

'. . but I have heard my father say - I remember it well, although I was but a lad - that there were seven hundred ships, less four, when they sailed from St Valery; and that there were besides these ships, boats and skiffs for the purpose of carrying the arms and harness. I have found it written (but I know not whether it be true) that there were in all three thousand vessel(47) bearing sails and masts. Any one will know that there must have been a great many men to have furnished out such vessels.'

It has been argued that Wace's father could not have the personal knowledge referred to in this paragraph, because of the time scale. If the text was written in 1160 it is more than likely that his father could have been a young man present at the time the Invasion departed. I believe that he could have related this to the young Wace in the early years of that century, without stretching credibility too far. Wace makes the point that he was a young lad at the time. Here is the first hand account of a witness who is in direct contradiction of what other earlier authorities have said. Rather than ignore this matter Wace makes the point that it is his father's word, leaving the conclusion to the reader. In any event the conclusion is correct that whether there were 696 ships or 3,000 this was a great event, by the standards of the day.

The story continues:

'They waited long at St.Valery for a fair wind, and the barons were greatly wearied(48). Then they prayed the convent to bring out the shrine of St.Valery, and set it on a carpet in the plain; and all came praying the holy relics, that they might be allowed to pass over sea. They offered so much money, that the relics were buried beneath it; and from that day forth, they had good weather and a fair wind. The Duke placed a lantern on the mast of his ship, that the other ships might see it, and hold their course after it. At the summit was a vane of brass, gilt. On the head of the ship, in the front, which mariners call the prow, there was a figure of a child in brass, bearing an arrow with a bended bow. His face was turned towards England, and thither he looked, as though he was about to shoot; so that which ever way the ship went, he seemed to aim onwards. '

Wace does not mention that the fleet sails at night, but does so indirectly referring to the fleet being able to follow the lantern. The text is further authenticated by the collaboration of the description of the child figurine with that shown on the poop (not the prow) in the Bayeux Tapestry. The same figurine is described in Taylor's anonymous manuscript(49) to have pointed to England with his right forefinger, and to have held to his mouth an ivory horn with his left. It is stated there that William's ship was called the Mora and was a gift from his wife Matilda. Which of these versions is correct may never be known, but it is in my view certain that William's personal ship was differentiated by a distinguishing figurine, or would otherwise have been differentiated in some other way.

Wace continues:

'The ships steered to one port; all arrived and reached the shore together; together they cast anchor, and ran on dry land; and together they discharged themselves. They arrived near Hastings, and there each ship ranged by the other's side. . . . . . . and they scoured the whole shore, but found not an armed man there.'

This text is in some ways more detailed than Poitiers or the Carmen, since it is making the point that the landing was in unison and probably organised that way, as well as being unopposed. As we discussed earlier this is the most likely way that an accomplished commander would arrange such a venture. Wace confirms that they landed as a great fleet in unison, that they all make to one port near Hastings and that they were tied up along side each other. In practice this means the landing took place over an extensive area of shore.

Upon the basis that at least 700 ships were involved, it would take over two miles of shore line, if each took only five meters when beached. On the assumption that the previous texts are correct the calm bay where this took place would also have to accommodate at least two miles of shore line.

At this point Wace writes:

'They formed together on the shore, each armed upon his warhorse. All had their swords girded on, and passed into the plain with their lances raised'

He clearly indicates that the area next to the Invasion site was flat. This appears to contradict the present Hastings Castle site, since it is a steep sided valley and the shore of the cove beneath the castle was too small to accommodate a large number of boats.

There then follows an important passage where Wace describes the landing procedure in great detail. It appears to be a first hand report from his father and confirms exactly the visual image given by the Bayeux Tapestry, a full analysis of which will follow:

'Then they cast out of the ships the materials, and drew them to land, all shaped framed and pierced to receive the pins which they had brought, cut and ready in large barrels; so that before evening had well set in, they had finished a fort. Then you might see them make their kitchens, light their fires, and cook their meat. The duke sat down to eat, and the barons and knights had food in plenty; for he had brought ample store. All ate and drank enough, and were right glad that they were ashore.'

The final statement that they were *'right glad'* that they were ashore confirms my belief that given the dangers of the crossing in such small craft the likelihood of re-embarkation was remote. Having survived the rigours of the voyage to re-embark would have been the height of folly. The story gives a clear impression that upon achieving a safe landing at the port of Hastings a meal was consumed to celebrate the event.

At this point Wace supports the Carmen claim that William ordered his ships to be incapacitated:

'(23a)Then he ordered proclamation to be made, and commanded the sailors that the ships should be dismantled, and drawn ashore and pierced, that the cowards might not have ships to flee.'

This is in my view a confirmation of the Carmen reference to rendering the fleet immobile and seems a prudent move, having left it under the protection of their fort. Whilst not apparent in the text it has been suggested by a colleague that the Bayeux Tapestry might show dismantled boats being used for the construction of the fort portrayed at the site(50). I agree that this is a possibility and believe this statement by Wace confirms the probable use of timbers for that purpose. Having sailed with at least 600 ships the obvious way to transport timbers for a fort was in the frames of the vessels carrying them.

Wace then makes a further point that due to so many things happening his chronology requires him to move backwards and forwards through events:

'All cannot be written at once; but, passing backwards and forwards to each matter in turn, I have now to tell the duke immediately after his arrival made all his host arm themselves.'

The implication being that we are being taken back to the point where they landed because there is an important element of the story that has been omitted. Lacking the power of word processing it appears that this has been added to allow the inclusion of the following paragraph:

'The first day they held their course along the seashore; and on the morrow came to a castle called Pevensey. The squires and foragers, and those who look out for booty, seized all the clothing and provisions they could find, lest what had been brought by the ships should fail them; and the English were to be seen fleeing before them, driving off their cattle, and quitting their houses. All took shelter in the cemeteries, and even there they were in grievous alarm.'

Wace claims that Pevensey was sacked the day after the landing. This reference to '*first day*' refers to the day of the landing, since there is no mistaking '*morrow*' meaning the following day when they went to Pevensey. This appears to be a wholly logical and probable explanation, given the failure of any other manuscript to provide a satisfactory explanation of how Pevensey features in the landings at all. Up until this point the only place named had been Hastings.

Scholars[51] have proposed in the past that Pevensey was probably sacked first and then the fleet moved on to Hastings in order to explain Poitiers and Jumieges account. I do not believe this to be the case, because there is overwhelming evidence pointing to the landing and camp at the port of Hastings. Wace provides the only logical and viable explanation of events, since the evidence indicates that the first day was spent consolidating the ground and erecting a fort. Having done this a raiding party would have consolidated their position with the nearest garrison and this is exactly what Wace reports them as doing. It is noticeable that he does not say how they got to Pevensey, but it was not with the 700 ships they brought with them, because by then most had already been beached or dismantled. It would most probably have been on horseback, detouring around the 30 mile estuary or via a small number of boats on the following day's tide. Given the difficulty of negotiating tide and wind between Hastings and Pevensey horseback would be wholly reliable and most likely, as it was the only form of warfare that most of these men knew. Sailing was not natural to the vast majority of the troops and so I believe it unlikely that they would willingly risk life and limb, on a further sea venture, after reaching their objective safely. Having secured a beach head the men would be ready to engage in the consolidation process that was second nature to men at arms of that time, plundering the neighbourhood on horseback, seeking provisions to feed the army.

Wace is the only Chronicler to provide a logistically plausible explanation as to how Pevensey and Hastings feature in the Invasion story. This is further endorsed by evidence provided in the Domesday Survey[52].

There now follows the story of how King Harold came to hear of the landings mentioned in the Carmen[28a]:

'*A knight of that country heard the noise and cry made by the peasants and villains when they saw the great fleet arrive. He well knew that the Normans were come, and that their object was to seize the land. He posted himself behind a hill, so that they should not see him, and tarried there, watching the arrival of the great fleet. He saw the archers come forth from the ships, and the knights follow. He saw the carpenters with their axes, and the host of people and troops. He saw the men throw the materials for the fort out of the ships. He saw them build up and enclose the fort, and dig a fosse[53] around it. He saw them land the shields and armour. And as he beheld all this, his spirit was troubled; and he girt his sword and took his lance, saying that he would go straightway to King Harold, and tell the news. Forthwith he set out on his way, resting late and rising early; and thus he journeyed on by night and by day to seek Harold his lord.*'

As stated earlier I believe this story has important implications for confirming the landing site, since both the Carmen and Wace recount the same event. Here is another witness account of the landing, with the building of what appears to be a transportable fort, since Wace tells us that '*the men throw the materials for the fort out of their ships*' and later '*barrels held the pins*' they used to assemble it. The fort was completed with a ditch and a hill near by. A remarkable feat of engineering for such primitive times confirming William's undoubted organisational skills.

The most important item that has been overlooked is the final three words of the paragraph '*Harold his lord*'. This gives a direct clue to the origin of the witness. It would be expected for the man to be a local of the area and to report to Harold his King[54]. Yet Wace uses the expression '*lord*' inferring a particular feudal lord and master relationship. I do not believe this to be purely coincidental, but an indication that the witness was a knight who knew Harold personally from a manor in the area where Harold was his actual lord, otherwise the text would have addressed Harold as his King. In these circumstances I interpret the use of the expression *'lord'* as significant. This new interpretation would give Harold a more detailed knowledge of the geography of the area than he had previously been given credit. The Domesday entry for the manor of Crowhurst confirms that Harold was the lord of that Manor in 1066:

'Lord in 1066: Earl Harold – Lords in 1086 Walo of Willingham; Walter son of Lambert.'

When the knight arrives at Harold's camp Wace restates the landing site:

'The Normans', he cried, *'are come! They have landed at Hastings. '*

There is no reference to Pevensey in this context and further justification for a Hastings landing site.

Wace now a starts detailed description of the events of the night before the battle, leading into the battle scene. The night before the battle is spent in the Normans camp:

'The priests had watched all night, and besought and called on God, and prayed to Him in their chapels which were fitted up throughout the host.'

Wace indicates that the camp was at this stage large enough to accommodate a number of chapels, most probably in the form of tents.

It goes on to say:

'The Duke stood on the hill, where he could best see his men.'

With this he confirms the Chronicle of Battle Abbey's conclusion that the site was a hill, rather than a ridge. After giving the pre-battle pep talk William gets into his armour and at that point is offered the hauberk the wrong way round:

'The hauberk which was turned wrong, and then set right by me, signifies that a change will arise out of the matter we are now moving. You shall see the name Duke changed to King.'

This is of course the same story that is told in the Chronicle of Battle Abbey.

Although Wace devoted numerous chapters to the actual battle there is nothing further of assistance to us relating to the landing site and camp. Wace names the site firstly at a port near Hastings and later at Hastings when the knight describes events to Harold. There appears to be a realistic indication that around 700 ships were used. This would mean that the landing site would need somewhere in the region of two miles of beach to accommodate such a number of ships for a unified landing allowing only 5 meters per ship. In common with the Carmen, part, if not all of the fleet, is decommissioned either by dismantling or drawing ashore. Wace maintains that they brought parts of a fort with them, but does not detail whether the timbers from the ships are used, even though there does appear to be a clue in the description of the ships as *'dismantled.'*

For the first time a plausible reason why Pevensey features in the story is given and the probability arises that the witness to the landings may be the resident of a manor with a personal knowledge of Harold as his lord. Wace gives a very detailed description of the landing that confirms events in the Bayeux Tapestry. Lastly Wace confirms that the site upon which the camp is held is a hill site, where the deed with the hauberk was witnessed being held the wrong way round, which is most probably the same hill site called Hedgeland in the Chronicle of Battle Abbey.

Chapter 7: THE DOMESDAY SURVEY (1085 - 1086)

(Author's Note October 2010: It should be remembered that this chapter was written when I had no understanding of how the battle site integrated into the Norman Invasion story. Looking at this evidence now it clearly shows the connection between the Invasion, battle and camp of William the Conqueror. However at the time of this investigation into the Domesday evidence my sole focus was trying to establish whether the data related to the wasted manors of Sussex would reveal the centre of Norman operation, when assessed with the local knowledge of road development that was available to me. As a side effect of that I wished to establish whether there was a solid foundation in the story that the Normans landed or camped at Pevensey. In consequence the chapter may be confusing to those who do not know the local area. I have therefore created a number of maps to show the lay of the land.

I have decided to include a study of the Domesday Survey[55] for the county of Sussex as a result of reference to the area around the Duke's camp being '*laid waste*' in the Poitiers and Carmen manuscripts. The same expression was frequently used in the Survey and is believed to describe manors that had suffered total loss, as a result of the plundering by the invading army. A cursory inspection of recent texts on this subject proved to be unsatisfactory, other authors whom I looked at were either relying on earlier works that could not be verified, or whose work appeared incomplete in relation to the whole area that we are interested in. In consequence I decided to look at all the manors in the Hastings and Pevensey areas, detailed in the Domesday Survey as the Rape[160] of Hastings and Rape of Pevensey respectively, applying the benefit of computerised graphics.

The survey was conducted upon William's instructions approximately 20 years after the Invasion. The Saxon Chronicle records that it took place in 1085, whilst other sources claim 1086. In either event it forms a remarkable written record of the state of the nation so soon after the Invasion. The whole exercise was conducted in less than a year and is now held in the Public Record Office. One of the regional versions, from Ely Abbey, tells us what the Commissioners were to ask. These questions appear to form the basis for the whole survey and were:

'*How many hides?*[56] *How many ploughs, both those in lordship and the men's? How many villagers, cottagers and slaves, how many free men and Freemen? How much woodland, meadow and pasture? How many mills and fishponds? How much has been added or taken away? What the total was and is? How much each free man or Freeman had or has? All threefold, before 1066, when King William gave it, and now; and if more can be had than at present?*'

The purpose was to find out who owned what and how much it was worth. It was called the Domesday Book by the landowners because it was the final authoritative register of rightful possession in the land; by analogy its judgement was as final as that of Domesday. Each manor is listed with its owner, with other details and in particular relates values of those manors before, during, and after the Invasion. These values provide valuable clues in the search for the Invasion landing site, when examined in relation to the areas of Pevensey and Hastings. The Invasion would have undoubtedly have inflicted a heavy burden upon the land surrounding the site during the time the army was in residence. This is endorsed by the fact that fifteen manors in the Hastings and Pevensey Rapes are described by the Commissioners to have been '*waste*' at the time of the Invasion.

Taking into account Poitiers and the Carmen's similar claim to the area immediately around the Norman's camp, it must be concluded that one of these manors is probably directly connected with the site of the camp.

The manors in the areas of Pevensey and Hastings fall into four distinct categories. These are:

1. Those who's value before, during and after the Invasion remained the same. It is concluded from this that the Normans are very unlikely to have been visited, let alone camped in the manor. In consequence these manors were eliminated from the search.

2. Those manors with a very low value where the total value was less than 5 shillings. These were eliminated from the search upon the basis that any increase or decrease in value by a very small amount could distort any reliable percentage fluctuation figures.

3. Those whose value decreased at the time of the Invasion and subsequently increased, recovering some or all of the lost value in the 20 year period. These values form the core data for the study, since the reduction in value shown at the time of the Invasion is assumed to be caused by the presence of the Norman army sustaining itself.

4. Those manors reported to be laid waste at the time of the Invasion. These form the most likely source for the Invasion landing site and Norman camp.

In order to evaluate the information supplied in the Domesday Survey it is necessary to look at the geographical spread of the manors in the Hastings and Pevensey Rapes at the time of Domesday

These are shown on the next page as MAP1(57).:

Chapter 8: MAP 1

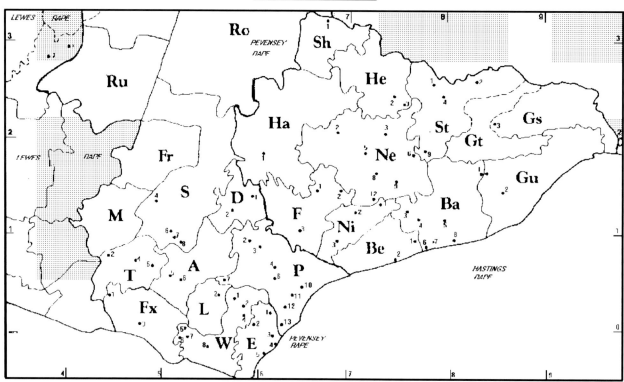

HASTINGS: BA 1 LIDHAM, 2 WESTFIELD, 3 CROWHURST, 4 WILTING, 5 HOLLINGTON, 6 CORTESLEY, 7 FILSHAM, 8 HASTINGS, BE 1 BULLINGTON, 2 BEXHILL, F1 FRANKWELL, 2 ASHBURNHAM, 3 HERSTMONCEUX, 4 WARTLING, GS 1 HEIGHTON, 2 IDEN, 3 GLOSSAMS, 4 PLAYDEN. EVEBENTONE, GT 1 KITCHENHAM, 2 UDIMORE, GU 1 RYE, 2 GUESTLING, HA 1 WARBLETON, HE 1 BURGHAM, 2 SALEHURST, 3 DRIGSELL, NE 1 EYELID, 2 BRIGHTLING, 3 MOUNTFIELD, 4 DALLINGTON, 5 NETHERFIELD, 6 WHATLINGTON, 7 PENHURST, 8 BEECH, 9 BATTLE, 10 UCKHAM, 11 BATHURST, 12 BROOMHAM, NI 1 CATSFIELD, 2 NINFIELD, 3 HOOE. MEDEHEI, SH 1 HAZELHURST, ST 1 BODIAM, 2 HIGHAM, 3 BELHURST, 4 EWEHURST, 5 WELLHEAD, 6 LORDINE, 7 FOOTLAND, 8 HURST, 9 SEDLESCOMBE. BASSINGHAM

PEVENSEY: A 1 SIDNOR, 2 SESSINGHAM, 3 SELMESTON, 4 ARLINGTON, 5 ALCISTON, 6 BERWICK, 7 WINTON, 8 ALFRISTON, D 1 HENDON, 2 HAWKRIDGE. PENGEST, E 1 YEVERINGTON, 2 BEVERINGTON, 3, EASTBOURNE, 4 EASTHALL, 5 CHOLLINGTON, FR 1 WORTH, 2 LITTLE HORSTED, FX 1 TARRING NEVILLE, 2 S. HEIGHTON, 3 BISHOPSTONE, 4

FROG FIRLE, G 7 BRAMBLETYE, HA 2 HARTFIELD. WILDENE, L 1 WILMINGTON, 2 FOLKINGTON, 3 BROUGHTON, M 1 S. MALLING, P 1 HAREBEATING, 2 HAILSHAM, 3 BEWLEY, 4 HORNS, 5 HOOE LEVEL, 6 HANKHAM, 7 WOOTON, 8 CUDNOR, 9 PEELINGS, 10 PEVENSEY, 11 RENCHING, 12 LANGNEY, 13 HORSEY. CHENENOLLE, RO 1 ALCHIN, 2 ROTHERFIELD, 3 MAYFIELD, RU 3 SHEFFIELD, 4 FLETCHING, 5 BARKHAM. INWOOD, S 1 ETCHINGWOOD, 2 WALDRON, 3 CHIDDINGLEY, 4 LAUGHTON, 5 STOCKINGHAM, 6 RIPE, 7 ECKINGTON, 8 CHELVINGTON, 9 CLAVERHAM, T 1 COMPTON, 2 BEDDINGHAM, 3 PRESTON, 4 W. FIRLE, 5 CHARLESTON, 6 SHERRINGTON, 7 TILTON, 8 ITFORD, W 1 WANNOCK, 2 WILLINGDON, 3 JEVINGTON, 4 RATTON, 5 CHARLSTON 6 ENCEAT, 7 W. DEAN, 8 BECHINGTON, 9 E. DEAN, 10 W. BURTON

All the manors are marked according to their geographical position. This is then expanded to MAP 2, which eliminates all those manors which do not satisfy the stated criteria[58].

Chapter 9: MAP 2

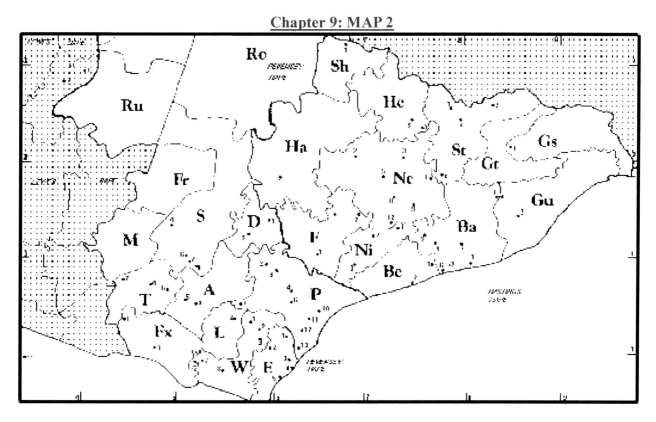

HASTINGS: BA 1 LIDHAM,, 3 CROWHURST, 4 WILTING, 5 HOLLINGTON, 6 CORTESLEY, 7 FILSHAM, 8 HASTINGS, BE 1 BULLINGTON, 2 BEXHILL, F1 FRANKWELL, 2 ASHBURNHAM, 3 HERSTMONCEUX, GS 3 GLOSSAMS, GT 1 KITCHENHAM, GU 2 GUESTLING, HA 1 WARBLETON, HE 2 SALEHURST, 3 DRIGSELL, NE 2 BRIGHTLING, 3 MOUNTFIELD,, 5 NETHERFIELD, 6 WHATLINGTON, 8 BEECH, 9 BATTLE, 12 BROOMHAM, NI 1 CATSFIELD, 2 NINFIELD, 3 HOOE. MEDEHEI, SH 1 HAZELHURST, ST 1 BODIAM, 2 HIGHAM, 4 EWEHURST, 9 SEDLESCOMBE. BASSINGHAM PEVENSEY: A 5 ALCISTON, 6 BERWICK, D 1 HENDON, 2 HAWKRIDGE. PENGEST, E 1 YEVERINGTON, 2 BEVERINGTON, 3, EASTBOURNE, 4 EASTHALL, 5 CHOLLINGTON, FX 1 TARRING NEVILLE, 3 BISHOPSTONE, G 7 BRAMBLETYE, HA 2 HARTFIELD. WILDENE, L, 2 FOLKINGTON, P 2 HAILSHAM, 3 BEWLEY, 4 HORNS, 6 HANKHAM, 7 WOOTON, 9 PEELINGS, 10 PEVENSEY, 11 RENCHING, 12 LANGNEY, 13 HORSEY. CHENENOLLE, S 4 LAUGHTON, 6 RIPE, 7 ECKINGTON, 8 CHELVINGTON, T 2 BEDDINGHAM, 4 W. FIRLE, 5 CHARLESTON, W 1 WANNOCK, 2 WILLINGDON 4 RATTON, 5 CHARLSTON 6 ENCEAT, 7 W. DEAN, 8 BECHINGTON,

Taking this plan I examined each of the manors shown on MAP 2 to see what the Survey reported their value to be at the time of the Invasion. This produced some interesting and surprising results .

MAP 3 is then produced shows the geographical spread of the study manors, with each manor given a value at the time of the Invasion. This value is then marked according to a band of values expressed as a percentage of the pre-invasion value.

There are six bands that I have drawn up to provide the reader with an easily understandable visual interpretation of the data.

These six value bands are:

1) WASTED - Where there is no value - Red

2) Where the value is up to 35% of the pre-invasion value Pink

3) Where the value is 36% to 50% of the previous value Yellow

4) Where the value is 51% to 65% - Pale Yellow

5) There the value is 66% to 80% - Pale Green

6) Where the value is 81% to 100% - Dark Green (virtually no wasting)

Chapter 10: MAP 3

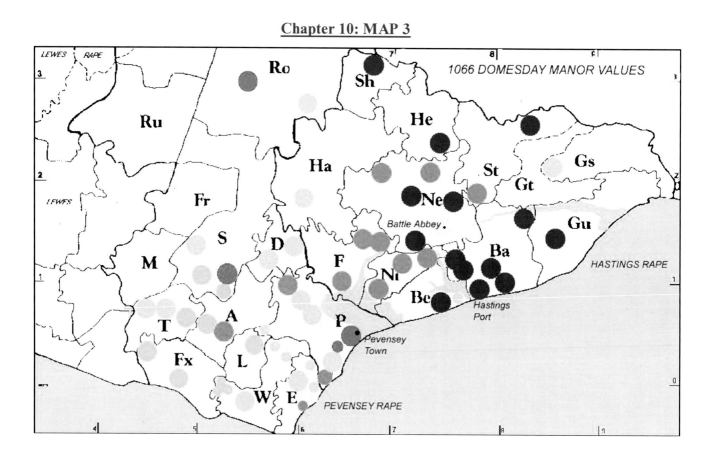

A table of values is provided giving the information upon which this diagram is based is provided later[59].

Chapter 11: DOMESDAY ANALYSIS

Maps and Graphs

GRAPH 1, which follows, shows the same information, but spread out in a linear format, in order of distance from Wilting manor. Wilting manor has been chosen as the centre of activity because I believe that it can later be shown that this manor, situated on the Combe Haven Valley, is the site of the old Port of Hastings[60]. The port that was operational at that time and continued to be used until the 14th century, when it was closed by the movement of a large shingle banks across its entrance, as a result of severe storms[61]. GRAPH1 follows:

GRAPH 1

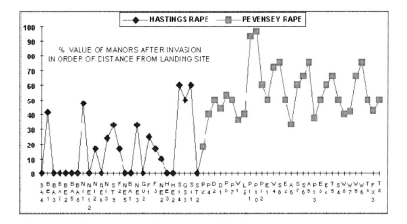

This shows all the manors adjacent to Wilting (BA4 on the immediate left) as wasted, with the exception of BE1 the manor of Bullington, which is on the immediate opposite shore of the Combe Haven valley from the proposed landing site. A more detailed geography of this valley and the evidence that it was at the time of the Invasion a large inland bay is provided in a later chapter. At this stage I seek the indulgence of the reader in accepting that according to my hypothesis Wilting is the correct manor to use as the centre of operations. This is evidenced by the manor value charts, provided in the Domesday Book.

Two things are immediately apparent from this visual display. Firstly almost all the manors in the Pevensey Rape (on the right – square markers), at the time of the Invasion, have much higher values than those in the Hastings Rape (on the left – diamond makers). Secondly the values appear to slowly increase the further away from Wilting (straight line distance) the manor is situated.

The graph shows values in relation to distance, regardless of direction from the site, but is defined by the local roads. In consequence blips occur in the middle area of the graph at Ewehurst (SI4). These are caused by the values to the north being different from those to the east and west, at a similar distance. It is therefore necessary when looking at the Invasion story to analyse the values of the manors from Wilting along the road to Pevensey to see what this produces on GRAPH 2. By doing this we will be able to see if there is any correlation between values and distance travelled along that specific road, without the distortion of manors between that were not situated on that road.

If current historical hypothesis is correct you would expect to see values immediately adjacent to Pevensey reduced dramatically if Jumieges, Poitiers and the Bayeux Tapestry are interpreted to mean that the Normans landed there. To be fair to the Bayeux Tapestry it does not state they landed at Pevensey and I shall examine this in the next chapter.

37

GRAPH 2

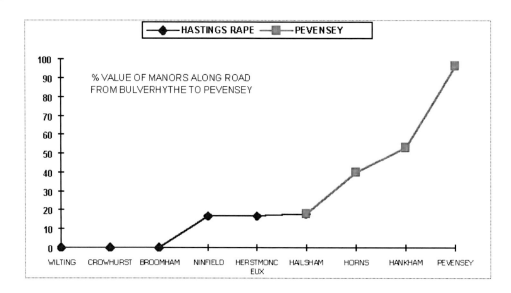

The route that I have used between Wilting and Pevensey would involve following what was then and now known as the London road out of Wilting (adjacent or at the Port of Hastings). It was nothing more than a track at the time of the Invasion, going to Battle through Crowhurst. Evidence of this track still exists going over Sandrock Hill in Crowhurst, through Blacksmiths Field and then along the eastern side of the Combe Haven inlet direct to where Crowhurst Church now stands. This route now exists as a footpath, as it has been superseded by the development of the fordable road route over Hye House hill. The London road from Hastings in those days passed where Crowhurst church now stands, heading up what is now Station Road, but was then the only track in existence, to the top of Telham Hill, where it went straight on to Battle through two steep valleys (now also a footpath that connects to the Tesco filling station at Battle, close to the Abbey).

MAP4

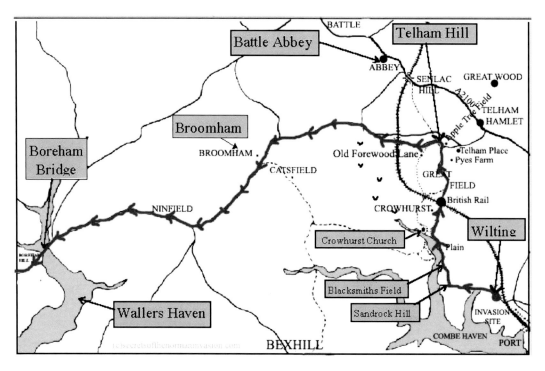

Map of route Normans took from Crowhurst to Boreham Hill showing Combe Haven Valley bottom right

I would recommend looking in detail at this map using the external web site if your reader has connectivity. The location is http://www.secretsofthenormaninvasion.com/map4.jpg. This road was the line of hamlet development before the introduction of the turnpike along the ridge, in the relatively recent 19th century, which provided a faster and safer route to Hastings. This turnpike bypassed the old London road at Telham Hill, which went through two particularly steep valleys, which made access by horse and cart almost impossible. If the ridge route between the Abbey and Hastings port, proposed by past historians, had in any way been developed, as a usable alternative prior to the turnpike, Crowhurst would not have been used as the main route for coaches prior to this. There would be at least a few properties with a history before the introduction of the turnpike, but there is no evidence of this. As further justification, the population centres at Crowhurst, Wilting and Hollington manors would not have developed, as they did, along the linear connections of this main road. A road that to this day is called the London Road.

Information of major significance, which has been omitted from the historical analysis to date, is the fact that Telham Hill was a major crossroad on the Hastings to London road. The left turn (travelling north) went directly off of the Hastings peninsular to Broomham and on to Boreham Bridge, without the need to go to Battle. Telham Hill should not be mistaken for Telham on the ridge. Telham hamlet is at the very top of the ridge and not the same place as Telham Hill, lower down to the west and marked on all Ordnance Survey maps. Colloquial and local spoken history concerning the Battle of Hastings refers to Telham Hill and many historians have made the mistake of assuming this means Telham on the ridge. Whilst Telham, as a name, does not feature in any of the manuscripts I have looked at, there is a strong argument that the inclusion of the name in spoken tradition indicates its importance in the events of that day. This matter and others I shall address in the second part of this book dealing with the Battle of Hastings.

Further confusion in understanding the names of these places is caused by those who do not know where Broomham Manor is, because Broomham in 1066 is now where the main road passes through Catsfield. In consequence whilst Catsfield is listed as a separate manor in Domesday, it is off the main road to Pevensey on the Crowhurst - Henley Down - Catsfield Road, starting in Crowhurst, on the far side of the inlet from where the invading army was positioned and therefore impossible for the Normans to access because the inlet was at that time flooded. They were camped on the wrong side of that inlet and consequently were forced to travel to Telham before being able to move west.

Supporting evidence for the route from Telham Hill through Broomham to Boreham Bridge, as the most direct route from Hastings to Pevensey, comes from the fact that Catsfield manor, was totally wasted. The road from Telham to Broomham skirted the effective southern boundary of what was to become the land of Battle Abbey, called "the Leuga". In consequence the road at that timemust have been well established. We must conclude from the evidence provided by the graphs that the Normans went to Pevensey via Broomham using this route. Travelling further north to Battle on the London road from Crowhurst would have missed Broomham completely. This would have been a much longer route to Pevensey, than the faster flatter route via Broomham, as can be seen on MAP4. It would have left that manor with much higher values. On the assumption that the Normans did go to Pevensey during the period of the Invasion, Domesday supports the Wilting - Telham - Broomham - Ninfield route as being the only completely logical one, which does not produce contradictions in the relative values.

MAP 5

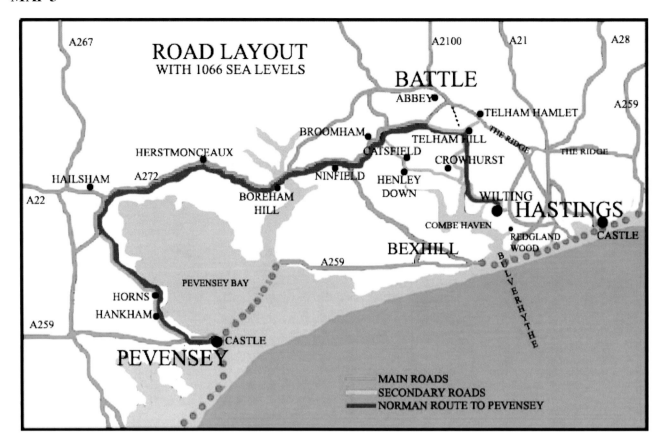

Map of Crowhurst to Pevensey

MAP5 above shows the present road layout with the coast line as it was in 1066, with the sea level shown up to the 5 meter line coloured light blue – the first available line on Ordnance Survey maps. This light blue area shows the amount of land that was in 1066 either sea or tidal marsh. The dark blue area is the sea now. The failure to understand this topography has led to assumptions in the past that could not possibly have been correct (such as the idea that the Normans marched along the coast to Pevensey – across a coastal bay).

Living in Crowhurst, at the centre of the area under discussion, I understand the Crowhurst, Broomham via Telham Hill, Ninfield route from Hastings to Pevensey to be the only possible route that the Normans took on foraging expeditions, given the geography as it was then. Catsfield manor was not wasted, because it was neither on the main route to Pevensey, nor on what was then the main through route along the coast from Hastings. The Combe Haven valley, marked blue next to the Hastings sign, provided a severe obstacle to the immediate west of Hastings and whilst it has been argued[62] that the town of Battle was the only place to exit from what was an effective peninsula, I disagree with this, as anyone could learn from a simple study of the five meter water line[63] in the area. The Normans did not need to go further north than Telham if they wanted to go to Pevensey from Hastings using the major available routes.

MAP 6

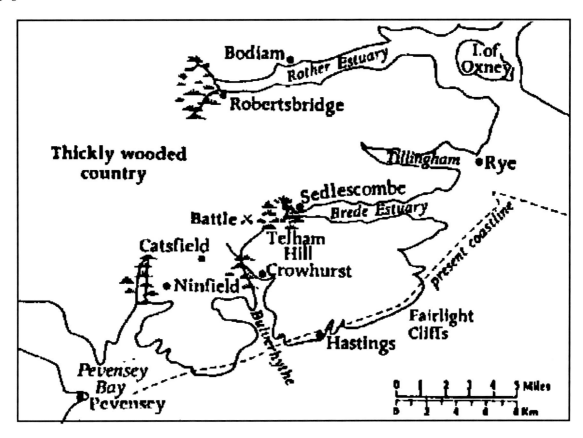

The Hastings District in 1066 from J. A Williamson: Evolution of England (Clarendon Press)

Williamson's map has been heavily relied upon by scholars to support the belief that Battle Abbey was then built at the head of the peninsula[64]. This hypothesis is convenient, but essentially flawed. The map is reproduced here and should be compared with current Ordnance Survey maps TQ60/70 and TQ 61/71 giving full details of elevation[65].

Examining Williamson's map it can be seen that Telham Hill is marked where the hamlet of Telham is situated, on the ridge to the northeast, rather than at the actual Telham Hill site directly north of the Crowhurst to Battle road(as seen on MAP5). The Combe Haven Valley/Bulverhythe is completely the wrong shape and all the contours of the coastline appear to have taken on an artistic licence far beyond the reliable, verging upon a distortion of known facts. The correct outline, or at least one that is a far more reliable one, is shown on the map we looked at earlier redrawn from the Ordnance Survey data, which I have created from scientific sea-level readings.

In my opinion Domesday supports the view that the invading army went through Ninfield on the way to Pevensey and as such must have either forded the inlet at the bottom of Boreham Hill, or used a bridge that already existed in some form or other. Any alternative route would have involved far greater logistical problems, because Waller's Haven, the name of the then tidal inlet to the west of Ninfield, at Boreham Bridge, divides north and west into a number of tributaries. This inlet requires crossing, whether you are travelling to or from Pevensey and Hastings. If this is the case the Abbey being built at the main access point of the peninsula argument falls away, since access to the mainland can be reached by ford or path along a 7 kilometre front from Boreham Hill to beyond Battle directly north-west of Hastings, using recognisable routes that subsequently developed into highways.

The main coast road from Pevensey to Hastings turned left at the junction at the top of Telham Hill to Broomham, without the need to go to Battle (which of course did not exist at that time), continuing to Ninfield and Herstmonceux on the edge of the Pevensey marsh. Without the existence of the town of

Battle no purpose was served by taking the northern route via Battle, when a simpler and perfectly satisfactory shorter route existed along the ridge parallel to the sea at Telham. From Herstmonceux it went through, or close to Hailsham, before turning round the bay to the small holdings of Horns and Hankham, where it reached Pevensey. This is an area that is remarkably flat, devoid of any potential camp sites situated at the bottom of a hill of any size.

It is clear from the values shown in Domesday that Pevensey suffered relatively little from the Invasion. In fact the Domesday entry for Pevensey indicates that the value before the Invasion was 76 shillings and 9 pence. There is no mention at all of loss in value, with the exception that when the Count of Mortain was given the manor, by William, there were only 27 burgesses instead of the previous 28. In consequence I am being gracious in accepting any loss in value. The entry adds that the value at the time of the survey, 20 years later, was then over three times as much, at 323 shilling and 9 pence. Clearly the people of Pevensey had done very well from the Invasion in the time that had elapsed. This is hardly consistent with the concept of the ravages of an invading army, as experienced in the Hastings area.

Not being a person versed in the wisdom of historical studies, outside this very narrow interest, I cannot understand how it can be argued that Pevensey could be either the landing site or William's camp site. An invading army has to establish a bridgehead and then consolidate its position. At the time in history that we are looking at there were no modern communications or back up systems. As soon as the men were on foreign soil they needed provisions. The larger the force the more provisions were needed.

According to Domesday there is no evidence that the town of Pevensey was in any way involved in providing William's army with provisions that subsequently reduced the values of the manorial holdings. All the evidence in that book points to the landing and camp being situated at Wilting, or possibly Crowhurst, on the Combe Haven valley, at the old Port of Hastings, where the reduction in value was greatest. In that area all the manors in a large swathe of countryside running to the east and west of the old London road, which ran north-west from Hastings, were laid waste. In effect all value was removed by the invading foragers in the time that they were camped there.

In conclusion the authoritative documentation of the Domesday Survey completely vindicates Wace's claim that Pevensey was little more than a raiding party on the day following the Invasion. The evidence of manorial values confirms that this pillage was not by boat, upon the formation of a landing bridgehead. Neither was it upon landing and then moving to Hastings via the Invasion fleet, in vessels that the army were unlikely to be accustomed to. The evidence of the Domesday Survey clearly shows the progressive lessening of the impact of the foraging army along the route from Hastings to Pevensey via what was then known as the coastal route. Pevensey seems to have escaped almost unscathed. It is known that the resident army of men held under duty from manors to the King - the Fryd - had been stood down after spending the summer manning the forts of the south coast. The geographical position of Pevensey made it a particularly unlikely landing site, since the castle almost totally covered the very small peninsula upon which it stood. To land anywhere in the immediate vicinity of that castle, upon the most probable basis that there would be an armed defence, would be a tactical disaster that no commander of William's ability would have made. Even if he had prior knowledge of the standing down of the guard I do not believe it credible, in an age where communication was so slow, that he would risk everything by allowing Harold to reoccupy a stronghold immediately adjacent to the proposed landing site, in the time it would take to receive the reconnaissance report. Whilst William would undoubtedly have had spies at the main ports the Channel formed a formidable obstacle to the passage of information. All the reports show it to be impassable for the fleet for some time prior to the Invasion due to the weather. Given these circumstances a prudent commander would seek to land upon an unfortified shore.

Those manors in the vicinity of Pevensey suffered moderate losses according to their original value and position in relation to the distance from the camp at Hastings, and position in relation to the main coastal route. There is no other possible explanation to the figures involved. Whilst loss of value was measurable in the Pevensey area it was nothing like the devastation suffered in the area to the north of the Combe Haven valley where there is hardly a manor left intact. The proposal that the invading army landed somewhere unknown near Pevensey, on the main bay area, does not stand up to scrutiny. All the manors around the bay show the same characteristics where loss is equated to distance from Hastings. If the proposal that Pevensey were the landing site was to be supported in any way there would be a sustainable deviation from the norm. This does not happen and I propose that the evidence of the Domesday Survey, taken with the absence of any archaeological evidence, of any kind illustrates that this story has no foundation whatsoever.

A study of the manors in the area immediately surrounding the Combe Haven valley is here:

GRAPH 3

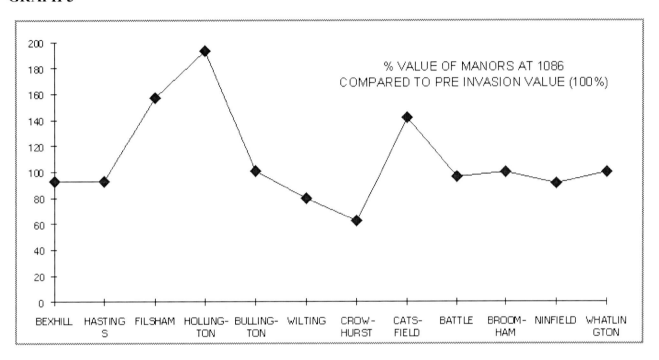

This graph clearly shows that even 20 years after the Battle of Hastings that Wilting and Crowhurst, the manors immediately to the north of the Combe Haven valley, are still the least well recovered of all the manors in Sussex. The reason for this is because these manors suffered the highest degree of ravaging by the invading army, and thus took the longest to recover. This is the logical and only explanation for the dip in the chart.

The Domesday Survey data proves conclusively that the town of Pevensey and the manors in the immediate vicinity could definitely not have been William's camp or landing site. It shows that the manors within the Hastings Rape were those that suffered the devastation. It shows Wilting and Crowhurst as the centre of this activity and supports unequivocally the concept of the landing and Invasion site being in one of those manors, both of which have extensive shore lines on what is known locally by the people of Crowhurst and Wilting as the Bulverhythe. This area was a large inland natural harbour, with accompanying bay of shallow, relatively still water. In consequence I shall now refer in this document to this bay as the Bulverhythe in the same sense as those who still live in the area, unlike many academics who site Bulverhythe at the entrance to the Combe Haven valley, which retains the name. It is my view that Bulverhythe, as a name still in use today, is an important element of the tradition of spoken history surviving boundary and name changes, the significance of which I shall address later.

Chapter 12: THE BAYEUX TAPESTRY approx 1077

The Bayeux Tapestry is a remarkable survivor of an age when little survives to describe the events of the time. It was made approximately ten years after the Invasion and was hung at the consecration of Bayeux cathedral in 1077. The Council of Arras had recommended in 1025 that the illiterate masses could be better educated by hanging suitable pictures in churches. It is therefore likely that this was part of the motivation for such a large undertaking. Its importance cannot be over stated, since unlike any other document that has survived from this time, there is some degree of certainty that William saw it at Bayeux. What I therefore propose is that its accuracy in all respects is unchallengeable and the difficulty faced with its interpretation is solely due to applying the scenes to the wrong location.

The Tapestry is slightly over 70 meters long by about half a meter wide. To be correct it is not technically a tapestry at all but an extensive piece of embroidery. It is unknown who commissioned it, or who did the actual work, but the current belief is that Bishop Odo, who at many points appears as the Tapestry's central figure, may have been responsible[66]. In France the Tapestry is known as Matilda's tapestry. Matilda was William's wife. William was one of the few monarchs who at that time remained faithful to his wife throughout his complete reign, enjoying a large family. A number of stories indicate a strong bond between William and Matilda that was uncommon for a monarch in a period when women played a minor role in affairs of state. It was Matilda who is said to have commissioned William's ship, said to be called the Mora, for the Invasion, as well as the Tapestry. It is therefore possible that although there appears to be no written evidence of Matilda's involvement, her influence was such that the Tapestry has acquired her name.

Recent analysis of the embroidery style and the use of spelling in the Saxon manner, as well as spelling mistakes in the Latin, suggest that contrary to past belief, it was probably made at Canterbury in Kent, England[67]. Canterbury was at that time one of Europe's leading embroidery schools and by way of circumstantial evidence Bishop Odo became Earl of Kent after the Conquest. The size and speed with which it was designed and completed indicates a considerable production process that could only have been completed at one of the major schools of embroidery.

The most remarkable element of the Tapestry is its authentic traceable pedigree and the faithful cartoon like description of events. There are many mysterious elements that historians have found impossible to equate. I believe that it is far more faithful to the events of the time than has previously been given credit. In particular I believe that the Tapestry is not only faithful to the types and style of dress and armour, but is also faithful in building and land descriptions. Dr Marjorie Chibnall, in her critique confirms that this view is supported by at least three other eminent historians, including Arnold Taylor's paper (Vol XIV) on 'Belrem', Derek Renn's (XVI) on 'Burgheat and gonfanon' and Nicholas Brooke's general survey in the first volume. This is contrary to current thinking and I shall demonstrate the accuracy of the text in relation to the landing site, in order to justify this position.

It can be reasonably argued that if the designer was so absolutely exact in relation to clothing and events, why should he then seek to ignore accuracy regarding the important matters of detail on the major factors, such as the buildings and the geographical nature of the terrain? Whilst it is noted that maps up to at least the 16th century were notoriously inaccurate the Bayeux Tapestry relates a story and in this respect portrays events in locations. The very cartoon nature of the pictures requires details of location to provide the setting for the story. Those locations where only known to those who attended and in consequence, if I am correct, provide a number of clues to the location of the landing and the camp that can only be correctly interpreted by application to the actual landing site. It might also be argued that anyone living at the time might have knowledge of dress, armour and ships of the time - but not of the geography local to the battle. It is this reason why the Bayeux Tapestry provides invaluable clues that cannot be ignored. Only someone who had been to the site would have included the correct details, which can only apply to the landing site, thus proving the designer had first hand knowledge of the events portrayed.

I believe it can be shown that the author of this work was just as careful when drawing the buildings and the terrain. The first plate we turn to PLATE 1 concerns the funeral of King Edward, where the body is taken to Westminster Abbey. Here is portrayed a building that closely resembles the known building of the time. Recent discoveries in the foundations at the Abbey confirm that the original building was as large as the one portrayed, closely resembling the image on the Tapestry:

Chapter 13: PLATE 1 Westminster Abbey

PLATE 2
St Michael's Mount

Mont Saint Michel monastery is shown on an uncultivated hill, at the top of the Tapestry, whilst the estuary is clearly shown in the foreground.

At Dol the Normans are shown attacking Conan's stronghold. Here again the terrain shows a hill with a fortification on top. Either side there is a mound with a view of a moat or defensive earthworks, with Conan escaping via a rope over the ravine, whilst the Normans attack on the side with a drawbridge. Two dove like birds are positioned in front of the mound to symbolise a peaceful surrender. The scene is correct in all detail including the barricading of the castle entrance with shields[68].

PLATE 4
Rennes

Next Rennes is shown as a central tower at the top of a hill surrounded by a palisade. Here again two mounds are shown but this time in a completely different style indicating a much steeper and difficult defence. This appears to be man made rather than a natural feature. The entrance is also shown in a way that indicates a rampart with animals beneath. It has been suggested that these are sheep grazing. It is my view that the style of the Tapestry suggests that the uniform ringlets in the area below the castle are the artist's way of indicating a regular man made fortification, whilst the previous hills each have definitive geographical differences in their portrayal.

Chapter 15: PLATE 5 Dinan

After Rennes the army pursues Conan to Dinan, north-west of Rennes. A cleverly constructed scene shows three stages of the attack in one sequence. On the left is the attack, with the drawbridge up. In the centre two knights set fire to the palisade, whilst on the right the surrender is shown with the keys to the city handed on a lance, as a token of surrender. Here again the ground is detailed with the two defensive mounds, a central tower and palisade holding the defending forces.

Throughout the Tapestry men and buildings are positioned on the ground except where there is a good reason to show some form of perspective. Where items are placed directly behind one and other the farthest item is raised off the ground. Similarly I believe that when an object is raised off the ground on its own, rather than in conjunction with others, this indicates that the object is actually higher in relation to the geography of the site in question. This is why Mont St Michael (shown on Plate 2) sits on its own above the action being shown to take place in the estuary below.

I would now like to examine the Tapestry in detail covering the period from the departure from Saint Valery through to leaving the camp on the morning of the battle. I shall only address those sections of the Tapestry that provide evidence as to the authenticity of the proposed site.

Chapter 16: PLATE 6 Boat making

At this stage the fleet is being prepared for the Invasion. The first apparent difficulty the Tapestry presents us with is the fact that the ships, as embroidered, appear very small. Four men are actually working upon their construction whilst a fifth appears to be holding one of the ships.

In the same sequence ships drawn to the same scale are shown being tied to the top of a high post. The men are shown with their ankles covered in water, whilst the man nearest the boat is up to his knees. The ships themselves are sitting high in the water with three planks above the water line, whilst the earlier frame shows the same ships with four planks. There are holes along the top edge of the ship, to take oars if necessary. I interpret this sequence to mean that at least some of the ships in question were exactly as drawn, being little larger than large war canoes.

A similar scene is used to show the men felling trees, just prior to this plate. I do not believe it was an accident that the trees are drawn approximately twice the size of the men felling them. This is the same scale confirmed by the carpenter working on the planks that have been cut. In the later section where the main fleet crosses the Channel the smaller ships are shown high in relation to the main subject matter. Each accommodates only four or five men with the crew clearly sitting down.

Chapter 17: PLATE 7 Tree felling

Here we can see the scale of the men and trees being cut down.

PLATE 8
Ships with small ships in rear

The fact that the men and horses are shown sitting further endorses the large war canoe concept. The masts were not a permanent fixture, since they are later shown being removed upon landing and are supported by four ties on each.

Chapter 18: PLATE 9 William's ship

The text states 'Here Duke William crosses over the sea and came to Pevensey' – with a picture of a big ship of similar construction, with the Viking style prow and characteristic low draught. The scale has changed, because the top of the prow is above the head line of the crew. This shows a ship that is larger than the previous ones and this time the mast is secured by six lines. There are ten men on board, with at least two standing up. At the head of the mast is the lantern, referred to in Poitiers description of the mid channel stopover, where they waited for the fleet to catch up.

At the rear of William's ship is the figure of a boy pointing with a banner and blowing a horn. Wace stated that the figure was of a child in brass, bearing an arrow with a bended bow, whilst Taylor's anonymous manuscript claims that the child pointed towards England and held an ivory horn to its mouth.

On Plate 9 we see the words **'AD PEVENESAE,'** which has been used to justify Pevensey as the landing point of the Invasion. I do not believe that these words alone, or taken with the Poitiers text, offer any conclusive support to those who support Pevensey town as the site of the landing. It is vital to view the Tapestry in context rather than on a plate by plate basis analysis. The text, when taken in conjunction with the scene before and after, breaks at this point, before starting the landing sequence. It indicates that the intention of the author was to portray the fleet making its way to Pevensey. The fleet is still in full sail when William's ship is shown graphically represented mid Channel, when seen in the context of the 70 meters of cloth. Taking the words *'Ad Pevensae,'* in isolation of the continuous story taking place around them, is misleading in the context of the Tapestry story. When seen as a whole the author's intention clearly shows that Pevensey was marked as the destination, not the landing site.

It must be remembered that the English coast was a formidable unmarked foreign land, to those who occupied the small vessels involved. Pevensey Castle was the only landmark of any significance in the area, yet no attempt is made to represent Pevensey castle in the story of the landing.

It is my belief that the inclusion of the word Pevensey in this and other texts indicates the common belief that Pevensey was the area of the intended site of the Invasion. William probably chose Hastings, because intelligence showed it to be unmanned, whilst the herring fleet was engaged in the annual catch at Yarmouth. Given the known flow of information across the Channel it is unlikely that all but William's inner circle would know the true destination until they arrived. Hence the Tapestry states in my view what every man knew at the time - namely that the destination was the area known as Pevensey, and that could be anywhere within the control of Pevensey castle.

Today we tend to forget that printed maps did not exist in this period of history. The only two fortifications of any merit on the south coast of England were at Dover and Pevensey - both with formidable castle defences. A consequence of this being that the Invasion location could only be known to the Normans by the nearest castle. In this case Pevensey. As we shall see it would be impossible for the army to land at Pevensey Castle or town and return along the coast in the time scale involved. The conclusion is therefore drawn that Pevensey in the context of the Bayeux Tapestry was *'the area of Pevensey'*. Once this simple observation is understood all the historical manuscripts become correct, with no ambiguity. The only ambiguity in those texts is in the misunderstandings of those who read them now, by drawing conclusions based upon modern understanding of Pevensey as a town, as opposed to the geographical area of the south coast of England in 1066.

Along the edge of the ship shown in Plate 9 we can see 8 shields are placed in the front half and 5 in the rear. The same shield formation is shown on the other ship in the same sequence, to the right of William's ship. In this and the other Invasion sections horses are shown inside the ships, with their heads below the level of the men transporting them, confirming that they must have been tethered and tied down.

On the basis that these matters, as portrayed, were accurate within the bounds of the ability of the designer of the Tapestry to portray them, the conclusion would be an estimate of the number of men involved based upon the ratio of men and horses to ships. The Tapestry shows 7 ships of the smaller 4/5 man type and 5 ships of the 13 shield type. Using the same ratio of ships and men to 696 ships (Wace's estimate) the total invasion task force would have consisted of 290 large and 406 small ships.

On the assumption that the 13 shield (large ships) hold 13 men the estimate works out as follows:

AS SHOWN ON TAPESTRY	AS SHOWN ON TAPESTRY	AS SHOWN ON TAPESTRY	AS PROJECTED WITH 696 ships	AS PROJECTED WITH 696 ships
LARGE	8	10	464	580
LARGE	8	8	464	464
LARGE	5	4	290	232
LARGE	10	-	580	-
LARGE	10	-	580	-
SMALL	2	3	116	174
SMALL	4	-	232	-
SMALL	5	-	290	-
SMALL	5	-	290	-
SMALL	2	4	116	232
SMALL	4	2	232	116
SMALL	4	2	232	116
TOTAL	67	33	3886	1914

This gives a total of approximately 3,886 men, with 1914 horses for knights. Alternatively if the Tapestry is portraying these scenes on the basis of shields, representing one man per shield and a similar number of shields are held along the unseen side of the ship, then the number of men increases by a further 1,160 men. This brings the total to 5,046 men with 1914 horses, assuming all other supplies were loaded in the vessels. This compares favourably with other authoritative estimates[69].

These numbers are further endorsed by the actual logistics of conducting a landing of this size in one day. Sir James Ramsay confirms in his book The Foundations of England[70] that in 1415 it took three days for Henry to land 8 - 10,000 men at Harfleur. It would therefore be reasonable to expect William's fleet to be smaller than this.

The ships themselves appear to be Viking in style and designed with detachable heads that fitted at the prow and stern. The Icelandic Law[71] prescribed that people approaching new lands from the sea should not have ships with heads on them. If they had heads fitted at sea they should be removed before landfall, in order not to frighten the land spirits.

The practice of removing the heads prior to landfall can be seen to be enacted within the Tapestry. It shows all the ships with removable heads and at the point of landfall the heads have been duly removed (see next chapter below). An excavation of what was believed to be a semi fossilised remains of a head was sent to the Maritime Museum. It was deemed to be too decayed to confirm. This is a photograph of the excavated item taken from the inlet where William is believed to have landed:

(50a)

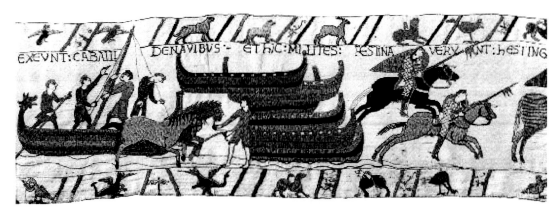

As the horses disembark the artist has deliberately drawn the lighter horse on the left leaving with one leg still in the ship, as the portable mast is removed. This is a clear indication that the horses needed to be tethered, with legs tied, in order to be able to make the journey in such small vessels. William was the first general of his day to bring his horses with him in this way without ramps and the sight of so many mounted knights must have come to the English as a great surprise. It was the English tradition to fight on foot, so bringing large numbers of mounted cavalry would have a great impact upon the balance of power in any assault. In consequence I believe it is correct to assume that the author of the Tapestry would ensure that the transportation method and delivery of this new and powerful concept of naval invasion, with horses, was correctly presented, when it was such an important factor in the success of the Invasion.

At this point the ships can be seen beached all in a line, side by side, exactly as described by Wace. This is where the landing happens with the words '. . . *the soldiers hurried to Hastings to requisition food*'. **Hastings is named as the Invasion site** at the point where the landing takes place.

Chapter 20: PLATE 11 Three houses/farm

The landing sequence shows the arrival of the Invasion force in an agricultural community. There are three houses shown high on the Tapestry possibly indicating that the site was low and overlooked by three properties(72). Each house has a different construction. One appears to be brick and tile, one wood lath and thatch with the third lath and tile. The presence of farm animals indicates landing in an agricultural area that is farmed.

Next follows the serving of the first meal, after the erection of the wooden fort that they are reported to have brought with them. This plate shows the first fort the Normans built, as two towers connected by a roof, which could be constructed from parts of the dismantled ships. This would support Wace's claim that the ships were dismantled. It would clearly be a logical thing to do, as the timbers from so many ships would form a readily accessible timber source, with which to build a fort. These defences can be seen with what may be the oar ports intact, in the cross section, exactly as portrayed earlier (Plate 9 and Plate 10) as white holes in black timber.

Placing the foot of the tower upon the base of the Tapestry leads me to believe this site to be at the bottom of the hill described in the Chronicle of Battle Abbey and Wace's Roman de Rou. The coloured curved strips, seen behind the fort, could also indicate a hill. These strips are I believe a diagrammatic way of showing the way that farmers sowed crops across fields, to allow ploughing by oxen, as demonstrated by strip farming in early agriculture. This seems a logical explanation, but does not satisfactorily explain the existence of a projection at the top of the curve. Whilst not apparent on most reproductions in print it is very obvious when viewed in person at the Bayeux gallery.

This 'nipple', as I shall call it, makes further inference to the fact that the strips may not have been meant to be interpreted as a hill, but some form of roof. The fact that it matches the planking on the Invasion boats may be just co-incidence. All that is certain is that the designers wished to draw this particular item to our attention.

There then follows a meal where two sets of people are dining:

The first, on the left of the above (not shown), are using their shields as a table raised above the normal ground level, illustrating the resourceful use of materials brought with them. The second dining scene shown above appears to be at a similar elevation, but this time in a circular room. This scene is very important in understanding the events of that day. It has been suggested that the presentation is of a circular table. I do not believe this is the case, as the artist is showing an important scene, which took place on the day of the landing, confirmed by Wace's manuscript. It illustrates a number of stages of the same meal in one picture, demonstrating the skill of the originators, to save time in production and achieve the maximum impact. The fact that the table is tapered indicates that it has been specifically designed to show some form of perspective, which in turn means in my view that the room was round, rather than the table.

The man in front is a servant with hand basin and towel for hand washing. Bishop Odo is the dominant figure blessing the food. The duke sits at the right of the Bishop, with one hand in a dish taking the meal. The man the other side of Odo is signalling that the meal is over and it is time to leave. There is only one implement on the table and that is a knife, the only eating implement of the age.

An important aspect of this section of the Tapestry is that the landing sequence, when seen in total, is a continuous event up to this point. Bishop Odo is shown with a fish on the table, together with fish in front of one or possibly two of the other guests. This provides almost conclusive evidence that these events took place on a Friday, when clerics abstained from meat; a tradition of the Catholic Church that persists to this day. Bishops may not always do so now, but they did then. The 29th September was the Friday in question, the day of the landing; therefore this meal must have been taken in the Norman camp on the first day or night of the Invasion, as also confirmed by Wace. The Saxon Chronicles, which we shall look at in the next chapter, provide very little evidence about the Invasion, other than confirming that the Normans left St Valery on the night of Thursday 28th September. This is confirmed in the Carmen, where it states:

'The feast of Michael(73) was about to be celebrated throughout the world when God granted everything according to your desire'.

The Bayeux Tapestry provides us with a unique detail that could easily be over looked. There was not enough time nor tide for the invaders to have landed in the morning at Pevensey town and then sailed or marched on to Hastings to arrive there on the same day as the landing (which was the Friday). The reason for showing the bishop eating fish, whilst the other men ate provisions, was to confirm the bishop's position as spiritual leader.

In many respects this picture in the Tapestry takes on the spiritual aspirations of the last supper, with Bishop Odo occupying the leading roll. The meal was a significant event, since Wace reports the same supper. It was known to everyone, at the time, that this took place on the day of the landing and this was a Friday. This is the reason for a fish on the table in front of the bishop, whilst the normal men ate chicken. The consequence of this analysis is that contrary to previous historical thinking the Bayeux Tapestry provides further unexpected and it could be argued incontrovertible proof, by virtue of the logistics of the day, that Hastings was the landing site.

Chapter 22: PLATE 13 Defences

The text here states: *'He ordered defences dug at Hastings'*. This time two fortifications can be seen. One is at the top of a hill, seen behind the men digging, consisting of two towers with what appears to be a wooden balustrade on the top of a hill. The style of the ground is illustrated in what is probably a strip farming format, as we have described previously. The men are digging at the bottom of this hill adjacent to a further picture of the two-towered fort. This has two windows in each tower, suggesting we are being shown the same fort that is illustrated at Plate 12, but later in the week, when they have consolidated their position, by building a second fortification at the top of the hill adjacent to them. Not only is this logical, but it confirms the reinstatement of forts (in the plural) mentioned in the Carmen text. One fort positioned at the bottom and one at the top of the same hill.

It is important to note that the defence work is being conducted at the lower fort, which was presumably close to the port. This is to the right of the lower fort, and at the bottom of the hill. It should also be noted that the diagrammatic view of the lower fort shows that the foot of the tower is terraced or has been earthed up, since the terracing does not cross the bottom of the tower. William is shown on an adjacent elevated dias indicating a commanding position over the site as he receives news of Harold.

The final scene that we shall look at in the Bayeux Tapestry shows a house being set on fire, with a woman and child escaping. It is worth pointing out that the graphical approach to the agricultural strips that appear on the main hill (Plate 13) also appear in the front middle section of this stylised house. The construction style of this building shown here, and the first house shown high up on the Tapestry, in Plate 11, seems unlikely to be coincidence. I believe it shows the burning of the first house (or manor house) at the top of the hill overlooking the site of the camp. The woman and child are illustrated as being shown safe in the bottom fort, which is under construction. The decorative top of the lower fort can be seen adjacent to the hands of the men with the torches. These same decorative features can be seen on the same image to their right, which I believe illustrates the same fort at a later stage of construction, at the centre of the image, at approximately the same elevation.

The lower fort is now shown after nearly two weeks occupation and enhancement. It is referred to in the Tapestry as Hastings. The Tapestry does not attempt to explain whether this is the town of Hastings. The attention of the designer is solely concerned with the events of the day at the camp and it is illustrated accordingly.

The two towers are shown in all their glory and we are shown an effective 3D view of the fort, in the only way the artist at that time knew how. Perspective was added, as has been done throughout the Tapestry, by the effect of slanting connecting roofs. In this case the large central tower, with a tile type of roof, is either at the front of the picture or the back depending upon how viewed. A large thinner tower is to the right, at the rear, with the main exit door adjacent to the right hand tower. The text reads:

'Here the soldiers left Hastings'

On the left side of the fort is a lower balustrade with the earth banked up against the wall at the foot of the tower. There is possible terracing where the door leaves the fort and in the centre of the main tower can be seen a mound, which I believe to be a mound that may be a grave site. I have as yet seen no logical explanation of this item.

All these matters are important for identification of the correct site of the forts and the authentication of the correct landing site.

In conclusion the Bayeux Tapestry provides a host of information that cannot be found anywhere else concerning the landing site. At the same time it endorses many aspects of the text already covered.

The main points are that the Invasion fleet came in two sizes of ships that were very much smaller than might be expected, with some not much larger than a big canoe. One of them could be expected to have the remains of a brass boy still affixed to either the stern or prow holding a bow, a trumpet or a horn. The ships themselves should be identifiable as having removable masts, with the appropriate fittings. If the masts were to be found one could have a brass lantern attached. The size of these ships would allow for horses to be able to disembark, without the use of ramps. They would have a hull that is four or five planks deep, with shallow draught in a Viking style. The site of the landing was at the bottom of a hill and at least three buildings or manors were close to the top of the hill overlooking the site.

The first fort that was built was reported to be mainly from the prefabricated assembly, which it is reported they brought with them. It was probably on an established farm and consisted of two towers with the later addition of a fosse or ditch. The dining area was raised and William's seat of residence on the site was in a position of authority. The towers of the lower fort had either been earthed up from the outside or terracing had been dug. Looking at the site from the perspective of the landing the fort was not directly below the hill, but situated at the bottom of the hill and slightly to the right, whilst the upper fort with a palisade was directly on top of the same hill.

Lastly a house was burnt and a grave may be situated inside the fort boundary, with the main exit on the right hand side looking from the same viewpoint as all the other pictures. The total expeditionary force may have been as little as 4,000 or 5,000 men with up to 2,000 horses. In consequence the camp would probably be smaller than previously anticipated. The most significant contribution that the Tapestry makes to our knowledge of the events of that time is the picture of Bishop Odo enjoying a fish supper on the day of the landing at Hastings. This would confirm the fact that the fleet arrived at Hastings on 29th September 1066, the day after their night-time departure from St Valery, making it impossible for the landing to have been in Pevensey earlier that same day. It confirms that any visit to Pevensey followed the Hastings landing, as confirmed by Wace in his manuscript description. Taken with the fact that Hastings is named at the point of the landing and no geographical or other features within the Tapestry identify with Pevensey, there can be no doubt that Hastings was in fact the landing site. This is information that may seem to be inconsequential to the common man, but logistics define what an army of 5000 men with 2,000 horses can do. The tide and time was against the version of events we have learnt in school. Now we find that the correct version given to us in six major manuscripts is authenticated by the Bayeux Tapestry.

Chapter 24: THE ANGLO-SAXON CHRONICLE (1042 -1154)

The Anglo-Saxon Chronicles are in fact a number of chronicles compiled progressively into what is known colloquially as The Anglo Saxon Chronicle. They are considered similar to each other to be thought as versions of the same source. They vary sufficiently from one to the other for each to warrant individual study.

The Chronicles that I have looked at are called the Abingdon, Worcester and Peterborough Chronicles. Since the Abingdon Chronicle ends before the Norman Invasion I have not taken it into account. The other two compress into less than a paragraph their version of events concerning the Norman Invasion. Taken in isolation there appears nothing to add that is not known. Taken with the evidence of the Bayeux Tapestry they provide further evidence that the Invasion took place at Hastings.

The Worcester Chronicle dated as the year 1066 states very little other than:

'The Count William came from Normandy to Pevensey on Michaelmas Eve, and as soon as they were able to move on they built a castle at Hastings.'

The first impression would appear to endorse Pevensey as a landing site, but this I believe is misleading. The Chronicle uses the expression *'came from Normandy'* in relation to making towards

Pevensey *'to Pevensey'*. It clearly does not say they landed at Pevensey and here a valuable distinction is made in the text. If the Chronicler had meant to say *'The Normans landed at Pevensey'* the structure of the description would have been completely different. The text confirms the Normans built a fortification at Hastings and almost by way of an excuse, as well as inference, says that they did not stay at Pevensey, if at all.

The important factor about the Worcester Chronicle is the confirmation that they came from Normandy on the eve of Michaelmas. Michaelmas was on Friday 29th September, confirming the Bayeux Tapestry evidence that the Normans departed from St Valery on the evening of Thursday 28th September 1066. Sailing over night they arrived at the English coast, upon the rising tide, between 9am and 12am the following morning.

Further confirmation is obtained from the Peterborough Chronicle which states: *'Meanwhile Count William landed at Hastings on Michaelmas Day'* giving the same set of events from a different perspective. In this version Hastings is directly named as the arrival point and the landing date is named as Michaelmas Day - the 29th September.

The Anglo Saxon Chronicle is considered by many to be the most reliable of documents, because more than one version exists and all are written from the point of view of the local inhabitants, rather than the invaders. Taken with the other highly credible version of events, portrayed in visual format by the Bayeux Tapestry, there can be no room for doubt that Hastings, and in particular the Port of Hastings, was the actual landing site. The evidence is highly suggestive that Pevensey may have been intended to be the landing site, but more than this does not stand up to close scrutiny, when cross referenced with other contemporary documents.

Florence of Worcester, a monk of the twelfth century, using the Anglo-Saxon Chronicles as a source, refers to the same event stating: *'It was reported that they had landed at Pevensey'*. Here a clear distinction has been made between this and the original Worcester text, inserting the reference to it being *'reported'*. This could be interpreted as meaning that the original reference was a report rather than a confirmed fact. This effectively amends and clarifies the earlier text, without undermining its supposed authenticity.

If the Anglo-Saxon Chronicles are to be believed, and I have no reason to doubt their authenticity, along with the Bayeux Tapestry, the Normans landed at Hastings on the morning of Michaelmas (Friday 29th September 1066). One Chronicle confirms this whilst the other is more ambiguous and has to date been misinterpreted. It was not possible, because of the tide, for the Normans to have landed at Pevensey and sailed on to Hastings in the same day. The tide was not only against them, but more importantly the wind was also. This had been described as favourable for the crossing and therefore from the southeast. The suggestion that Pevensey could be the landing site is an historical fallacy, used to try to support one line of text by William of Poitiers, whose source is unclear. That support is out of step with all the other historical reports and based upon a misunderstanding of the medieval use of the term Pevensey to mean the area between the castles of Pevensey and Dover. Apart from this one item in Poitiers and the totally unreliable Jumieges text, suggesting Pevensey as the landing site, there are no other contradictions.

It is my belief that the evidence of spoken word, as opposed to the written word, is what has taken the Pevensey argument to where it is today. Poitiers copied what he heard, stating that *'they all reached Pevensey, and there without opposition they freely disembarked'*. If Pevensey was the stated destination there was no reason to believe that this was not what actually happened. The text goes on to state *'Rejoicing greatly at having secured a safe landing, the Normans seized and fortified first Pevensey and then Hastings'* It is my understanding that this sentence is one of the most misunderstood statements in English History. It has been taken by historians to endorse the earlier statement of Pevensey as the landing site, yet this is not what Poitiers actually says. Firstly he states that they (the Normans) secured a safe landing place (omitting to say that this is in fact Hastings). After this he states that they *'fortified Pevensey and then Hastings.'* Taken with Wace's description this is almost certainly correct. The morning after the Invasion was the day upon which Pevensey was attacked according to Wace.

At that time the Hastings landing was not consolidated and in consequence the order of events given by Poitiers is completely correct, without undermining any other version we have discussed. The paragraph in question relates to the act of fortifying the area. This was concluded at Pevensey first, because the castle at Pevensey was already in existence. At Hastings the consolidation process took some two weeks prior to the battle. It is therefore not valid to support Poitiers over Wace or Wace over the Carmen. Each has a valid statement to make based upon what they believed to be true. If there is any element of doubt it is in Poitiers for being out of step with all the others, making an ambiguous report.

The further we are removed from the events of the time the more difficult it is to prove one way or the other and hence the importance of correcting past misinterpretation. It is my belief that the written manuscript evidence we have studied provides the only correct basis upon which to base a hypothesis. If that hypothesis is true it will be borne out by the archaeological and geographic evidence. It simply is not satisfactory to rely upon the statement that no evidence of this nature exists, because a thousand years has elapsed. The Invasion took place in 1066 and as every schoolboy knows man leaves traces where ever he goes and under all circumstances. Any thesis based upon the reliance of theory without practical, material evidence is not worth the paper upon which it is written and I rest my case for the manuscript evidence, with that over-riding proviso.

Chapter 25: CONCLUSION OF SITE REQUIREMENTS

According to Manuscript Study

The eight manuscripts that we have looked at were all written within 150 years of the Invasion. They were written in days when the written word was almost exclusively the province of kings and the clergy. In consequence oral history in the form of spoken tradition, poems and song formed an important link in the way an important story, such as the events of the landing, were handed from generation to generation. In view of this it is to be expected that details that commenced as certain facts in the course of time get changed as they pass from generation to generation.

This has been assumed to account for the discrepancies between the Jumieges and Poitiers texts, regarding the naming of the site as Pevensey. This I believe is a false assumption based upon relatively recent understanding of the way information is passed. Details held in the great libraries were studiously copied and sources recited word for word the stories their fathers told. The art of story telling was at that time considered one of the great arts, handed down in a pure and lasting form.

This explains why Wace's manuscript written so long after Poitiers' contains far more detail. Not only do I believe the detail to be remarkably correct, given the number of years between the source and its creator, but there are many facets that contribute information that is not available anywhere else. Recent English 'thinking' has put an interpretation upon this to infer Wace's 'unreliability'. I believe that the evidence of all the manuscripts prove conclusively that in almost all respects, regarding the actual Invasion site, all the writers where correct in all material detail. This is quite remarkable by today's standard, where a newsletter can change completely before it has had time to travel around the world.

In this respect it must be remembered that we cannot make reasoned judgements as to 'reliability' or otherwise regarding these manuscripts, applying rules of the twentieth century. We are simply out of time and historians who make assumptions upon beliefs based upon today's logic can become severely unstuck. The Norman Invasion is a subject upon which almost all historians of any note have a limited knowledge. They have probably read Poitiers and possibly one or two of the other sources, dismissing the other texts as 'unreliable', without keeping up with recent developments, or addressing the issue from another perspective. It simply is not acceptable for an author to have his work discredited in one country, because the story as told does not fit a current historian's thesis, yet in another country, such as France, to be considered the absolute authority.

In consequence I do not believe that any of the manuscripts that we have looked at can be dismissed as 'unreliable'. The reasons given in the past were unfounded and based upon inaccuracies now corrected. Since this is the case I have not considered relevant the comments, or considerable discussion that this subject has raised in the Victorian era. I have certainly excluded any reference to recent authors who have not taken into account all the available sources, although they are listed in the bibliography at the end of the first part of this book.

Applying pure logic, the documents we have looked at must contain the key to the mystery of where the Invasion took place. History to date has got it wrong. How do I know this? The answer is for all to see, should they care enough to look for their own proof. They will find, as I did, that there is no physical proof of substance one way or the other of either the Invasion site or the site of the Battle of Hastings. No weapons, no wooden fort, no ships, no archaeological remains of the Invasion in Pevensey or Hastings. In fact there are no real artefacts at all, leading to wonder whether the Invasion actually took place. Of course this does not mean that none exist. The hypothesis that this text promotes relies upon the firm belief that if you look in the right place archaeological evidence must be found. If I am correct the long missing evidence will be found. If not the arguments presented here will be proven worthless and in due course pass the way of all unproven theses.

Having retained a degree of decorum in presenting my reasoned argument to date I cannot resist a slight dig, if that is the right word, at the established view that Norman remains disintegrate in the acid soil of the region. This is of course convenient poppycock, since archaeologists have been removing remains and relics from the soil of the area dating back to the Iron Age. Proof of events in the past is not confined to the sole retrieval of iron objects, which certainly may have decayed a considerable amount. It is well known that even iron objects, particularly larger ones, such as axe heads and boat parts, leave an easily recoverable image in the soil, as the ions migrate and are replaced by phosphates. The fact that none have been found at Hastings or Pevensey adds weight to the inevitable conclusion that no one has looked in the right place.

Prior to publication I sent the manuscript of this book to a number of eminent historians in order to make sure that the facts as presented where correct. I was surprised to be taken to task over the fact that I could not list those eminent historians who may have looked for artefacts at the recognised sites, but failed to find any. It appeared to me that this was taking the onus of proof too far and missing the over all point. Namely if evidence was there to be found it could only be found at the landing and battle site. I am certain that many hundreds of qualified people have looked over the years, but with nothing to report they could not publish their results. There have been exhaustive digs at both Hastings and Pevensey castle, not to mention Battle Abbey. Yet it is my clear understanding that there is not one archaeological item that can be dated to the landing or battle.

It might be wise at this juncture to remind my readers that the writer is not, as I stated earlier, an academic. In consequence perhaps I have a sceptical nature that demands something more than theory, before accepting what I have been told. Without wishing to trivialise the enormous amount of work involved in this project, or indeed undermine the seriousness of the work of those noble men who spend their lives digging in ancient soil, it would seem appropriate for a media person such as myself to draw the reader's attention to the words of the world's most famous fictional archaeologist of all time. Our hero Indiana Jones in the Temple of Doom is confronted by a question about archaeology. There he states that 90% of archaeology is research in libraries and manuscripts. If that general conclusion is correct the work examined so far provides the reader with a good basis to start the real hunt for our *'Holy Grail'*. With that in mind I would now like to produce a summary of all the matters revealed in the source documents in a numbered list:

1) UNOPPOSED LANDING

The Bayeux Tapestry, The Carmen, Poitiers and Wace all agree that the landing was unopposed. This supports the theory that the landing was not at a town. It would be logical to conclude that if the landing were at a town site the devastation would have taken place to the fortifications and have been recorded. This did not happen and provides major support for landing in a rural environment

2) TOWN OF LANDING

According to Jumieges the Normans landed *'at Pevensey'* whilst Poitiers says they *'reached Pevensey'*. Neither uses the expression *'town of'* or similar explanation, leaving the conclusion that the area of Pevensey was a probable meaning. Poitiers extends the same sentence to say that they *'seized Pevensey and then Hastings'*. Both statements would be correct if the Normans knew the area between Pevensey castle and the Bulverhythe as Pevensey, along with the marsh. The Bulverhythe formed a natural boundary leaving Hastings in control of the peninsula to the east. In consequence it is possible to interpret both these documents in a way that supports a site that is neither in Hastings or Pevensey, but somewhere between the two.

If you take the view that Jumieges and Poitiers both meant the town of Pevensey then it can be seen that they are the only manuscripts of the era to propose this. Poitiers own qualification that they *'secured a safe landing place'* before the reference to seizing and fortifying Pevensey and Hastings weakens Pevensey as a possible site. In my view the total available manuscript evidence completely destroys the credibility of Poitiers claim that the Normans landed at the town of Pevensey.

Lined up in support of Hastings on the other side of the equation are six major works of the time. The Carmen says the camp site is at Hastings. The Chronicle of Battle Abbey says that the camp was *'at the port of Hastings'*. Wace confirms the landing *'near Hastings'* with Pevensey being visited the day after the landing. The Bayeux Tapestry names Hastings at the point of landing and finally we have the Saxon Chronicles detailing Hastings in one version with Pevensey in another.

Given that this Pevensey report is then amended by Florence of Worcester the weight of evidence is balanced in favour of a site that was at the port of Hastings.

3) CAMP BY OR NEAR SEA
Confirmed in Poitiers text as well as the references to a port by Wace, the Carmen and the Chronicle of Battle Abbey. It is logical to assume a port is by or near the sea.

4) CAMP AT A PORT
The Carmen names William's camp at *'the port of Hastings'*. The Chronicle of Battle Abbey does the same, whilst Wace says they *'steered to one port'*. As stated above Hastings holds more weight of manuscript evidence and is indirectly confirmed by a later Saxon Chronicle entry stating that *'right in front of the port'* where William's fleet landed *' stood a Castle handsome and strong'* and that William allowed knights to enter therein and garrison it for two years(74). Although not a direct confirmation of events it leads to a logical conclusion that the camp and castle were on the same site, when taken in conjunction with the Bayeux Tapestry evidence.

5) PORT CAPABLE OF HOLDING AT LEAST 696 SHIPS
Jumieges says 3,000 ships were involved over all, whilst Wace is more conservative with *'700 less four'*. Either proposal established an enormous undertaking for the resources of the day. In any event the port needed to be of a considerable size. It needed to be far larger than the area known as the port of Hastings, which is generally accepted to have been situated under the cliffs of the castle that survive to this day. It is assumed that as a result of the coastal erosion in the 12th and 13th centuries the old port can no longer be found. I dispute this, as I shall show later that the port of Hastings was located in the Combe Haven valley at least until 1094. This valley held the largest natural harbour in the south coast, second only to Poole harbour.

6) CAMP AT SITE OF A CALM BAY
The Carmen provides a number of clues to suggest a calm bay. Firstly they *'leave the sea behind them'*. This infers a passage into a waterway that was not part of the sea. Secondly the shores where guarded, suggesting more than one shore, which would be appropriate to a bay. Thirdly the same chronicle refers to a final landing place in a calm bay. Given the three separate references I do not believe this to be either a mistake by the author or an error in translation.

7) CAMP ADJACENT TO A LARGE SHORE

The Chronicle of Battle Abbey uses the expression *'extensively along the shore'* to describe where the ships were beached. The assumption that at least 696 ships were used in the Invasion fleet (and possibly 3,000) requires a very large shore. If each occupied only five meters and they were beached in a continuous line, without a break, the total shore line would be a minimum of three and a half kilometres, or possibly fifteen kilometres, if Jumieges estimate were correct.

8) THE SHIPS WERE SIDE BY SIDE
Wace says that they *'arrived and reached the shore together'*. The Bayeux Tapestry endorses this showing all the ships on the shore together at the point of landing. This ties in with the above point 7) confirming at least two miles of landing site required.

9) THEY BUILT A WOODEN FORT
Three manuscripts confirm this major point. These are The Chronicle of Battle Abbey, Wace and the Bayeux Tapestry. Wace even goes into great detail about the pins and frames that hold the fort together. At the time of the Invasion only Pevensey had a well established castle of stone construction. Evidence collected by Charles Dawson(75) in his book History of Hastings Castle makes this clear and is endorsed by J. H. Round in his article The Castles of the Conquest(76).

10) THE FORT HAD A DITCH (FOSSE)
The Bayeux Tapestry shows the construction of a ditch at the site of the lower fort. This is also confirmed by Wace as an event that takes place after the raid on Pevensey.

11) THERE WERE PREVIOUS FORTS AT THE SITE
This important observation is made by the Carmen. The Carmen's reference to *'dismantled forts'* at the site of the Invasion confirms the existence of more than one fort. The Bayeux Tapestry surprisingly confirms our new interpretation of the existence of two forts (in the plural) on the same site, further backing up the Carmen reference.

12) THE FORT WAS ON A HILL SITE
The formation of the Norman camp and Invasion site at a hill is one of the most certain facts concerning the events of the day. Four independent sources confirm this. The Chronicle of Battle Abbey names the camp at a *'hill called Hedgeland'*. The Bayeux Tapestry shows a hill behind the lower fort, with a further hill below the upper fort. Wace describes a hill nearby when describing the episode with the English spy who reports to Harold. He also confirms that the duke addressed

his men, whilst in their camp, from a hill. This conclusive cross referencing shows the camp and Invasion site to be next to a hill that cannot be found in the Pevensey Bay area. It is an area devoid of hills of any note and certainly none with a fort at the top and bottom.

13) THE SHIPS WERE EARTHED UP
This item, together with the following two items appear to be in direct contradiction, one with the other. Only the actual site of the Invasion will resolve the mystery of how three separate accounts of what happened to the Invasion fleet can all be correct. There is no conflict in each account, since they are all correct. The Carmen claims that the ships were earthed up presumably to avoid desertion.

14) THE SHIPS WERE DISMANTLED
Wace makes the claim that the ships were *'dismantled and drawn ashore'*. This appears to have some possible confirmation in the way that the forts are drawn in the Bayeux Tapestry. The oar ports on the ships being reproduced as part of the construction on the new forts.

15) THE SHIPS WERE BURNT
The Chronicle of Battle Abbey records a further version where William has ordered *'most of the ships'* to be burnt. This appears to be a rather unlikely turn of events. Timber ships would have an intrinsic value for construction purposes, when faced with the logistics of supplying food and shelter to a large invasion force. To burn such a rich source of available material would not appear to be very sensible and in consequence an observation that you would expect to be flawed. It would be expected that such an observation was made to supply a reason why no ships from the Invasion fleet had until now been found. However he may well have burnt his own boat as a symbolic statement to his men that they would not return without winning.

16) THE SHIPS WERE SMALL
The Bayeux Tapestry provides a number of visual clues that provide evidence to support the fact that the main ships used in the Invasion were small by current day standards.

17) WILLIAM'S SHIP HAD A FIGURINE
The Bayeux Tapestry and Wace both confirm this point, although they differ as to which end of the ship the figurine was attached. Taylor's manuscript confirms the same point, indicating the inevitable conclusion that if this figurine could be identified the actual landing site would be proven.

18) THE SHIPS HAD VIKING TYPE PROWS
The Bayeux Tapestry is a unique witness to the Viking style of the ships and appears to bear out what was known to be the likely seafaring roots of the Invaders.

19) THE PROWS HAD REMOVABLE HEADS
The Bayeux Tapestry also confirms that the heads on the prow of the Invasion ships were removable. The tradition of removing them before landfall was established through Icelandic law, popular throughout the Scandinavian countries. The Normans being descended from the North Men of Scandinavia inherited both the law and the design of their ships.

20) THE CAMP WAS NEXT TO OR AT A MANOR HELD BY THE KING
This conclusion is a new interpretation of the Wace story, where the knight who reports the Invasion does so to Harold *'his lord'*.

21) THE INITIAL LANDING SITE WAS SMALL
The Carmen makes the point that the initial landing place was small by virtue of the fact that they *'gained control over no great space'*.

22) THERE WAS A PLAIN NEAR BY THE LANDING SITE/ WATER SUPPLY
Wace says that they *'passed into the plain with their lances raised'* upon landing. The form of the plain is not expanded upon, but it is reasonable to expect that the relatively large number of men and horses would require such a place to be fed and watered. It would also be essential for there to be fresh water, enough to sustain this force at any such site. This observation, if correct, would also disqualify the traditional Hastings Castle site, since it could never be described as a plain. The most recent survey of the cricket ground[77], commissioned by Hastings Borough Council in order to build the Hastings Shopping Centre, confirms that the area below the castle was in fact a fresh water marsh, which is now and always has been behind a shingle bank. It seems highly unlikely that a port would be built on land that was in front of marshy ground. The hypothesis that the port was washed away by erosion is confirmed by this report to be nonsense. To camp on such a site would be wholly illogical. Whilst it may suit the Hastings Council to commission such a report to validate building a shopping centre on the site, it does nothing to further the historic claim that this was the place William the Conqueror originally landed and camped.

23) THE NEIGHBOURHOOD WAS LAID TO WASTE

The Carmen and Poitiers both use the expression *'laid to waste'* when describing the area around the camp. I do not believe it is coincidence that both texts, originating so close to the time of the Invasion, should use the same phraseology. The fact that this same phrase is used consistently in the Domesday Survey provides conclusive evidence that the area around the Norman camp suffered severe destruction.

24) THE GROUND WAS UNEVEN AND WATERLOGGED

Poitiers remarks on the roughness of the ground at William's camp. The conclusion as to water logging was as a consequence of the need to dismount upon returning to camp, together with Wace's story about William falling at the landing site. This would be expected, as a result of at least three weeks bad weather prior to departure from St Valery.

25) ONE CAMP WAS AT THE BOTTOM OF AN AGRICULTURAL FIELD

The Bayeux Tapestry in my opinion shows two camps. This is a new interpretation of the evidence presented by the Bayeux Tapestry. The one at the bottom of the hill has agricultural strips behind it in two different places when showing the same site. The confirmation of the site being a working farm is shown by reference to the farm animals at the scene of the landing. This is also indirectly supported by the universal confirmation that the landing was unopposed, since an unopposed landing would infer land with a low inhabitation density - such as agricultural land.

26) THE OTHER CAMP WAS AT THE TOP OF THE SAME FIELD

The Bayeux Tapestry shows a second camp with a balustrade running between two towers on the top of the same hill, with agricultural strips below it.

27) THE BOTTOM CAMP WAS TO THE RIGHT OF THE BOTTOM OF THE HILL

The Bayeux Tapestry shows the camp at the bottom of the hill, to the right of the main hill, as seen from the landing site perspective. The landing site is to the left of the lower camp.

28) THE FORT AT THE BOTTOM OF THE HILL HAD TWO TOWERS

The Bayeux Tapestry shows the main fort at the bottom of the hill with two towers connected by a balustrade.

29) THERE WAS A MOUND BETWEEN THE TWO TOWERS

The Bayeux Tapestry shows a mound between the two towers at the bottom fort. This could possibly be a grave site.

30) THE TOWERS AND FORT WALLS HAD A TERRACED BOTTOM

The Bayeux Tapestry consistently shows the construction of the bottom fort with terracing at the bottom of the walls.

31) THERE WAS A CIRCULAR DINING ROOM

The Bayeux Tapestry shows the first dining scene described by Wace. In it William and his entourage are eating their first meal in a circular dining room.

32) THE EXIT WAS TO THE RIGHT OF THE FORT LOOKING FROM THE SEA

The Bayeux Tapestry shows the main exit from the lower fort (which is called *'Hastings'* in the text) is on the right hand side, as seen from the same perspective as all the rest of the Tapestry, looking towards the shore from the sea.

33) THE DUKE'S QUARTERS WERE ELEVATED AT THE SITE

The Bayeux Tapestry shows William's position seated at the main camp in a raised position.

34) THE CAMP AT THE TOP OF THE HILL HAD TWO TOWERS AND A CONNECTING PALISADE

The Bayeux Tapestry shows the camp at the top of the hill to have two towers connected by a balustrade.

35) THE CAMP HAD CHAPELS IN ADJACENT FIELDS UPON DEPARTURE.

Wace observes that chapels were set up the night prior to departure to battle.

36) THE LANDING SITE WAS LOW DOWN BELOW THREE HOUSES

The Bayeux Tapestry shows the landing site to be low down, below three houses laid in a row, either together or upon a ridge. These may be a diagrammatic way of showing the site of the landing to be adjacent to or within the view of three manors or manor houses.

37) THERE IS A GRAVE AT THE SITE

Two major sources confirm a burial at the site of the Norman camp for both Harold and the Normans killed at the battle.

These sources are Poitiers and the Carmen, with Wace stating that he does not know if the story that Harold was taken to Waltham was true.

38) THE GRAVE HAS A MARKER STONE
Poitiers and the Carmen independently describe in almost the same words the inscription on the stone placed upon Harold's grave.

39) THE CAMP IS IN THE MANOR OF CROWHURST OR WILTING
The Domesday Survey provides conclusive evidence that the most likely manors for the Norman camp site were where the value of the manor recovered least in the 20 years since the Invasion. This suggests the greatest damage by the invading army was at either Crowhurst or Wilting.

40) THE SITE IS CALLED HEDGELAND
The Chronicle of Battle Abbey names William's camp as being at a place called Hedgeland.

The analysis of these eight manuscripts produces forty separately identifiable clues to the correct landing site. After examining the geographical and archaeological evidence we shall re-examine these forty points to establish how many have validity in relation to the proposed site.

Chapter 26: INCONSISTENCIES

Having examined a number of translations of historical documents relating to the Norman Invasion it cannot have escaped the reader's notice that each account studied appears to contain material that is at best inconsistent with the others, or at worst contains elements that must be invention, intentional or otherwise. The Invasion fleet could not have landed at Pevensey and subsequently built a fort there (Jumieges and Poitiers) if Wace and the Carmen are correct in naming the fort and landing at Hastings. The evidence of six major documents point conclusively to Hastings, yet history has dictated, in recent years, the acceptance of Jumieges and Poitiers account as the correct version. It would therefore be a good idea to ask the question why this has happened.

The answer, like all good mysteries, appears to be because each element of each manuscript is open to question at a number of different levels. Until the nineteenth century no-one appears to have taken much interest[78] in the matter. The monks at Battle Abbey had written their version nearly eight hundred years before. The Abbey had grown upon the false charters[79], flourished and died. The town of Battle grew around the Abbey, perpetuating the myth embodied in the Abbey chronicle. Meanwhile the Normans took over Pevensey after the Invasion and built a fine keep within the walls of the far more ancient castle. The castle at Hastings on the other hand was commissioned by the Count of Eu, with the new town of Hastings developed within its protection. Over the following half millennium these objects of Norman power faded into virtual oblivion, leaving a heritage that the Battle Abbey document supported long after the Normans had gone. During those eight centuries that passed, from the Duke landing until the Victorian age, little changed or mattered. Only when the enquiring minds of the Victorians arrived on the scene did the issue of who did what and when arise.

In 1846 the railway came to Hastings and was connected to London. This was the age of enlightenment and like all good commercial enterprises of the day the railway owners realised the exploitation value that Hastings provided. Suddenly Hastings became the province of railway marketing, to a nation that had little in the way of education, and no ability to question the claims made by the tourist industry. The railway was by the standards of the day big business and it was not long before a branch line was installed from Battle Abbey, through Crowhurst, to Bexhill as well as along the coast to Pevensey.

Such was the commercial success of the railway enterprise that when a whale beached itself near Pevensey in 1865 the publicity department of the London and Brighton and South Coast railway immediately advertised the fact in the local paper, accompanied by the legend that this was at a place known as Norman's Bay. This, according to British Rail, was the actual place where William the Conqueror landed – Norman was an appropriate name for the whale. A station was hurriedly built at the site to accommodate the masses of visitors who initially came to see the whale and who now could experience history at first hand. Thus we owe British Rail the honour of fooling a gullible Victorian nation into parting with its hard earned money, as a result of a marketing campaign built upon a total invention. This may be nothing new, by modern standards, but was never suspected in 1846. No-one ever considered that Norman's Bay was in the middle of an area that was under water in 1066 and to the visitors of the day this was not a matter for query. As the tourist industry grew in Pevensey, Hastings and Battle the marketing legend slowly became fact, not only in the minds of the public, but also the academics of the day.

In 1879 Freeman wrote what he believed was the first definitive history of the Norman Conquest[80]. This initiated a furious debate concerning which source documents he had used were reliable by academics of the time[81]. In his enthusiasm for the subject Freeman appeared to expand texts from the manuscripts that he had studied to suit his particular view of history. In so doing Freeman did more to undermine, what had previously been considered the most authentic source documents of the period, than any other. One striking example of Freeman's audacity was to rename the Battle of Hastings the battle of Senlac. The authority for this name was provided by Orderic, a monk who lived in Normandy. Orderic reported the name some time after the Invasion. Whilst there appears to be no known reason why Orderic named the site as Senlac, Freeman used this unsubstantiated observation to make his own mark on history, by changing the name in one stroke.

Like many such circumstances time has a way of levelling out the inconsistencies and putting the record straight. This happened some thirty years later when J. H. Round launched his blistering attacks in the pages of the Sussex Archaeological Collection between the years 1895 and 1899. Round appeared to win the day due to his methodical analysis of Freeman's texts, conducted in vitriolic fashion, tearing apart each small inconsistency without the slightest consideration as to those that appeared in the documents which he held to be valid (Poitiers in particular). In consequence Round drew the inconsistencies in Freeman's writings to the attention of the Victorian academics who sought to know the historical truth. In so doing the fact that Freeman supported the Wace and Carmen texts resulted in Round's criticism of Freeman destroying the credibility of Wace and the Carmen, purely as a by-product of what now looks like nothing more than personal envy. Round rested his case squarely upon the fact that Freeman had drawn extensively upon the Wace manuscript, which is the most complete account of the events of the landing. Round took the view that there was one major error in Wace's work, which could never be reconciled. This being that upon the night of the battle each camp was in sight of the other. Everyone who had ever visited the site at Battle Abbey knew this could not be possible, since the geography could not allow each army to see the other from their respective camps, one at Hastings by the current castle and one the other side of Battle ridge. If such an obvious error could be made it was clear to Round that the Wace manuscript could not be authentic, since the detail that surrounded the events of the night before the battle are extended over many pages. This led Round to the conclusion that the whole of the Wace document was fiction and in consequence Freeman's writings were not worth the paper written on. This is a logical and powerful argument, but only provided the two camps were not within sight. I shall show in part two of this document that Round was mistaken in this matter and in consequence the whole basis of his criticism of Freeman was flawed. Now, with the benefit of modern archaeological methods it will be shown that Wace was correct. Wace will take his position as the pre-eminent authority on the Battle of Hastings and Round, like his archenemy, will find his works removed from the shelves in what will appear to be a re-enactment of perfect Karma.

I do not wish to cloud the issue at this stage by being sidetracked into validating any one manuscript as opposed to another. What makes the work in front of you so compulsive in it's argument, after you have seen all the evidence, is that there is not one inconsistency that cannot be explained, given the identification of the correct camp site. I shall therefore address the matters relating to the landing until the time is right to reveal the answers to the above conundrum.

Given the evidence and arguments presented at the end of the nineteenth century historians had no alternative but to accept the Chronicle of Battle Abbey, Jumieges and Poitiers versions as the only reliable documents. These endorsed popular opinion and at the same time had a single consistency in that they name Pevensey. The fact that you needed to turn a blind eye to other glaring errors or inconsistencies between the different accounts was of no concern. J. H. Round had won his day and was hardly likely to draw attention to such matters. Pevensey could be supported by the use of the words '*dismantled forts*' by the Carmen, but at the same time the same document could be dismissed as unreliable when naming Hastings as the landing site.

As stated earlier much has happened since the beginning of the century in the world of academic research into the manuscripts involved. It is now held that the Carmen is not the fake that it was thought to be. This in turn raises the question as to whether the same may be true of Wace. I believe this to be the case for the reasons stated above. If I am correct historians must be prepared for the worst, since there is a logical conclusion that does not bear contemplation. This being that William the Conqueror did not engage Harold Godwinson on the other side of the ridge at Battle. The fact that not one single archaeological artefact has ever been found there might cause concern. None the less I shall put the evidence in front of you and leave it to you and others more qualified than I to adjudicate.

It may appear that the claims of this last paragraph may be too much to bear for those who only know the truth according to written history. At this stage it might be as well to remind them that until this very year Bosworth Field was commemorated in the wrong field and so those familiar with History (with a big H) will know that she has made a habit over the years of leading us astray, until such time as she seeks to reveal herself in all her glory. It is my view that the inconsistencies that we have looked at are History's way of telling us that all is not what it seems. Half the reports cannot be all correct and half all wrong. This is neither logical nor probable. History has drawn our attention to these matters in order that the error may be corrected. As stated earlier, time is a great leveller, and science an even better one.

I shall now look at the correct position of the Port of Hastings at the time of the Norman Invasion in order to support the claim that this is where the Norman landing site and camp is situated.

Chapter 27: THE PORT OF HASTINGS

It is my opinion that having personally examined the historical record of the most eminent sources relating to Hastings Castle and the town of Hasting[82], there is no conclusive evidence whatsoever that Hastings Port has ever been located in the area of land immediately below the current Hastings Castle. It is a matter of historic record that all these most eminent sources substantiate their claims by the words *'most probably located'* below Hastings Castle or words to this effect.

Charles Dawson, who wrote the most detailed study of the Castle and History of Hastings[83] states:

'there can be no question that harbours once existed at Pevensey, Bulverhythe, and Hastings, which have now vanished. **These points need critical examination. . .** '

He goes on further to confirm:

'In the absence of any detailed record, *it is impossible to give a precise description of the appearance of Hastings in early and medieval times. . . '.*

Dawson goes on to study all the known historical documents prior to the Invasion. He draws attention to the Charter of Offa dated as early as AD.795 making the point that it may possibly be a forgery, but confirming that:

'. . the ports of my possession which are in the same neighbourhood on the sea, Hastings and Pevensey, **with their salt works***'*

Further confirmation is found in the Confirmation of King Aedelwulfus AD.857 in which it is stated:

'that a monk of St. Denis had bitterly complained of the injuries which the kings men had miserably inflicted on the followers of the Saint in England, especially at Rotherfield, and in Hastings and Pevensey, **at their salt works***.* '

On their own these reports account for little, since they do not say one way or the other where the port in question is. The fact that they locate salt works in one and possibly two separate accounts confirms that the port in question could not be an open sea port, since salt works require draining. In fact these reports strongly suggest that the port of Hastings must have been located at the Combe Haven valley, adjacent to the Bulverhythe, where the only known salt works in the immediate district have ever been located.

The first report of Hastings Castle or Ceastra occurs in the Saxon Chronicle in 1050[84], when there is a reference to *'the men of Hastinga-Caestra'*. This should not be misinterpreted to mean a stone castle. Prior to the Normans the word *'Ceastra'* more likely referred to a fortified residence of the local chief, made of wood. In consequence the British Museum manuscript throws no further light on where this was located.

Dawson examined all the evidence prior to the Invasion, which was known, but still had to assume that the castle was the one drawn in the Bayeux Tapestry. He registered his own doubts[85] about the inconsistencies, but faced with no other apparent alternative concluded that they must be one and the same.

Having re-examined the record, as a result of the archaeological work, which I shall report later, I must conclude that Dawson drew the wrong conclusion, albeit for the best intention. He should have known that salt works could not geographically have been located where he proposed that the port was located at the time of the Invasion. Alarm bells should have registered when he wrote:

'That there were at Bulverhythe pertaining to the said barony at Hastings - 20 acres of salt pasture[86] worth per annum 6s 8d. '

Further alarm bells should have sounded when he reported that:

'Jeakes, in his annotations on the Cinque Ports Charters, speaking of the neighbouring spot called Bulverhythe, sets forth that it was not only the original haven of Hastings, but as such the then supposed place where William the Conqueror landed.' [87]

Yet Dawson chose to ignore the implications that these independent observations would have. Did he prefer to ignore them because they may undermine the authority upon which his book was based? I do not know, but what struck me was that the more I looked into these matters the more likely it seemed that Bulverhythe may have been the site of the original port at the time of the Invasion. It looked to me like Jeakes was right. As reported earlier Dawson registered doubts about the authenticity of the mound at Hastings being of Norman origin[88], but chose to take the traditional view, most probably for fear of critical attack. To his credit he reported all the anomalies, whilst he could have easily ignored them. None the less it is my understanding that the assumptions he made were flawed, because they had no basis in hard facts. In my view a tragedy given the scope and detail of the works involved.

As soon as you are alerted to the possibility that prior to the Norman Invasion the port of Hastings may have been located at Bulverhythe it is possible to put all the documents of the time into perspective without contradiction. First this explains the charters naming salt works at the port. Secondly it explains the various reports that the Normans landed at the port by virtue of the geography of the area, as well as the confirming documentation that we have studied earlier in some depth. Thirdly it explains why some 200 years later Pope Nicholas IV granted a one year and forty day relaxation of penance for pilgrims to visit the Chapel at Bulverhythe. The question must be asked why pilgrims should ever want to visit such a site. Bulverhythe had no apparent historical importance except for the report that William the Conqueror landed there. This is evidence that only the Vatican record can confirm. Indeed the Bulverhythe Point was considered of some strategic value, since it was reported at the time of the Armada to be a place where the Spanish could also land[89].

The spoken tradition in the Hastings area today states that the original Hastings harbour was located below the castle cliffs, on the site of the current town. This is not substantiated by the written record in any way, but has developed most probably because historians have sought to place it there without any archaeological record to back up such a thesis. W. H. Dyer, a well known local lecturer, states *'Hastings was a busy port in Saxon times, but it is not known whether any fortifications stood on the eminence where later the castle was erected'*, indirectly confirming the uncertainty about knowledge of the site at that time. Interestingly enough the spoken tradition in the Combe Haven valley[90] places the original Hastings harbour at Bulverhythe. Barry Funnell reporting for the Hastings Area Archaeological Research Group (HAARG) on the America Ground[91] in 1989 states: *'the early chronicles describe Hastings as having the best natural seaport in south-east England.'* This is only true of Bulverhythe, which was at that time a flooded inland harbour, second only to Poole as the largest natural harbour on the south coast.

A further study of other writings on this subject produces many examples of cross-referenced support for Bulverhythe, as the original port of Hastings, at the time of the Norman Invasion. E. M. Ward in his detailed study The Evolution of the Hastings Coastline[92] states: '*Bulverhythe, as a 13th century port was of some importance*'. Straker and Lewis[93] make the point that '*the haven of Bulverhythe was possibly used as an iron port*' for the Romans. Millward and Robinson[94] confirm that '*Bulverhythe was probably an important Saxon port and was later a member of the Cinque ports.*' Lastly the Patent Rolls still mention the importance of Bulverhythe as a port as late as AD 1500[95].

Whilst these later examples are mostly qualified by the use of the word '*probably*' they each show for different reasons why Bulverhythe played a strategic roll in the history of the area. Geographically it represented an inland harbour that may have extended to several square miles of calm water. In consequence the Romans, the Saxons and the Normans would each have identified a use for such a strategic resource. The surrounding land provided a perfect landing site for anything up to several thousand small craft. It is my contention that William used this to his advantage.

One final clue arises to confirm the fact that Hastings port pre 1066 was almost certainly situated on the Bulverhythe within the natural harbour area. This is that Hastings enjoyed a pre-eminent position in relation to the Cinque Ports. These five ports, Hastings, Romney, Hythe, Dover and Sandwich received special privileges, most probably because they were the only source of ships in the absence of a navy in the early days of English history.

The first reference to the Cinque Ports is in a charter of Henry II according to the eminent historian, and ex-curator of Hastings Museum, John Manwaring Baines. In his book entitled Historic Hastings[96] Mr Manwaring Baines makes the point that whilst each of these ports enjoyed a special relationship with the crown Hastings appeared to enjoy special favours. He notes that '*all freemen of the ports were called 'Barons*' and *although not en-nobled by that title, their representatives were recognised as being almost on the level with peerage barons.*' They were exempt from taxation and trading dues and had the right to be tried by their own courts. These were extraordinary privileges. Hastings appeared to enjoy a special privilege, which many attribute to its roll as head Cinque Port. This was the right to provide barons to carry the canopy of the King and Queen in procession at the coronation. Further, at the banquet after the coronation they sat at the right hand side of the king, in the place of honour.

It is my opinion that these honours were special and bestowed upon the people of Hastings, because of their special relationship with the crown, dating back to the time of William. This explains why these privileges were granted, but also provides a logical explanation based upon the fact that the port of Hastings was the largest and most influential of all the ports in the south of England. The honours bestowed matched the status of the port and could only be located at Bulverhythe.

It is logical that the town of Hastings should have developed where the port was. I shall seek to propose an answer to where Hastings was located that is both logical and is supported in part by documentary evidence.

Chapter 28: HASTINGS TOWN

The general belief that Hastings Town was situated in the valley on the western side of the current Hastings castle, at the time of the Norman Invasion, with a port somewhere to the south of the cliff, has no archaeological basis whatsoever. Critical examination of the available documentary record leads to the inevitable conclusion that Hastings pre-Invasion was not where it is claimed to have been located. Applying the rules of evidence as used in a court of Law, the proposal that the accused *probably* did this or *presumably* did that, would be thrown out at the first hurdle.

The reason for such action is simply because what evidence there is regarding the distant history of Hastings is so incomplete. Most conclusions must ultimately be qualified as guesswork. The fact that the current castle is of Norman construction is not denied, and it is assumed that the town of Hastings would be immediately adjacent to the fortification, for this reason alone. This supposition amounts to a critical error, when examining the history of Hastings, because of its unique position in English History. To assume that because other towns developed in this manner means that Hastings did the same does not take into account that Saxon Hastings, or what there was of it, was destroyed at the time of the Norman Invasion. This is clearly one interpretation of the Bayeux Tapestry[97]. Further evidence is provided by the fact that there is no entry at all for Hastings in the Doomsday Survey. This is most remarkable and an omission that most people find incredulous when their attention is drawn to it. How could the king's messengers fail to record the entry for such a famous town, the very town where they landed and camped, if it was not a deliberate act?

Dawson states with some irony[98]:

'There is no omission more curious than the absence of all direct mention of Hastings Castle or the town.'

This is where an obvious truth is clouded by intellectual reasoning, or put into more colloquial English, the eminent historian cannot see the wood for the trees. Those who have taken time to study the Doomsday survey put forward the argument that other towns were omitted from the survey. In consequence a blank page may simply indicate that Hastings was intended to be added at a later stage. It is reasoned from this that missing Hastings from the list must therefore have been an oversight. There is of course a far more obvious answer in that Hastings, as a Saxon town, no longer existed, having been destroyed in the course of the occupation: hence the blank page.

This proposal is actually supported by historical evidence hidden in the Guestling entry for Doomsday. This states:

In this manor is the new burg, and there are 64 burgesses returning £8, less 2 shillings. In Hastings 4 burgesses and 14 borders return 63 shillings. Of this manor Robertus de Hastings holds. . . . . '

Here is a direct reference to a '*new burg*', part held by Robert of Hastings. Dawson accepts the point that it is not impossible that this refers to the new town of Hastings, to the east of the castle, in the Bourne valley, which forms part of the present manor of Brede. Further support for this case is the reference to '*Nove Hasting*' in the Pipe Rolls of 1182[99], discussing work at the castle of Hastings. This is a clear reference to a '*new Hastings*', as opposed to the one that stood before somewhere else.

In the absence of any other contrary evidence there seems to be a clear case that confirms the existence for a new town of Hastings, at the time the Doomsday information was collected (1085/6). This is subsequently confirmed by the evidence in the Pipe Rolls, but more importantly confirmed by the actual development of the buildings and infrastructure within the town.

MAPS

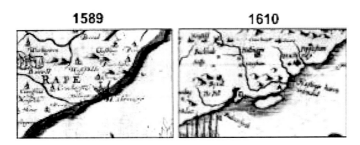

The earliest reliable maps showing the town of Hastings are dated 1589[100] and 1610[101]. These two show very little detail, with a Church and the town situated between the second and third of three river outlets. The later of the two maps, by John Speede (above right), more clearly positioning the town nearer the third river on the eastern side. This is exactly where the Bourne stream runs today and is known as '*the old town*'.

All the old properties of Hastings are located in the Bourne, including the High Street and a section of the old town wall (located adjacent to the third river on the right of the maps). It would appear to be a logical conclusion that since the oldest properties are located in this valley this is where the roots of Hastings post Invasion were located. In the Priory Stream valley to the west of the castle (the centre river of the three) there are no buildings pre 1795, other than the Priory. It is therefore most likely that the Priory controlled the whole Priory valley, from the date of its construction, thus excluding any development until such time as it was destroyed. It was not uncommon for religious houses of the time to exclude the public from their land. The lack of development in the Priory valley indicates this to be the case in Hastings.

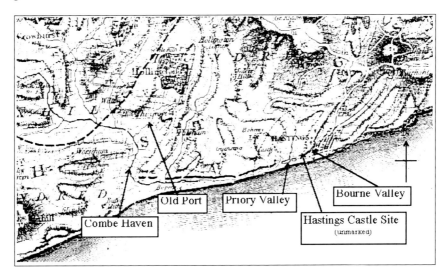

Yeakell and Gardener's map of Sussex dated 1795

Documentary confirmation that Hastings developed in the Bourne valley is found in the Yeakell and Gardener's map of Sussex dated 1795 two hundred years later (shown above). This is the first reliable map, drawn to approximate scale of 1' to the mile, carefully detailing all properties known at that time. Each property has been meticulously drawn as a black square, showing the development of an active population centre in the Bourne valley. The Priory valley to the west, on the other hand shows a few scattered properties, where the priory stood, together with two ponds behind the beach immediately below the castle. There is no other development in the Priory valley and nothing to indicate that there ever was. The ponds themselves form no evidence of the harbour, as archaeological excavations[102] show the water to be an accumulation of drainage water from the Priory stream, which was trapped by shingle moving down the coast. This formed a marsh, which had probably been in existence since at least the 13th century, when the shingle was formed by storms, but may have always been like this.

This raises the question where to look, as there is no doubt that Hastings existed pre 1066. There are several references in the Saxon Chronicle to the '*Burgh*' of Hastings under the name of '*Hastings Ceastre*', as well as the edict of Greatley[103] dated 928. The use of the word '*Ceastre*' does not necessarily mean castle, as stated earlier, but is more likely to mean a fortified place. There is no record of any lord or chief, other than the King or Earl of Kent, with jurisdiction in the area. In consequence the likelihood that a true castle existed pre invasion is very small.

This conclusion is supported primarily by archaeological evidence conducted in the nineteenth century and reported in full in Dawson's History of Hastings Castle. He states throughout his book[104] in a number of places that there is an absence of any Anglo-Saxon masonry. He states that the castle curtain wall '*probably dates from shortly after the time when the Castelany, or Castlery, was given to Robert, Count of Eu*'. This was after the Invasion.

Other difficulties arise in relation to what construction work there was. No evidence of the mandatory Norman keep was found, other than a small hard mortar floor near the cliff[105], on level ground, rather than on the traditional mound. This throws further doubt on the claim that this was the first English castle which William built. The fact that lime was impossible to locate at the time of the Invasion[106] and evidence in the Pipe Rolls shows '*lime and stone for the work at Hastings*' in the reign of Henry II, provides strong evidence that building work did not start at Hastings Castle until somewhere between 1089 and 1095, a quarter of a century after the Invasion and after the death of the Conqueror.

Prior to this time Hastings Castle was I believe located at the old port of Hastings, thus providing a consistent authentic documented record. It is my claim that the Hastings Castle and port of Hastings prior to 1094 or possibly 1095 at the latest, were both located at the place now known as Bulverhythe.

I shall seek to show the reader evidence to support this claim, which will provide sufficient interest to warrant a full archaeological investigation, by the necessary authorities. This evidence takes the form of photographs of the site in question, together with photographs of elementary excavations, sufficient to uncover enough proof to warrant independent examination. All excavations were reinstated and nothing has been removed from the site. Such is the age and dilapidation of those artefacts, which still exist in the ground, that recovery can usually now only be achieved by expert archaeological recovery methods.

The claim that Hastings town, port and castle, were situated on the Bulverhythe prior to approximately 1090, is indirectly supported by the documentary evidence. The castle prior to this date was made of wood. The mistake that historians to this time have made is to assume that the references to castle or Ceastre prior to this date are all at the same site as the stone castle of today.

One of the prime cases for the belief that Hastings castle was built at the site of William's camp is given in text by William of Poitiers, who tells us that the Duke '*gave the defence of Hastings to an active commander before departing for Romney*'. We are also told in the Orderic Vitalis manuscript that this is Humphrey of Tilleul '*who had undertaken the custody of the Castle of Hastings **from the day of it's building.** '

Two interesting points arise from this text, which at first may not be apparent and depend upon the understanding of the chronology of events. There appears to be corroboration of the claim that a castle was built post Invasion, since the named Norman Humphrey of Tilleul could not have been at the start of the building unless it started after the Invasion. This means that there was probably no castle, as we know it, made of stone prior to this point, but Humphrey was put in charge of the defence, as Poitiers informs us, most probably of the town of Hastings. This may at the time have been known as a castle, because it was made of wood, exactly as portrayed in the Wace account, but further fortified to accommodate the needs of the day. It was only at the end of the 11th century that castles of stone came into existence, so it is wholly consistent for the first Norman castle to be made of wood located at the then port.

If this is the case something must have happened to cause Hastings to move from its original site by the Bulverhythe, to the Bourne valley, east of the current castle on the rocky headland overlooking the current town. Clues as to what caused this can be found if you understand the course of events:

William landed with a huge flotilla of small ships in the large inland bay, which was then known as the port of Hastings. This was accessed through a relatively small tidal entrance opening upon calm water with several miles of shore and adjacent saltpans. This shore was low lying with few advantage points. It had two deep water anchorages immediately adjacent to a semi-fortified area that may well have fallen into disrepair (*dismantled forts - Carmen*). This had wooden buildings scattered along the shore for several miles. The occupants of these buildings fled upon the arrival of the Normans, but in all respects they had landed at what was then known as Hastings.

When the Normans arrived they dug a ditch to defend their position and erected their own fort, which William brought with him, made of wood. This was built on a natural mound overlooking the bay and harbour the day of the landing. On the following day a raiding party was sent to Pevensey to consolidate their position. Later the area around the port was fortified and the existing fortifications reinstated. William spent almost a month at Hastings, in which time he built a second fortification at the top of the hill adjacent to his camp giving command of the London road, this became known as the Castle at Hastings after the one by the sea was destroyed.

After the battle William left for London via Rye and Dover having spent just over two weeks at the port after the battle, but not until he had placed his commander Humphrey in charge of the port area, where the camp and '*castle*' stood. The Chronicles state '*There right in front of the port*' where William's fleet '*landed stood a Castle handsome and strong*' and William allowed knights to enter therein and garrison it for two years[107]. The expression '*There right in front of the port*' can only make sense when applied to the Hastings port at Bulverhythe, since this is the only place where a castle could stand in a way that you would consider to be in front of the port. It is not correct to dismiss this statement as an error, but provides supportive evidence for Bulverhythe.

The great Council in the time of William Rufus was held in 1094 at Hastings Castle. In attendance were the most powerful men in the land. These included Anselm, Bishop of Canterbury, as well as the Bishops and the new King. This gathering was brought together to dedicate Battle Abbey, as it reached completion 28 years after the Invasion, and after the death of the Conqueror in 1087. The register of Battle Abbey records '*The Castle then stood below the cliff, on ground since overflowed by the sea*'. This can likewise only refer to Bulverhythe, as the erosion of the coastline referred to by many writers, is only recorded to have occurred two centuries later in the late 13th century.

There is an inescapable logic that when William decided to build an Abbey at Battle his main representatives, religious or otherwise, who were acting for William, would be accommodated at the site of the camp and castle at the port. This was less than an hour's walk from the Abbey and perfectly secure. The people there would oversee the project through till completion. At the point of completion of the abbey the reason for the site at Bulverhythe would cease. In common with Norman policy of the time the then lord of the manor, Count Eu, decided to build his own stone castle on the headland. This overlooked and intimidated his citizens in the new borough, now being built in the Bourne valley. The site that he chose was impressive and in perfect tune with Norman thinking.

It is only at this stage, after the death of the first Count William of Eu[108] that his son takes the decision to build a new stone castle on the headland. Once this decision is implemented the area of the wooden castle next to the Bulverhythe would revert to agricultural use, which in turn would have a long-term negative effect on the adjacent port. As the Bourne Valley grew in importance, the wealthier inhabitants migrated down the coast, under the security and watchful eye of their lord. Thus when the great storms of 1294 struck the coast, sweeping across the Bulverhythe entrance, the fate of Hastings port was sealed. The land reverted to agricultural use and for 700 years the original port of Hastings was lost to the world.

The last six paragraphs are an attempt to explain what may have happened, given the information that I have found. I believe this to be the only explanation that can successfully account for all the discrepancies that occur when taking the traditional approach. None of this is worth a pinch of salt if I cannot now show you the site in question. I shall therefore seek to explain the various facets of the site and ultimately compare these to what we should find, if all the documents studied carry the correct information. As stated previously this can only apply to the correct site.

Chapter 29: GEOGRAPHY

We have seen from the first maps of Hastings by Christopher Saxon in 1589 and John Speede in 1610 that little can be gleaned as to where Hastings might have been located as early as 1066. Even though these two maps are recognised as inaccurate, they do throw a little light on the question of where the original port was located.

When Dawson examined the historical record of the castle in 1909 he explored the issues relating to tidal drift and the viability of the site of the current cricket ground (now Hastings shopping center)as a port(109). In these records he noted a number of anomalies in relation to the maps, including the mysterious island shown south-east of Hastings in the l610. I have reproduced them again here(110).

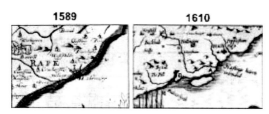

I believe there is a logical explanation for this island, which can be explained in relation to the events of the 13th century. Up until that time it is my contention that Bulverhythe was the main port of Hastings. I believe it is for this reason that Saxton (the left hand map) places the 'Hastings' title level with the left hand river of the three rivers at Hastings. The same process is carried out at Pevensey Haven. On the Speede map, only twenty years later, the island appears to the southeast whilst Bulverhythe is drawn to the west showing a large inland lagoon, in the shape of an inverted boot.

This is clearly a mistake, as the third river (A), and the lagoon, with tributary running east (B), are one and the same. In fact the lagoon exactly matches the shape of the harbour and entrance at Bulverhythe. It is marked on the map as Bulverhythe and therefore must be the third river, of the three, not the fourth as marked, since there are only three in this area. The fact that the tributary running off the lagoon follows the same route as the Hollington - Crowhurst stream confirms that these two rivers have been duplicated and the lagoon should really have been drawn where that river (A) is drawn.

The answer as to why an island is shown does not lie in any mysterious sandbank, which has subsequently been washed away, since it is still clearly visible today. In the 13th century the headland west of Bulverhythe was reduced by marine erosion. This caused shingle to move across the Bulverhythe entrance. Eventually the Bulverhythe port entrance was closed, as the authorities lost the battle and will to keep it open. Once it was closed the water backed up along the Combe Haven valley, forming the marsh that has developed into the wetlands that are there today. In the meantime, the river found a way out to the sea through the eastern entrance that now forms the exit for the Combe Haven stream. It is my proposal that at some stage, possibly between the years 1598 and 1610 both the eastern and western entrances to the Combe Haven valley (marked E and F on the plan on the following page) could have been open. In consequence any sailor of the day navigating along the coast would have recognised this entrance as having an island situated exactly where indicated on the Speede map, between the third and fourth entrance travelling west past Hastings.

Once this sequence of events is understood and a physical examination of the coast at this point is undertaken, there is no need to explain the map in terms of eroded coastline, with mysterious islands long since lost to the sea. Anyone living on the coast road between Glynne Gap and West Marina at Harley Shute knows that the land under them was once an island.

MAP OF BULVERHYTHE ENTRANCE

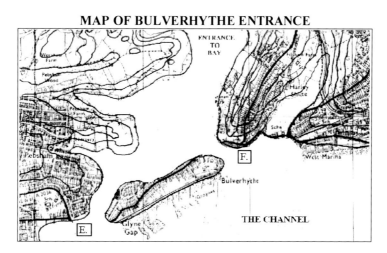

I bring the matter of the maps to the attention of the reader, not because it plays any major part in verifying the site of the old Hastings Port, but to show how historians often work with paper and in so doing do not have the experience of living on the land about which they write. Sometimes the answer may be plain to see, by those who live in the area, yet it will remain an historical mystery simply because the research is carried out in books, rather than on the actual ground. This particular example shows how facts are muddied to suit the evidence. Since no island is recorded on the official Ordnance Survey record it is claimed the island must have been eroded by the sea[111] (an argument also used for Hastings Port). Although there is no evidence to support this hypothesis it is constantly stated as true with many books coming to the same conclusion, without ever re-examining the case. It is upon exactly this premise that Hastings has developed a fictitious port below the castle. It was in fact at Bulverhythe all the time.

I shall now identify the location of the original Hastings Port, together with the historical infrastructure that in turn supports the case for listing the complete site as a national monument.

Chapter 30: LOCATION

Having discussed in some detail the reasons, both historical and theoretical, why the site of the port of Hastings was located on the Bulverhythe, it is now necessary to identify the pertinent features that still remain, together with those elements that can be identified as those connected with the immense amount of history concerning the port and the Norman Invasion in particular. These are each limited in their individual element by the large amount of time which has passed. Modern archaeologists will be able to confirm these finds, provided the necessary expertise is available, together with an adequate investment in human resources and the technology required to preserve any artefacts that may still exist.

I believe the site of the old port of Hastings is located on the northern shore of the Combe Haven valley at Ordnance Survey site TQ 778103 adjacent to Redgeland Wood opposite the old entrance to the Combe Haven valley. The site of the wooden castle pre 1094 is immediately next to this, overlooking the harbour and entrance to the sea, on the TQ 61/71 1:25,000 Survey map.

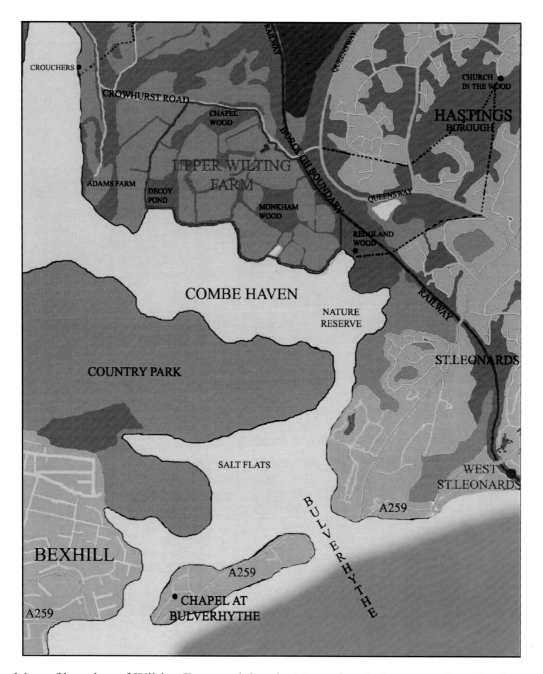

Map of location of Wilting Farm and Combe Haven in relation to modern Hastings

The Invasion site occupies the whole of what was known at the time as Wilting Manor, substantiating the Domesday evidence previously examined. This consists today of some 200 acres of land known as Upper Wilting Farm on the north side of the Combe Haven valley between TQ 767106 at Decoy Pond (whown on the above map), along the flood plain to the port at TQ778103(to the east), and north as far as Chapel Wood located at TQ 771111. The land adjoins the western borough boundary of the present day Hastings, which approximately follows the line of the London to Hastings railway (brown line on plan above).

The whole 200 acres is one very large hill, at the end of one of the south-western branches of the Ridge around the town, exactly as described in the documents that we have examined. The land rises from sea level by the shore, to a peak at almost 40 meters at Wilting Hill, occupying a brilliantly strategic position overlooking the main London to Hastings road[112] of the time, adjacent to the manor house. This road ran along what developed into the old coach road running from Wilting, through Crowhurst, up to Telham Hill and on to Robertsbridge and London via Battle.

The manor of Wilting has a continuous recorded history as an agricultural site that goes as far back as Domesday. It will come as no surprise to find that the first sheriffs of Hastings, appointed by William's first landlord the Count of Eu, were installed at Wilting Manor[113]. This is not a mere coincidence, but an indication of the importance of the site. Given that Wilting is recorded in Domesday as the second most wasted manor 20 years after the Invasion, by virtue of its poor recovery, why would the first sheriffs of Hastings be located there unless there was a very good reason? In terms of travel in those days, Wilting was by comparison well removed from the 'new burgh' of the Bourne Valley. I propose that it was because the Normans were based at Wilting in the early years following the Conquest, therefore it was a natural inheritance for the first sheriffs to occupy the same property.

[Author's note: The evidence being presented to the Inspector at this stage needed to refer to the line of the road which at that time was planned to be built. Several summers had been spent examining evidence on the edge of the marsh at Wilting Manor. However at that time this chapter was written (end of 1994) it was still not possible to conclude that the Normans landed at Wilting Manor. What could be speculated was that this was probably the landing site. All I could tell the Inspector was that the evidence that I had seen showed that the continuous archaeological record indicated there was evidence that supported my belief. Some might consider this an understatement, but it must be remembered that if I overstated the claim at this point in time, without evidence to support my belief, the lawyers who represented the Highways Agency would have destroyed the case at the Inquiry that would follow. In consequence I concluded my geographical study as follows:]

This site is designated as part of the line order for the A259 Bexhill and Hastings Western Bypass. The effects of this line order can be seen in Document Reference 29 Sheet 7 /8 (Section C/D) reference 10059/RC/046/A of the Highways Agency papers. Put into layman's terms the new proposed bypass will totally destroy the integrity of this site and would represent a national archaeological disaster, unparalleled in the history of this country.

To build a road through one of the greatest historical and archaeological treasures of the land, when it has remained hidden for nearly a millennium, at a time when it has only just been discovered, would amount to a monstrous act that the public would never accept. Any civil servant or politician in receipt of this knowledge who approved such an act, without first qualifying every aspect of the claims I lay before you, would be a very brave man indeed. Bearing this in mind I propose that we look at the archaeological evidence.

What we find at the old Hastings port, at Bulverhythe, is a continuous archaeological record dating back to the Bronze Age, when civilisation first started in the Combe Haven valley. This evidence supports the proposal that the site in question was a unique centre for civilisation in the area. There existed an infrastructure, which developed into the Saxon port, which William subsequently took by force.

Chapter 31: BRONZE AND IRON AGE DEVELOPMENT

The evidence for development during this period takes the form of Bronze Age scrapers spread over an extensive area, together with burnt and worked flints dating through to the Iron Age[161]. The report prepared by the Oxford Archaeology Unit during November 1992 was commissioned by Chris Blandford Associates on behalf of the Department of Transport. It states[114]:

'A brief assessment noted the presence of late Neolithic and early Bronze Age elements, a date which is reasonable for the assemblage as a whole.'

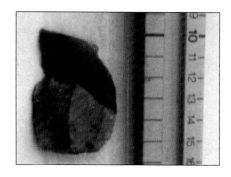

Bronze Age Scraper found on site

This is expanded to support Iron Age activity in relation to the burnt flints found on part of the site in question. Here the report confirms the existence of industrial activities:

Thirty pieces of fire-cracked flint were recovered from the field survey. Such material, being the by-product of direct and prolonged heat, such as produced by a kiln, furnace or bonfire and not from more general activities such as stubble burning, is a good indicator of past settlement or industrial activities, especially, in the latter case, when it is associated with slag or other metallurgical waste product (115).'

As well as flints the team conducting the field survey found tiles and bricks where,

'A few pieces may be assigned a Roman date on the basis of their fabric. '

This supports the proposal that having developed as a Bronze and Iron Age centre of civilisation the Romans used the port as part of the continuous occupation. This led to the growth of Hastings into the leading port in the south-east and subsequently the lead Cinque port.

It is noted in the report that,

'None of the slag retrieved was blast furnace slag which has a glassy appearance and was produced after 1496 (116).'

The consequence of this observation being that the huge amounts of slag found on the Wilting site supports the possibility of a major industrialised area, where the origins have yet to be identified, but are dateable prior to 1496 (117).

The report in question only covered the area in immediate contact with the proposed new road and therefore represents only a small part of the over all site. The author does not beat about the bush in the Summary and directly confirms,

'When these results are considered with the data gained from the desktop survey and other field evaluations, they point to possible archaeological features, which require further investigation (118).'

This should confirm to those who remain sceptical that there is something worthy of investigation at the Wilting site. Even if the reader is not yet convinced of any Norman involvement it must be noted that the archaeological survey conducted by the Department of Transport covered the complete route of the new road. Over the whole route there are no sites that the survey unit considered worthy of comment, with the sole exception of evidence at Wilting Manor (119). It is not in my opinion a coincidence, but solid archaeological confirmation of the importance of the site.

Further evidence of Iron and Bronze Age inhabitation are found in the immediate port area, in field number 5143 of 4.1 acres. This takes the form of a circular settlement shown bellow:

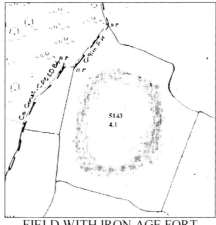
FIELD WITH IRON AGE FORT

Evidence to support Iron Age and Bronze Age development takes the form of a resistivity survey conducted during the summer of 1992/3 by myself and a colleague. The results of this survey are published later in the chapter dedicated to that. This shows the characteristic light and dark areas of ditches consistent with earthworks of the period. Visual examination of the area of hill on which this is found confirms likely Iron Age activity, by the outline of a circular settlement (shown on the plan above). Large circles in adjacent fields (shown on aerial photographs)[122] also confirm this opinion. A proper evaluation of this field, and the adjacent fields, is required by appropriate authorities.

Chapter 32: ROMAN DEVELOPMENT

Development of Infrastructure

During the early part of the first and second centuries the Romans developed an infrastructure at the port of Hastings. Evidence to support this statement is provided by the Department of Transport Field Survey, finding Roman pottery on the site at Wilting. Further confirmation can be obtained by examining other visual evidence, which can be demonstrated to exist by adopting the methods of the pre-eminent Roman road researcher I. D. Margary, who wrote the definitive study[123] on the matter.

Ivan Margary took a pro-active research approach to locating how Roman roads could be found. In 1932 he joined the Sussex Archaeological Society. It is recognised that his greatest work was identifying Roman roads which had long been lost. He did this using aerial photos and evidence gathered on the ground from detailed examination of hedgerows and undisturbed areas along routes that had previously escaped detection of Roman infrastructure. Details on his work can be found on the Felbridge and District History Group web site. I read the detail of how he achieved his results. This led me to embark on the mammoth task of tracing a huge number of tracks leading from the port site, including two that led directly to the two largest bloomeries[124] in the area, at Beauport Park and Crowhurst Park (less than three miles away).

[Author's note: Whilst examining the Ordnance Survey map of the manor boundaries I recognised that the area in the heel of the inverted boot of the inlet, where the port was most likely to be located, was called Redgeland Wood. This seemed too great a coincidence, since we had seen earlier that the Chronicle of Battle Abbey named the port as being at a place called Hedgeland, which was a hill. Whilst not conclusive it confirmed to me that I was close to finding the correct site of the Norman Invasion. Redgeland was not only located on the Bulverhythe marsh, where a port would be expected to be located, but was also at the foot of quite a large hill upon which Wilting Manor was built. My attention therefore moved to Wilting Manor and the issue of how the Roman roads integrated into the probable port structure. The work on these roads, whilst taking an immense amount of time to uncover showed the existence of a massive Roman infrastructure that simply would not exist if the port was not there in Roman times. If that were the case it would confirm that after the Romans left Britain the port would have been left in the same location for Saxon use and development. Upon this supposition the

port of Hastings could probably be confirmed to be located at Wilting by virtue of the Roman road infrastructure used to support the production and shipment of iron ore by the Romans.]

The tracks in question can be identified by the visual recognition techniques employed by Margery and are most evident in hedgerows and along footpaths that are no longer in existence. Within the port site these are further substantiated by the resistivity data, which we shall examine later.

The most striking evidence of Roman occupation is the remains of earthen jetties adjacent to deep water berths(125) on the east and west of the port site (marked C and D on the plan below). These are large earthen structures in the region of 100 meters in length, running along the shore, most probably designed to provide access for loading iron ore.

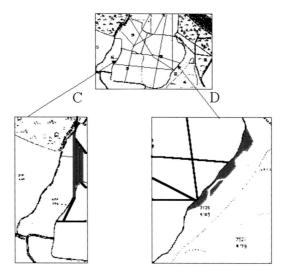

These were found during the summer when tracing the routes of the tracks on the ground from aerial photos. The tracks disappeared off the edge of the field on both the left and right of the lower fields (seen in the above plans). When these places were examined on the ground the field levels dropped between one and two meters. This posed the question *"where did they go"*, since upon first examination they appear simply to disappear into high marsh grass and overgrown undergrowth. Climbing down onto the marsh and into the undergrowth revealed the so called *"jetties"*. Earthen structures, which I assume were connected to the field levels by wooden structures of some sort, to bring them in line with the tracks.

Photograph of Wessex excavation at Redgeland jetty

Photograph showing charcoal layer 18inches thick extending from next to jetty.

Site C on the western side of the lower field has three different levels of terrace, one running almost the complete length of the inlet. Site D on the other hand, adjacent to the Redgeland Wood area, appears to contain an island jetty, which allows vessels to birth and turn with the minimum effort. These sites are currently completely overgrown with vegetation, needing clearance and detailed examination.

Each of these jetties, as I have called them, is connected to the other by a series of tracks, forming a veritable network of inter-connections. These lead from each berth to the other and from there via a number of routes to the local bloomeries, where iron ore was extracted.

Route of Roman track to the Hastings port

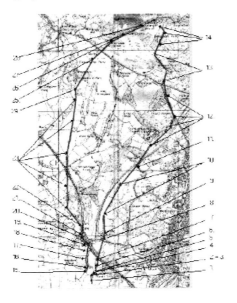

This map shows the route taken from Beauport Park via Crowhurst Park and the Ridge to the deep-water berths at Bulverhythe. As well as visual evidence provided using the Margery method, further evidence can be provided by study of the 1844 tithe map of Hollington.

There are a number of visible reference points as follows:

1. Crop shows track marking in early summer in Sandrock Field (see photo in Annex).
2. Entrance through field boundary cut through side of field.
3. Paving of ironstone and smelted waste (see photos on page 78).
4. Terrace crosses field (see photo in Annex).
5. Remains of track crosses pond before entering hedge.
6. Gap in hedge where track crosses.
7. Track cuts across edge of pond, rampart collapsed into pond.
8. Crossroads at Mayfield Farm, southern track now abandoned.
9. Track passes Mayfield Farm connecting with old ridge footpath.
10. Track follows field boundaries.
11. Excavation reveals cinder type material at approx. 18inch.
12. Track follows field boundaries to Beauport Park golf club.
13. Track lost on golf course.
14. Track runs through woods to bloomery.
15. Cuts down side of embankment.
16. Can be seen approx. five yards past field boundary as you enter Monkham Wood.
17. Track follows right hand side of stream crossing 10yds north of fork with agger type mound running out through undergrowth.
18. Terrace crosses field. (See photo in Annex)
19. Mound as track crosses edge of field and through hedge.
20. Terrace parallel to railway joining old track.
21. Terrace through wood.
22. Roman track carries on to top of mound then forks left to join footpath at bottom of valley, detouring steep ravine.
23. Track follows field boundary to Crowhurst Park.
24. Earthen terrace visible at rear southern side of caravan park.
25. Remains of metalling scattered through soil by ploughing.
26. Track is visible between two more recent access routes.
27. Track runs through edge of fairway approx. 3 yards into wood, wagon ruts still visible.
28. Enters excavation at west end of site.

From a Parish map compiled by David Padgham

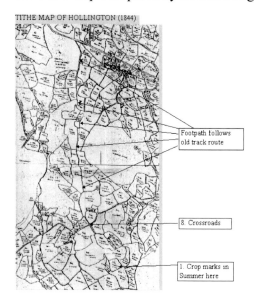

This map shows the existence of the ancient footpaths that once followed the same routes as the Roman tracks in the last chapter. Even though many have since disappeared, enough are still present on the first tithe map in 1844, to back up the visual evidence. In particular the cross road is still clearly visible at Mayfield Farm, where the main route from the Bulverhythe port crossed the London to Hastings road, although at some stage in the past it appears to have moved from east to west of Mayfield Farm.

Taking the tithe map evidence together with the visual evidence I believe that it can be shown that the two tracks connected Beauport Park and Crowhurst Park, with the loading bays at the old Hastings port. This indicates that, contrary to the previously held belief, the Romans took the smelted iron south towards the deep water port at Hastings, rather than the much longer haul eastwards towards Icklesham and Winchelsea , even though the latter was down hill all the way from Beauport Park. Loading at the Hastings port meant that they did not need to transfer loads from one boat to another in shallow water. Whilst a short part of the journey going towards Bulverhythe from Beauport bloomery is uphill, I do not really believe this consideration would be important when employing what was probably a slave labour force. Only one bloomery (Beauport Park) was the other side of the Ridge, whereas three were the Hastings port side (Crowhurst, Bynes Farm and Crowhurst Park). Speed of delivery would have been a more important consideration than amount of effort. In any event those other three bloomeries needed coastal access too. No-one has ever confirmed where they delivered their ore. The conclusion from this study is that all four bloomeries delivered their ore to the port of Hastings, using the same network of tracks.

Once the tracks reached the port area they were so designed as to allow the cargo to be loaded at either of the bays, without necessarily needing to turn the boats around. The carts could also be returned to either bloomery for reloading without the need to turn them, since the track network could accommodate this.

At the top of the low lying headland, central to all this activity, two buildings controlled the area concerned. These now appear as two ponds, but a few building stones can be seen adjacent to the gap in the mound, where the old track to the headland passed through. The fact that this track is there indicates that more evidence may be hidden from view in the thick undergrowth at the bottom of this field. These two buildings are shown on the map in the following chapter.

Henry Cleere and David Crossley, in their book The Iron Industry of the Weald, make the point that a case can be made for Beauport Park as '*some kind of headquarters*' because of the size of the excavations. Beauport and Crowhurst between them accounted for just under half of all iron production from the six major Roman iron production sites in the Weald[126]. This would require some considerable infrastructure in order to ship 40,000 tons of iron during the Roman occupation. It is my contention that the considerable effort required to construct the tracks and jetties confirms beyond doubt that the iron from these bloomeries was shipped south, using the facilities built at the port of Hastings on the Bulverhythe.

Whilst the port area was almost certainly industrialised, by the standards of the day, bloomery activity took place on all three hills, occupying the northern side of the Combe Haven valley, from Wilting in the east to Bynes Farm in the west.

Each of these hills, Wilting, Adams Farm and Bynes Farm has a characteristic quarry, exactly the same as Beauport, situated on the crest of each hill. Bynes Farm is situated on the western side of the Crowhurst valley and is unusual because the quarry is even larger than that at Beauport, but this appears to have remained unreported. Whilst a bloomery site was examined at Bynes earlier this century it was located lower down on the slopes of the valley, where a cinders field is located. The size of the excavation at the top of the hill suggests that this site needs further examination and the small excavation in Cinders Field, where it is located, did not I believe reveal the true extent of the activities there.

Jennings and Smyth Bore holes in the Combe Haven valley

The reason that Bynes is important in our investigation is that smelted iron was loaded into boats south east of Cinders Field. This means that when the Romans were exploiting this site (AD 140), the Combe Haven valley must have been flooded or navigable up to this point.

If you look at the map provided by the leading experts on the Combe Haven valley Jennings and Smyth, used in conjunction with their study in 1987, you can see the layout of Bynes, Adams and Wilting, in relation to the valley. The Bynes loading bay was located in the crook of the bend north of where borehole 16 is located. This is over 3 kilometres west of the Wilting port to the right of borehole number 5.

There is no evidence of any major change in the flora and fauna of the valley from the time of the Roman occupation, through to the period when the 13th century storms cut off the sea from the inland waterway[127]. In consequence it must be logical to assume that the valley was flooded and or tidal until that time. Taking sea level information into account, the floor of the current valley is located below both the present day sea level and also that at the time of the Norman Invasion. If the shingle bank is removed, or partly opened, it would be impossible for the valley to remain dry. Consequently it would be navigable to shallow draft boats and barges even today.

Evidence that confirmed this was provided by Simon Jennings and Christine Smyth, who are experts in analysis of sedimentary deposits and stratigraphic levels. Those stratigraphic levels were confirmed by accurate spot height measurements. Their evidence confirms this was a saline environment at the time of the Norman Invasion, meaning the valley was open to the tide.

Thus the concept of a large inland waterway becomes a reality by virtue of science, rather than hypothesis. Even with the development of marsh grasses it is certain that it was possible to navigate this waterway as far as Bynes. Therefore the landing site at Wilting is supported by the geographical and sedimentary information.

Adjacent to the Monkham Wood inlet there is a field with the only square corner on the whole Combe Haven valley, indicating man made intervention, called '*Sandrock field*'. This can be seen on the drawing below and the aerial photograph in chapter 37 This field appears to contain a possible defence of some description. In the spring each year a large square can be identified in the crop, with smaller squares in each corner (top photograph). I believe this may be a garrison fort, because of its shape and position, defending the major entrance to the port area. The tracks from the bloomeries converge at this point and run right down to where the water once stood.

PLAN OF SANDROCK FIELD

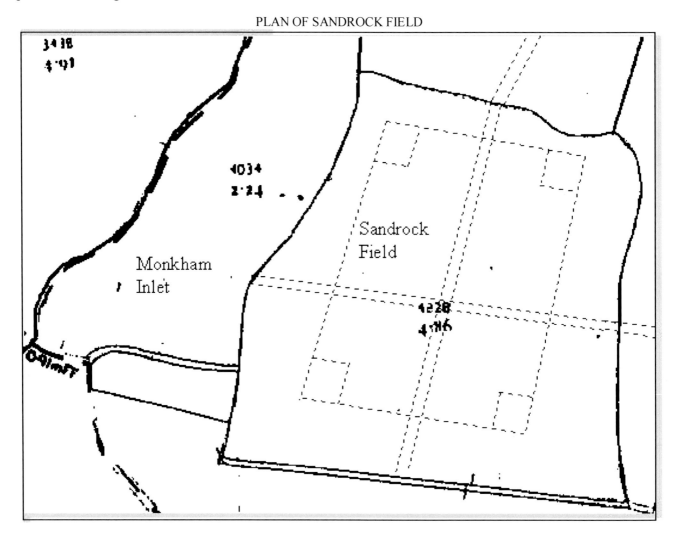

At the entrance to Sandrock field (on the northern side) the boundary is raised in the region of four feet (just over 1 meter). At that point the track to the bloomery is still visible as it cuts between the levels of the two field. At this point an excavation revealed an area of the slope that appeared to be some form of '*cobbled*' construction. It looked just like cobbles, with a root pushing up from underneath. Proper examination of this site is required by experts.

Close up of cobbles showing flat edges

Close up photo showing how cobbles are laid in a section between the two fields

Picture showing location of '*cobbles*' in field boundary, with tree root pushing up centre from below.

Chapter 34: PORT AREA

Finally I have produced a plan of the port area showing all the elements of the Roman period in the port area. These include the interconnecting tracks, the fort, the jetties (or loading bays), together with the sites of identifiable buildings.

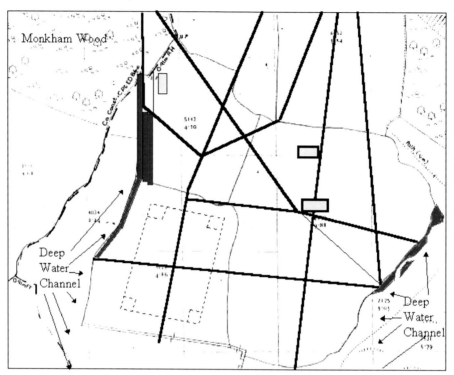

The complete Roman port site at Hastings

These confirm the existence of a flourishing community, which had to be housed and accommodated in the immediate vicinity. As yet the exact site of this additional community has not been identified and a huge amount of work remains to be done to excavate and identify the salient features of the site as a whole.

The manor house at Wilting is situated on the top of the hill and has an immense strategic advantage, by virtue of its control of the then main route to London. The view from the hilltop gives command over all the immediate area and would allow at least an hour's warning of any attack, if implemented on foot, as well as giving full view of the sea and shore. It is therefore highly likely that the area immediately adjacent to the manor house holds archaeological secrets worthy of investigation. Aerial photographs reinforce this conclusion and will be examined in more detail later.

The environmental and archaeological survey, conducted by the Department of Transport, relating to the Wilting site, has failed to identify specific features under the small area of land designated for the road.

Given the development of the port, the subsequent occupation by the Norman sheriffs and the strategic position that the top of the hill occupies, the manor house area needs extensive investigation, far beyond that employed to date. Without the benefit of the research contained in this document, those conducting the investigations have been working in the dark and without the resources to identify remains[128] that may have no iron left in them. I do not believe there has been any reference to aerial photographs[129] of the Wilting site commissioned for the report. It relies almost exclusively upon a geophysical study of the route, which does not cover all the specific fields that will be affected and should be discounted because of the delicate nature of any relics that may still exist.

I believe that it can be demonstrated beyond reasonable doubt that the site in question at Wilting had a Bronze Age settlement over an extensive area within the 200 acres, by virtue of the large number of flint instruments found there. It is reasonable to conclude that development of the site continued into the Iron Age and contributed to the forest clearance[130] of the valley. This then resulted in a Roman occupation of an area that became known as a port, which eventually became the port of Hastings, as a result of the occupation by the ancient tribe called the Hastingas (which we shall look at in the next chapter).

As discussed in some depth earlier there is no evidence of a port at any other site other than Bulverhythe, which could be called the original Hastings Port. This new evidence confirms the existence of a Bronze Age and Iron Age settlement adjacent to that port, which the Romans occupied for almost a century. If this port was the same one that William landed at, nearly six hundred years later, the question must be asked '*what happened in the time in between*'?

I believe that the settlement along the Combe Haven valley was not abandoned by its inhabitants when the Romans returned to Rome. The valley has a **record of continuous development** since the beginning of man's occupation of the area. When the Romans left the Hastingas tribe occupied it, whether that was before, after or during the Roman occupation cannot be determined. What is certain is that the port was the centre of growth, turning from a broad based settlement along the shores of the valley into the site of original Hastings Ceastra (castle), referred to in the ancient manuscripts.

If this assumption is correct, as I believe it is, evidence of the Saxon and Norman occupation must still exist, since the original town must have been located next to the port. Unbelievable as it may appear to those connected with research of this nature, evidence can be found. This evidence is within the boundary of the original port area, thus fulfilling the requirements of The Carmen ('*You restored the dismantled forts which once stood there*').

Chapter 35: THE HASTINGAS

Little is known of Hastings prior to the Norman Invasion, other than the fact that the Hastingas tribe occupied the area. The Chronicle of Simeon of Durham in 771 records[131]:

'*In these days Offa, King of the Mercians, subdued by force of arms the Race of Hastings.* '

Later the Charter of Offa to the Abbey of St. Denis in 795 describes Hastings as a seaport. No further mention is made until the edict of Greatley in the year 928 when the Hastings coinage began.

The people who occupied Hastings were different in some way from those in other settlements in Sussex. Peter Brandon, in his book The Sussex Landscape explains:

'*The third element in the old kingdom of Sussex was the hinterland of Hastings. In its place-name vocabulary, it's dispersed hamlet settlement and paucity of evidence concerning common fields, the district has strong affinities with Kent. The origin of these peculiarities seems to be the settlement of the area by the Hastingas, the tribal followers of Haesta. This name is still preserved in Hastings, a folk name, current before the creation of administrative units like the shire, hundred and rape, when the pattern of early settlement was still dominated by wild nature and other physical barriers. The Hastingas selected the dry land between Romney and Pevensey marshes and, hemmed in by the sparsely inhabited forest inland, were able to preserve their identity within these natural frontiers even until the eleventh century. They have the distinction of being the only early English to make significant inroads into the Wealden forest, so breaking its long and almost impenetrable obscurity. Even so, they mainly settled the coastal margins, particularly the heads of the then several valleys which were great inlets of the sea south of the upland known as Battle Ridge.*'

In the Anglo-Saxon Chronicle the Hastingas were mentioned in 1011 (132), relating to the Invasion of the Danes, who had over-run the area. The conclusion being that Hastings was effectively at that time a separate kingdom, even though the name of the dynasty attached to it is still unknown. The name Hastingas was omitted from the earlier *Tribal Hideage*, indicating that the forest of the Weald may well have protected them from the attention of the other lords, until much later.

The written evidence of manuscripts confirming this involvement at a place that later became known as Hastings, must be incorporated into the archaeology at the port of Hastings, in order for a consistent picture of the past to be substantiated. This evidence can be found in a number of places along the northern shore of the Combe Haven valley, when observed from the air. I therefore decided to search out any available aerial photographs of the area in question, with a view to looking for the tell tale signs of inhabitation which would back up the hypothesis to date. Most serious archaeologists accept that aerial surveys are an essential tool in validating any site prior to serious archaeological study on the ground. It is therefore with some satisfaction that I can produce aerial studies confirming all details previously reported. The significance of this I leave to the reader in evaluating the plausibility or otherwise of the proposal in hand.

(Authors note: Since this original document was written Google, provide desk top images now of almost all the locations in this document. These images are taken recently, but do not always display the elements that reveal the hidden signs of man's involvement in the past. Most frequently these images are taken in summer when crops are in the ground, removing the ability for photographs to reveal the subtle changes in colour that will show a long lost track or a ditch dug two thousand years before. None the less the addition of Google maps to a serious research project such as this is invaluable in that some of the features still jump out and have the benefit of being taken by the new digital cameras, which are far more sensitive than these original colour photographs.)

Chapter 36: AERIAL SURVEYS

Redgeland Wood

In order to research the history of the site I decided to look at the aerial photographs available. The best data available comes from the National Library of Air Photographs (NLAP), held by the Royal Commission on the Historical Monuments of England. These are crown copyright and go back as far as 1946 for our purposes. The quality of the earlier studies was extremely poor due to the low quality film and difficult means of obtaining them. We tend to forget that it was not so long ago that men hung out of the back of the aircraft with a box brownie to get what nowadays we take for granted. We are very lucky to have access to such a record. This allows us to look back beyond the developments of the last forty years, which might otherwise obliterate the more difficult to see items.

Those who study this document should be aware that much of the finer detail has been lost in the transfer from original source documents into computer graphics files, available for all to read. The drop in quality is unavoidable, but allows those without access to the original documents to make a reasoned judgement.

In presenting this evidence I have decided that the best approach is to study the photographs available in date order, starting with the earliest and working through to those taken last summer *[1994]*. In order to achieve the best reproduction I have copied them (as internet versions on my web site) as large as is practical, with accompanying explanatory text. All photographs are shown looking north unless stated otherwise.

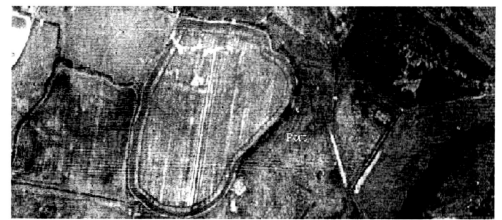

NLAP Film 3G/TUD/UK149 frame 5356 370% part enlargement 16th April 1946

The first photograph shows Sandrock Field on the left, Five Acre Field in the middle, with the deep water port area centre right adjacent to Redgeland Wood, next to the London to Hastings railway. The Roman tracks can be seen running east to west as a pale line from the kinks in the boundary with the port. The Roman track from the Five Acre field headland running north is clearly visible as a dark line. This photograph should be compared with the plan in the chapter earlier concerning the Roman era.

Five Acre field, centre of the photograph, reveals what is probably the first intimations of the tell tale signs of a Saxon camp, with ditches, an inner and an outer wall. The central white feature is the remains of the Roman building. The Saxon element is circular in nature with the eastern side more noticeable, showing as darker lines on the print. There are also a number of poor quality circular features which indicate possible early building sites

On the right of the port (in the top right hand corner of the photograph) can be seen what may be the remains of an earlier defence in Redgeland Wood. This structure is on private land owned by British Rail. It has been fenced in for many years and until recently completely impossible to get to. The London to Hastings railway passes within 20 meters on an embankment immediately next to it, cutting the site off from the general populace since the line was electrified.

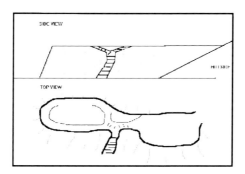

Defensive structure in Redgeland Wood

I cannot at this time establish exactly what the structure in question is. It is nearly ten feet high and covered in tightly packed stones. These appear to have been laid rather like a wall, but without any bonding material. It is oblong in shape with a depression in the middle dropping half a meter, as if the top carried a defensive fence. There are steps, or something similar rising from the front and it appears to be in a position to control access to the port from the north-east. The whole site is completely overgrown with dense briars and vegetation.

Immediately in front of this structure, running into the marsh, is an irregular raised boundary, which encloses an area of land crossed by the footpath. A large stone slab, similar to that used in the construction of Battle Abbey, marks the entrance from the south. The question as to how this stone got there immediately springs to mind. This enclosure also has an earthen raised edge and can just be seen on the aerial photographs as a dark outline with a rectangular shape in the southern corner.

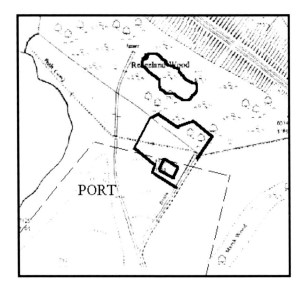

Redgeland Wood structure position

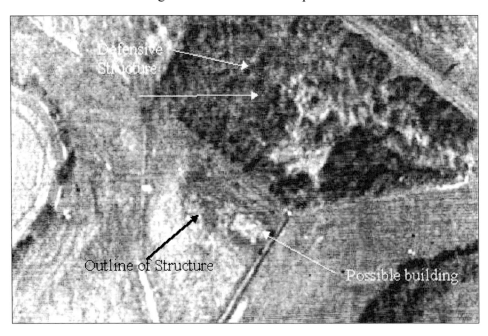

Enhancement of port area

I believe this may be the remains of an ancient building and that the structure may relate to the castle referred to in the Chronicle of Battle Abbey when it stated '*The castle then stood below the cliff, on ground since overflowed by the sea*'. The ground in question has undoubtedly at some stage been flooded by the sea. It is also located immediately below a headland that also was a cliff many years ago. If you look carefully at the photo you can clearly see the outline of the circular mound identified where the arrows point.

The statement in the Chronicle has always baffled historians. Here there appears to be the potential for an answer that interfaces with all the other elements of the puzzle. Whilst I cannot say with knowledge that these items are linked to the story of the Invasion I am certain that they relate to the port and are of great antiquity. Further investigation is essential in order for others to provide the necessary explanation. This land is the property of the railway.

Chapter 37: Sandrock Field

NLAP Film 541/532 frame 3059 400% part enlargement 23rd May 1950

This photograph was taken later in the year towards the end of May in 1950. It features Sandrock field with its distinctive square corner in the bottom left. It is distinctive because it is the only open field corner on the Combe Haven valley which is not rounded by the action of the waterways. The poor quality of the source material does little to enlighten the viewer, but raises the possibility of features within the field, which do not show on other prints.

Chapter 38: Monkham Inlet

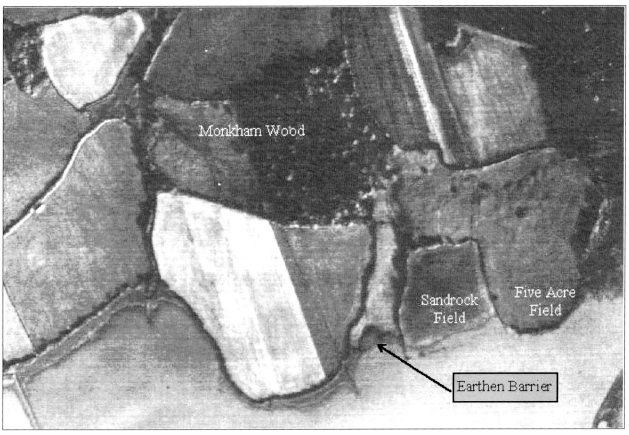

NLAP film 58/RAF/3915 frame 0178 f22 150% part enlargement 5th November 1960

This photograph shows a much larger area of the landing site to the east of Sandrock field and south of Monkham Wood. This was taken in November 1960 in the very early morning, when the mist was still lying on the valley floor. The field contours are more pronounced in Five Acre Field to the right, where the original Saxon hamlet was situated. Immediately to the north of this, in the field shown top right, a light grey streak reveals yet another Roman track, which has not shown on previous photographs. Compare this to the plan of the port area shown earlier.

In the centre of the picture is a field where half has been ploughed, hence the colour difference. Within this field there are a number of circles, which are more apparent on later prints. This field and the one to the left has a series of circular marks, indicating an early settlement all along the north shore of the valley. *(Authors note: these circles created by long established huts are very easy to see on Google maps)*.

Off centre of this photograph can be seen the Monkham inlet. Due to the earthen barrier, which we shall discuss later, the low level of the sun has accentuated the damming effect by keeping the mist out of the inlet and producing a shadow across the entrance where the arrow points. This effect is produced solely by the different level of the marsh and is not visible without a close inspection on the ground, yet appears quite apparent from this photograph.

Chapter 39: Roman Tracks

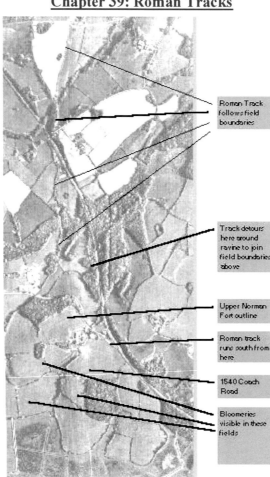

NLAP film MAL/75025 frame 070 136% part enlargement 30th April 1970

This shows the left hand fork of the plan of the Roman track running from the port area to Beauport Park bloomery. Clearly visible is the outline of the Upper Norman Fort, the 1540 coach road from Upper Wilting farm to Monkham Wood, with the parallel Roman track on the other side of the same field.

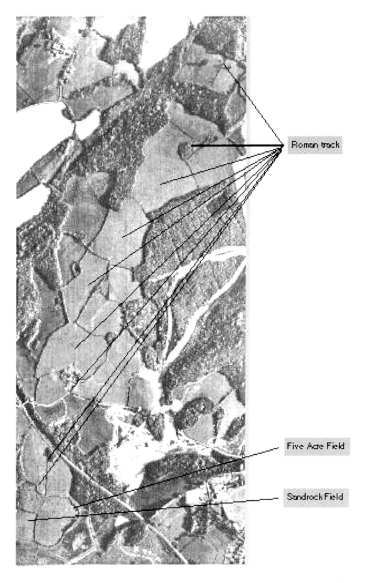

Roman track

Five Acre Field

Sandrock Field

NLAP film MAL/75025 frame 070 136% part enlargement 30th April 1970

This follows the right hand fork of the Roman track along the ridge to Beauport. The photograph was taken before the track was obliterated by the Queensway(133) new road in 1970. The new crop clearly shows the line of the old track following the old ridge road.

This is the aerial photograph that shows the field at the top of the hill at Wilting Farm. It clearly shows the outline of the upper fort in Chapel Field and the 1540 coach road. In the second photograph close examination shows that the earlier Roman road is still visible as a terrace across the edge of the field to the east of the manor house.

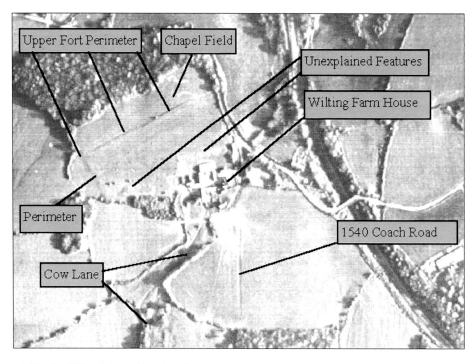

NLAP Film MAL/75025 frame 070 part enlargement 30th April 1975

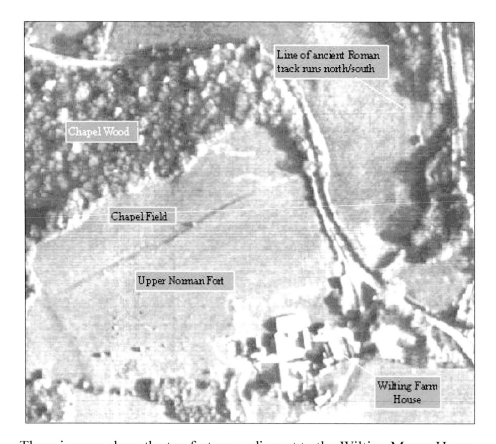

These images show the top fort area adjacent to the Wilting Manor House.

Chapter 41: Jetties and Lower Fields

These images show the aerial photographs of the jetties on both sides of the lower fields.

This image shows the jetties on the edge of the marsh at Redgeland Wood, which we looked at earlier.

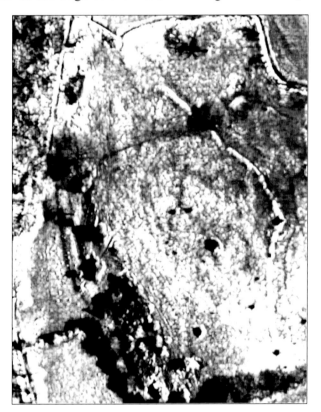

NLAP Film MAL/80006 frame 1961 48% part enlargement 4th April 1980

This image shows the jetties adjacent to Monkham Inlet on the other side of Sandrock Field to the west with the field where the Iron Age fort is located.

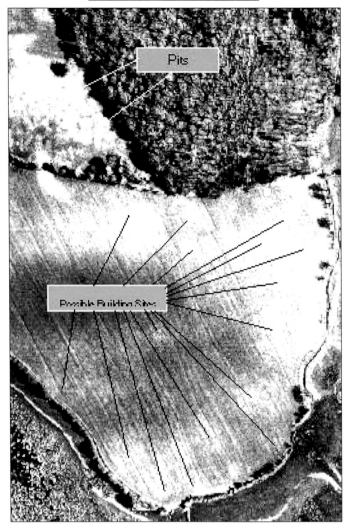

NLAP Film MAL/80006 frame 196 148% part enlargement 4th April 1980

This picture shows the field to the west of the Monkham inlet before the crops have been sown. Large white circles can be seen on the photographs running along the edge of the inlet suggesting buildings existed on the site at some stage in the past. The field to the west of Monkham wood is completely covered with pits, which show as white circles. These were most probably used for iron extraction and indicate a huge industrialisation process, far greater than has ever been imagined to exist in this area before. The size and extent of the ground markings is so great as to indicate the existence of a very large community, which has to date been completely lost to history. Further on-site examination is essential in order that these markings can be fully investigated and the potential for the site investigated.

NLAP Film MAL/80006 frame 196 148% part enlargement 4th April 1980

The final photograph from the National Library of Air Photographs shows the three features, Saxon, Iron Age and Roman elements all together. The Norman element has still to be discussed and this can be found within the Iron Age element north of Sandrock Field. The front perimeter is shown as an irregular white line (the ditch) in the top left hand corner of the picture.

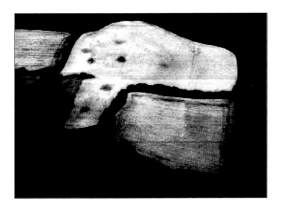

Aerial 2 August 1994

This photograph is the first of four taken from a helicopter in the summer of 1994 and is therefore the most recent. The prints are colour source material, hence the poor reproduction in black and white. We are looking due east towards Hastings at Sandrock and Five Acre fields from above Monkham inlet. The Roman track running from top to bottom of the photograph is clearly visible as a streak running down the image (above the "*1994*" above), although the computer scanning lines running across the bottom of the picture should be ignored. The dark brown patches in Five Acre field were in a doughnut type circle shape. This appeared as an inner and outer ring of slightly grey material spread throughout the soil. Fortunately the ground at the time had just been cleared and although the image was clear from the air the photograph does not do it justice.

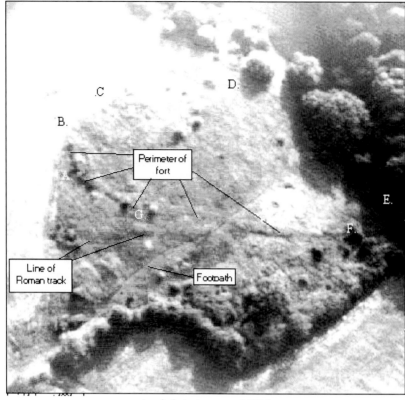

Aerial 4 August 1994

This shows the lower Norman fort area looking towards Bexhill in the south-west. The inlet can be seen in the top right with the first trees of Monkham Wood in the corner. Whilst the quality of the reproduction is poor it is still possible to see the distinctive shape of the ditch together with the line of the Roman track connecting the edge of Monkham Wood with the eastern port area. The circular light coloured feature next to the letter F is a prominent mound and the letters drawn on the photograph mark the approximate perimeter of the fort.

Aerial 3 August 1994 colour

We have looked at a lot of aerial photographs, but none give a better view of the scale of the site than the last one. It was taken looking east towards the metropolitan area of Hastings. The sea is in the background to the right. The light coloured field in the distant centre is Five Acre Field, adjacent to the old port, edging onto the marsh. The field in the foreground corresponds to that shown earlier and even with crops in the ground the markings of the early inhabitation are still evident from this distance.

The advantage of seeing these fields in this context is to make the reader aware that the port and the landing site covered a huge tract of land, able to absorb the number of boats and men required to do the job. This photograph covers only about half of the site we are examining, bringing home the scale of the total site and putting a perspective upon how big the Combe Haven waterway would have been in 1066.

Aerial 1 August 1994

The last of the aerial photographs gives a better picture of the 'Saxon doughnut' as it appeared to me on my 30 second flight around the site in the summer of 1994. The grey scale has reduced the visibility on the black and white prints, due to the different shades of brown being interpreted by the computer as similar greys, whereas the human eye can make great differentiation in colour. None the less these photographs provide conclusive evidence, to even the untrained eye, that these are no ordinary fields. The record shows that they have been in agricultural use since 1086(134) and yet clear markings of human habitation still exist today. The only conclusion this can support is that the claims made in this document are possibly true and therefore must be investigated by archaeologists with the necessary qualifications. After all this is no ordinary claim, it is a claim that hits at the heart of our English heritage and appears to be backed up by real evidence, both written and physical. Could anyone afford to ignore the possibility that here in the heart of rural Sussex lies an archaeological treasure of huge significance, hidden for almost a millennium?

At the time this document was written there is no archaeological record of the actual Invasion, only the subsequent occupation. Now I shall put before you the evidence to support the conclusion that it awaits discovery.

The land upon which the lower fort stands is truly remarkable, since it appears to have been left undisturbed by all the occupants of Wilting Manor, from the time of the Invasion until today. It is also a coincidence that the ownership of the Manor is also the same, in that it was transferred to the sheriff of Hastings after the Invasion, and it is now owned by Hastings Borough Council (the mayor being the nearest equivalent to sheriff today). Recent attempts to cultivate the area, with the aid of a tractor, were thwarted by the existence of a sandstone outcrop, thus ensuring its continual survival. It is as if a reason exists for its survival and each generation has unconsciously preserved the site intact. This is a map of the layout of post holes I have discovered:

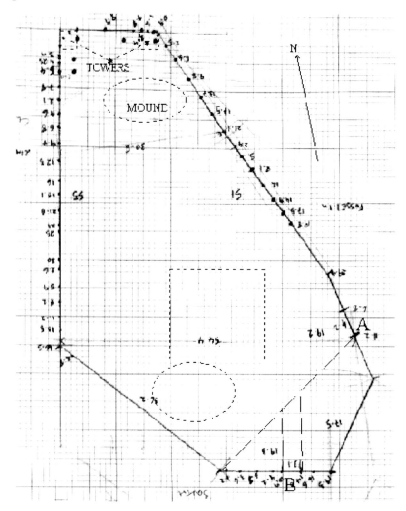

MAP OF POST HOLES

These post holes are created when a post is driven into the subsoil. The subsoil on this land is clay and only a few inches from the surface. Consequently when posts were erected for the fort the subsoil was moved out of the way by the post. Later when the post was either taken away, or disintegrated through decay, a hole was left, which filled with darker organic material. Those holes, where the posts once stood, can therefore now be detected.

The Norman fort was seven sided, with two identifiable entrances (drawn on the plan as A and B) on the east and south sides. Overall the fort measures 77 meters in length, running on an axis north/south, with a width of 56 meters. Post holes have been located at the points marked on the plan.

The soil on the site is very thin at the southern end, with blue/grey clay, less than six inches from the surface. In consequence, postholes can be located in some places, where the hole caused by a small wooden stake has been filled by organic debris. The stakes in question were small compared to what I, as a layman, would expect, being of various sizes from 1' to 1.5' in diameter. In many respects the same sort of support that would be expected for a relatively simple barricade. These stakes run completely round the site, at semi-regular intervals, and all are located on the top of a small mound, presumably caused by fill from the adjacent ditch.

At the northern end of the site there is an accumulation of sandy soil to a depth of between 80cm and 1meter, where wind has moved the soil down the slope towards the sea. This has been held back by some form of mound, covered with flat stones. These stones have an ironstone quality about them and appear to have been laid systematically in a large oblong circle. This oblong is app. 10 meters long by 4 meters wide. The mound takes the appearance of a possible burial mound and in consequence I decided to make an experimental excavation. I needed to provide myself with evidence that this really was something worth pursuing, since all the research done so far was of an academic nature.

Could this mound be the same mound referred to by Poitiers and the Carmen? The mound where Harold was buried? or is it the mound where William buried his own men, referred to in Poitiers, neither of which has ever been identified.

The excavation in question was in the middle of a briar, in excess of 12 meters in diameter. Having cleared a reasonable area, an excavation was started in the region of 2 meters long by one meter wide.

At a depth of 80 centimetres the sandy soil changed into a compact version of the same with the appearance of images in the soil. These were cleared with a small brush over a period of several weeks in the summer of 1993. The following pictures were taken to record the items uncovered.

There were three items in all:

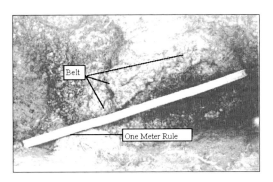

1) A BELT?

A belt type object was uncovered, shown immediately above the ruler. The age of the item was indicated as very old, since all recognisable magnetic signature has been lost when examined under a metal detector.

2) AN AXE HEAD?

This item took on the well-defined image of a possible axe head. It was rust coloured (more so than evident from the picture) and appeared solid metal.

Shown within area marked white

3) A KEY TYPE OBJECT

The key type object was located at the eastern end of the excavation and rested upon something that could possibly have been organic in nature. To my untrained eye it appeared like leather, but was solid in nature and not extractable.

As a consequence of these observations I concluded that I was not qualified to take any further action and refilled the excavation with a view to getting professional help. What I am convinced about is that the mound in question is of great antiquity, having excavated many sites previous to this one looking for clues. It may relate to any of the periods that cover the history of this site, but it has particular interest in that the clues that led me there were hidden in documents, which identify Harold's burial at the Norman camp. If the site of the Norman camp is proven to be correct, this may be the site of the burial of the last Saxon King of England, exactly as portrayed by Wace, under a pile of stones on a headland overlooking the shore and the sea.

The western side of the fort runs along the top of the side of what was once a sea inlet, which opens on to the Bulverhythe. This inlet once had a cliff side to it, thus making any attack on this side impossible. The southern sides of the fort were also protected by the proximity of the sea and were connected to the Monkham Inlet by a man made track.

On the north and western sides there is a ditch, since this was the open front, from which any attack might be expected. The ditch is still in existence today, showing as a well-defined indent, with earth piled behind where the palisade once stood. No excavation has yet been undertaken, since none was necessary to identify the feature.

Picture of the ditch at the lower camp

104

The picture shows the ditch running from the top right (north) to the bottom left (south) behind the oak tree. That tree has now been cleared from the site. In the background behind the oak tree you can see the mound with briar still intact.

SITE PICTURE

This picture shows the position of the camp in relation to its position on the edge of the Bulverhythe. The field in front is still ploughed in strips by the farmer. In times before mechanisation fields were ploughed by oxen. In consequence fields were ploughed in strips horizontally in order to avoid the need for the oxen to plough up hill.

Position of camp in relation to Wilting Hill

The same view taken looking north shows the strips in the same way as the Bayeux Tapestry (Plate 12) shows strips behind the fort. Now with the benefit of mechanisation the strips run the other way.

At the main entrance on the eastern side of the fort (A), there is an entrance leading on to the main plain. The earth has been levelled out at this point and within the perimeter there are definite signs of partitioning into various sub-areas, by the use of earthen ditches with attendant mounds. In the centre is a raised circular area, also in common with the picture shown in the Bayeux Tapestry.

The position of the fort coincides exactly with the parameters set out in our summary(135) of documentary evidence I therefore decided that sufficient evidence now exists to warrant a full resistivity survey of the field in question, since it is important to establish whether any features are hidden in the soil, which has been deposited there over the centuries.

This Wessex trench confirmed ditches located at the site of Lower Norman fort, exactly where it is claimed a ditch is shown being dug in the Bayeux Tapestry.

A resistivity study needed to be the next step, since this would reveal the existence, or otherwise, of any solid building structures, together with ditches or other features which produce differences in soil resistivity not visible to the naked eye. The advantage of doing a resistivity study is that the underlying archaeological material could be revealed without destroying the site. At the same time the raw data can provide a good visual image of the underlying geology together with any human involvement when removed by computer filtering.

Chapter 44: RESISTIVITY SURVEY

A number of surveys were carried out between August 1993 and summer 1994 by some willing and not so willing helpers, for whom I am most grateful. Most of this was done in the autumn before the valley flooded and spring after the water levels had dropped. During the high winter months the ground around the campsite was almost completely waterlogged. In fact one November day I managed to get the tractor carrying our equipment completely stuck in the entrance to the fort field. Even when a huge farm tractor came to our rescue, three hours later, there was a period of at least an hour when it looked like we were both in need of rescue. As we sat there wondering what to do, stuck in the middle of no-where, my mind went back to that event in Poitiers manuscript where William dismounted because of '*the difficulty of the ground*' at their camp site. Three hours soaked to the skin in two feet of mud brings home the meaning of those words with a vengeance.

The surveys were conducted using an RM4 resistivity survey kit, kindly loaned to me by the Hastings Area Archaeological Research Group. The plot was mapped out in twenty meter squares with one reading to each meter. The survey site was 560 meters long by 320 meters wide covering the complete Norman fort area. There is an additional section below the hedge line in Sandrock Field, to the south, which was 60 meters by 60 meters. This later segment was only recently added and still requires completing. Where appropriate I have shown on my web site two plans of each plot. One is the print from the computer and one where the feature we are looking at is marked. In common with the photographic prints there is a loss of quality that is attributable to the transfer process, but most features can easily be seen.

RES1

Shade Plot (Clip) Min -1 Max -1 Contrast. 1 Units Std. Dev

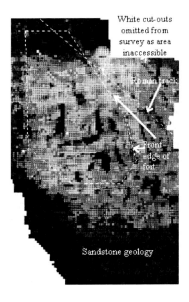

All the plots are looking north to coincide with the photographs earlier. The first plot (RES1) above shows the raw resistivity data with underlying geology. Dark areas are high resistivity indicating the sandstone outcrop which surrounds the site. High resistivity is the characteristic, which we are looking for since hidden artefacts produce the same dark image. It is therefore necessary to process the data to remove natural high resistivity using computer filters. The central area shows the main ditch of the fort (lighter line) cutting through the area of high resistivity in the top right hand corner of the fort area. Lighter areas demonstrate low resistivity. These indicate an absence of background readings, with ditches producing the lowest readings on a site. The presence of light areas provides a good method of identifying man made ditch construction. Surprisingly there is an area of high resistivity shown in the central area of the fort, which looks like the clear outline of a building of some kind, even though there is absolutely no indication of anything on the surface. Three sides of a wall exist with possible rubble on the north side. The area just below the bottom right hand corner of the fort appears to contain something, although at this stage the data is not reliable. On the screen version the Roman track crossing the top right hand side of the fort is clearly visible and appears on the print as a line of speckled squares.

These results are very exciting, since they provide conclusive scientific proof of the existence of a man made structure. Close examination shows the first signs of ditches running parallel to the front edge of the fort running along the eastern and southern boundaries. Further data processing now needs to be carried out. I therefore applied a high pass filter to remove the high readings caused by the background geology.

What is certain from this work is that the Lower Norman fort area holds many mysteries still to be revealed. The resistivity surveys confirm ditches and buildings showing occupation by man in an area that has previously been devoid of any reported activity since the Domesday Book was written. The outer ditches adjacent to the Lower Norman Fort confirm the probability that this was at some stage an Iron Age hill fort, which has subsequently been altered. The resistivity survey confirms the existence of the Roman tracks running across the site and under the perimeter walls. This indicates that the perimeter must have been built after the Roman occupation, confirming the probability that this is the first Norman camp. Whilst the possibility exists that this might be Saxon I have little doubt that the absence of the normal circular features associated with Saxon towns of the period makes this highly unlikely.

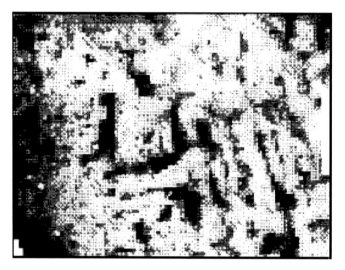

Enlargement of central area of Norman fort.

The central building located on the surveys in the centre of the lower field, shown above, comes as the biggest surprise of all. No one could have guessed its existence from a visual survey. This feature is the hallmark of all Norman defensive thinking - the Keep. This concept later developed into stone structures, designed to intimidate the nation into submission. If correct it would come as no surprise to historians to find that William built one at his first camp on the shores of Hastings port. The big surprise is that if correct it has been found after nearly a thousand years.

As a result of studying the information received from the resistivity survey it must be concluded that the probability that this is the first camp of William the Conqueror has increased immeasurably, purely because the data supports all the circumstantial historical evidence to date. Unlike the other evidence we have looked at, the resistivity data is not circumstantial, it is hard scientific fact, which requires extensive archaeological investigation to determine whether artefacts exist to support my hypothesis.

Assuming that the hypothesis is correct, the inlet and bay immediately adjacent to the camp must hold the Invasion boats themselves. These would form conclusive evidence that even the most hardened sceptic must reluctantly accept as proof of the authenticity of the site. With this in mind I decided to investigate the inlet with a view to locating remains of the Invasion flotilla and William's boat the Mora in particular.

The Monkham inlet is situated directly south of Monkham Wood and is marked on the 1844 tithe map of Hollington, drawn by David Padgham, as part of Piglands Brook(137). It is divided into three separate areas (A) the upper enclosure, (B) the beach area and (C) the harbour, separated from the marsh by reed bed (D). These are marked on the plan below.

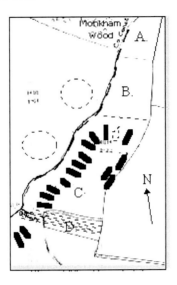

The first area (A) can be approached from Monkham Wood walking south through the wood. There is a wide uneven stream towards the southern end of the wood, which rapidly disappears underground as soon as it enters the open inlet. This area is flat, with a steep eastern side, which was probably a sheer cliff at some stage in the past. It shows signs of collapse and has been covered with earth, forming the jetties, which we discussed earlier, at the lower levels.

Picture of earthen jetty running into inlet looking south from Monkham Wood

The inlet is approximately 20 feet below the top field level, on the eastern side, where the Norman camp is situated. Thus ensuring no possible attack could be mounted from this side once the landing had been completed and the fort built.

View of terraces which form the jetty on eastern side of inlet from position (A).

The top section of the inlet nearest the wood is flat, but very wet most of the year. It is separated from the beach area (B) by a hedge. It is approximately a quarter of the way down the inlet looking towards the marsh. Both of the above pictures are looking south.

View of terrace above lower jetty approximately half way along inlet.

As you pass through the hedge you become aware of a beach section in front of you, together with the remarkable beauty of this totally isolated site. Until now I have confined myself to mostly factual matters. However it needs to be said that this inlet is a very special place. It has in fact been designated a SSSI, Site of Special Scientific Interest, because of the flora and fauna of the area, along with the marsh. Once you are in the inlet no civilisation can be seen or heard and it is true to say that the integrity of the site has been maintained, either by design or accident, since the days of the landing. The view is of what was once a beach; opening on to the marsh, which was once open water. In the front of the marsh, where the harbour area (C on the plan) meets the marsh (D), the reeds hide an irrigation ditch cutting across the inlet in front of an earthen bank. This earthen bank cannot be seen from the beach area, because the reeds, which are some eight to ten feet tall in places, totally obscure the front of the marsh and appear to go right back into it, if viewed from the beach.

110

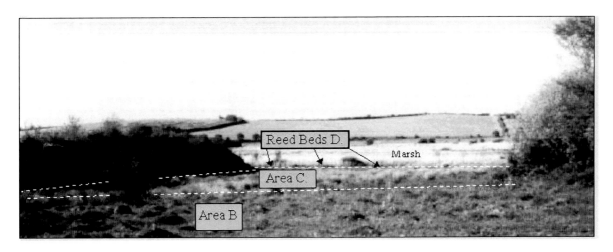

The view of the inlet, looking south towards the marsh. The hill in the distance hides the sea.

On the eastern side of the inlet the earthen terraces hidden inside the hedge line are very obviously man made, in that a series of three earthen terraces run along the northern section, from about half way connecting the upper and lower levels. These are only evident in certain areas where the undergrowth has been cleared.

View of three terraces with paths connecting

The Beach area (B) is now covered with water resistant grassland and large numbers of termite mounds, consistent with pastureland that has remained virgin for centuries. The eastern side of the inlet seems to be wetter, with grasses that thrive in wetlands. There is a well-defined beach line, marked by the dotted line on the picture on the earlier photograph, which sweeps across the inlet forming a small bay. At this point the floor level drops by at least half a meter. During the winter months this area (C) is virtually impassable due to it being positioned at the water table level. The slightest rain in the area turns the whole inlet into a lake, as the marsh acts as a giant reservoir for two

111

different tributaries of the Asten stream. A drainage ditch has been cut across the front of the inlet and cuts through the reeds at the front on the right hand side (looking south).

I looked for Norman boats drawn up along the front of the beach area. Investigation in the harbour area revealed at least nine similar slight mounds that could be boats along the western shore of area (C) and at least three in the central area. The mounds of the western shore were drawn on to the beach with between two and three meters between them, in a roughly parallel formation. Interestingly those on the other side of the inlet (the eastern side) were all parallel to the shore. Subsequent investigation by Simon Jennings and Christine Smyth of the Archaeology Department of the University of London confirmed to me that this inlet appeared to have a deep-water berth on the eastern side and a shallow shelving hard-core beach on the western side. This would account for the different positions of these boats.

Wace reports:

As the ships were drawn ashore, the Duke first landed, he fell by chance upon his two hands. Forthwith all raised a loud cry of distress, 'An evil sign,' said they, 'is here. ' But he cried out lustily, 'See, seignors, by the splendour of God! I have seized England with my two hands. . '

If this is the place where William stepped ashore and promptly fell in the mud, then it is highly logical that William's boat would be at the centre of this inlet. He is reported to have stepped ashore first, which would indicate a prominent position for the boat. According to the Battle Abbey Chronicle the boats were soon destroyed (burnt) after they landed[140], none the less the site of the boat would still remain. This sounds like I might be offering a rather lame excuse for finding the site of a boat, but hedging my bets in case it is later found that there is nothing there more than a pile of cinders. This is not the case; I most certainly believe the boats in question are there. If I did not believe this I would not have spent so many years investigating what appears till now to have been a historical myth.

Chapter 46: NORMAN BOAT PARTS

I therefore decided that an exploratory archaeological investigation was in order to establish whether there was any scientific validity the belief this inlet held the remains of ancient boats. I conducted an elementary surface clearance, removing the top six to nine inches of soil. Immediately a pattern appeared which bore no relation to anything that I had ever seen before.

Boat parts revealed at the site of the Mora?

I was surprised to find something so close to the surface. Digging further into the inlet revealed that the grey sediment layer of river mud is only just below the surface in some areas. The geomorphology of the inlet appears to have caused the top layers, which would normally have collected over the centuries, to move.

The picture above shows what I have called boat parts. The image that was revealed in the soil after two weeks of very slow clearance was of no assistance to me, other than to prove to me that something from ancient history is there. The parts are metal in origin showing as slight rust colour, but now completely replaced, making handling or removal impossible. The conditions reminded me of those experienced in Sutton Hoo, where the giant Saxon long boat was found. There too, no metal parts were recovered, yet perfect images of the metal parts were recovered by experts. The images consisted of struts, flanges and overlapping sections, which clearly could be anything nautical or otherwise. Needless to say expert evaluation is required. I believe it possible that the image above is connected with the rear of the boat and may have been fixed to the stern.

Chapter 47: THE EARTHEN BANK

After the elementary excavation in the summer of 1993 the site was covered in soil and a closer examination made of the geology of the inlet. Only relatively late in this investigation did I realise the fact that the inlet was in fact closed from the estuary by an earthen bank. This is drawn on the plan below as (D) part of the larger plan.(shown in Chapter 45) It is positioned right under a huge bed of reeds, which runs across the entrance. I had spent half a year or so wandering around this site, but had never seen the earthen bank. This is because you have to be on the marsh side of the inlet to be able to see it, or have to have walked to the very end of Sandrock Field. Even then it is not easily recognised, because the reed bed hides the different height levels of the marsh and the inlet. Walking on the marsh is only possible in high summer and then extremely dangerous, since the area is bog and quagmire, quite capable of killing anyone who falls in on their own.

I had assumed upon casual inspection that the ditch across the inlet was something to do with the modern drainage ditches running throughout the marsh region. This could not be so, because checking the tithe maps showed the drainage ditch alongside the bank followed the same route in 1844.

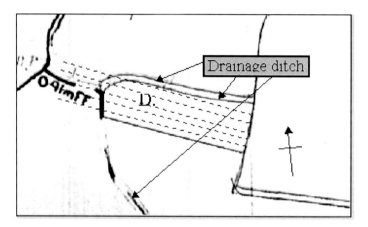

The ditch ran across the front inside of the inlet completely contrary to logic if installing normal drainage. The conclusion is that the earth bank must have been in existence when the drainage was put in, because it would otherwise not have been necessary to run the ditch across the front inside edge. If the bank had not been there previously then the drainage would have been directly through the centre of the bank or more likely down the eastern side of the inlet, where the water runs deepest. The western side must have been chosen by the engineers of the time because this was where the water ran out of the inlet, because the bank was lowest on this side, causing the water from the stream to come out there. Only when the ditch was dug did they realise that the marsh inside the inlet needed additional drainage, requiring an extension of the ditch along the inside.

Looking north into Monkham inlet mid summer.

The earthen bank is not of the same construction as the other drainage ditches on the marsh. It is lower and more weathered. At this time I have no conclusive evidence that confirms its age. Simon Jennings and Christine Smyth of the Archaeology Department of the University of London have conducted borehole tests to see if an age can be obtained. They are currently seeking a grant to do this work in conjunction with other work connected with the discoveries relating to industrialisation of the valley.

View of earth bank at Monkham inlet from marsh side looking northeast

The significance of this bank is that it provides the answer to one of history's great dilemmas: to explain how William was supposed to have burnt his boats (the Battle Abbey Chronicle) and yet earthed them up or decommissioned them (the Carmen). This anomaly has always forced historians to conclude that one version must have been an invention, forcing historians into separate camps, as to which version was authentic. The discovery of charcoal at the site of the '*boat parts*' leads to the conclusion that William may have burnt his boat, as well as some of the commanders, as a token of their commitment. The very low mounds that are present along the western shore of the Combe Haven, suggest that this is not true of the complete fleet. It is therefore quite likely that this mystery can be explained by the fact that the Battle Abbey record referred only to William's boat, whereas the inlet was earthed up, confirming the Carmen version of events. The consequence of this observation being that for the first time in history a hypothesis can be rendered concerning the events of the Invasion that show both manuscripts to be a completely truthful version of the events, with the inference that each is equally authentic. The interpretation has been incorrect to date, because the complete circumstances were unknown, as well as the location.

The full extent of the landing site is shown on the diagram on the next page, stretching westwards from the inlet as far as Decoy Pond, at the end of field numbers 841 and 842 on the Highways Agency plans of the proposed road route. This area is all designated SSSI and virtually impossible to obtain access to by the public. A lane has been built from this main landing site, which runs from the crook in the bay, directly to Wilting Manor house. This is called Cow Lane, most probably because it is used to deliver the cows to and from the marsh each year for grazing.

Aerial photo of complete Wilting site showing location of Cow Lane and main landing site

Cow Lane has a far more significant use, since it was undoubtedly the main access route for the Invasion force for provisions and support. The hedgerow leading to the marsh along Cow Lane can be established as very old, due to the large number of plant species[141] found there dating the lane to around the time of the Invasion. The explanation that this roadway came into existence for the cows alone now appears unlikely. It runs directly to the centre of the main landing site, and from there to the upper fort. Its age and location lead to the inevitable conclusion that it and the upper fort are directly linked.

Chapter 49: UPPER NORMAN FORT

As a result of studying the Wilting Manor site for several years in the lower port area, I was led to the conclusion that there may be a second fortification on the top of the hill, where the manor house now stands. In particular the visual evidence of a second fortification in the Bayeux Tapestry and the connection of the main landing area by the strangely named Cow Lane justified further examination.

The top field at Wilting, on the very summit of the land, where the manor house now stands, is called Chapel Field and is 4.52 acres. The view from this site is astounding, since there is a clear view over much of East Sussex to the west, as far as Beachy Head. It gives a commander occupying this site forewarning of any impending attack. To the north there is also a clear view of Telham Hill, where the London Road crosses the Ridge, thus alerting any watch of troops arriving from London, whilst giving the defenders at least half an hour's warning, in a day when half an hour could mean the difference between life and death.

Chapel Field sits strategically in a crook of the old Hastings to London road at Wilting, where it passes over the Hastings perimeter ridge. The HAARG study in 1987 identified the hedge between Chapel Field and the road as having a species count of 10, confirming an age of at least 1,000 years[142]. The hill is marked on the Ordnance Survey map as being approximately 40 meters in height, with relatively

116

steep slopes to the west and south. The current Hastings road skirts through the southern boundary of Chapel Wood, however examination of the ground inside the wood to the north of Chapel Field shows that previously it went a different route.

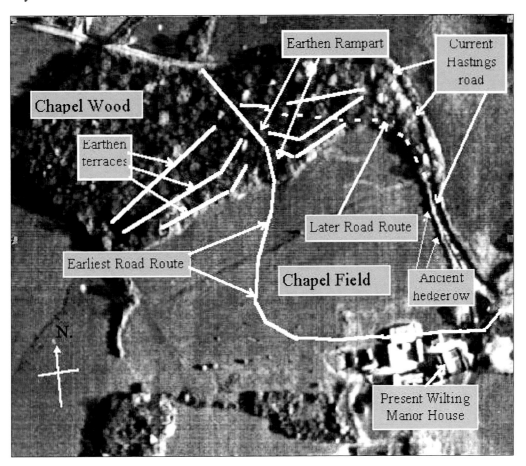

Aerial view of Upper Wilting Manor House and adjacent fields

There is a geological fault line that marks the boundary of Chapel Wood, as it passes into Chapel Field. This means that it is likely that at the time of the Conquest the northern end of Chapel Field was a cliff along most of the northern boundary. This would make access through the wood impossible, except via the old road. This can be seen from the evidence inside Chapel Wood, where the old road appears to have originally passed directly into the wood and up through the centre into Chapel Field. The evidence for this is the existence of a large earthen ramp leading from the bottom road up through the centre of the cliff area, where the fault line is located.

To the left and right of this ramp there are also earthen terraces cut into the hillside, which are now completely overgrown with trees and very dilapidated. However there are enough remains for verification that this structure did not get there by accident. It suggests that a huge amount of earth has been moved at some stage in the past. I could not hazard a guess at what time period, but leave this to persons more qualified than myself.

It can also be seen that the road later followed a route, more synchronous with the existing route, but further towards the centre of the wood. This is marked as a dotted line on the plan above. There are distinct track marks along most of this route, together with heavy ruts along the section below the cliff. This is evidently a more recent route, because of its ease of identification and lack of degradation. It could be assumed to be the route used prior to the modern tarmac road(141a.)

The question this raises is 'are the earthworks connected to the Norman Invasion?' I believe it is probable that the answer is yes and no. The Carmen reports that they reinstated the forts (in the plural) that were there. It is most likely that this referred to Iron Age defences, simply because the Saxon developments were unlikely to be in need of reinstatement. It is also unlikely that the Normans, no matter how inventive, could have moved the amount of earth required in the short time that they were in England. I am certain that these defences played a part in the Invasion plan, since strategically it would be impossible, from a military point of view, to occupy the lower fort and not occupy a similar one on the high ground overlooking the site.

Running through the centre of Chapel Field, just above the sign for the name on the photograph above is a grey line running approximately east/west. This is a huge earthen rampart. This is marked on the HAARG map in their 1987 report[143] as a lynchet separating Chapel Field from the top half (which was titled in the report House Meadow). The Oxford English Dictionary defines a lynchet as a derivative of Linchet – '*a strip of green land between two pieces of ploughed land or a slope or terrace along the face of a chalk down*'.

I believe that the earthworks in Chapel Field are man made and most likely to be of Norman origin. The lynchet is in fact the defensive front line of the fort, which the Normans installed at the top of this hill. There are clear signs that the field has been levelled into a rectangular shape. This is not something that can happen in nature and is also unlikely to relate to ancient defences. The Bayeux Tapestry shows a straight fronted fort with two towers at the top of the hill above the Norman camp at the port. I believe these earthworks marks the spot and traditional archaeological methods can verify this from posthole evidence, which should remain.

View of northern section of rampart separating lower and higher levels of Chapel Field looking east

It can be seen from the picture that this is a regular feature, which ensures any attacker would be put at a severe disadvantage. The defensive wall would be located at the top of the rampart and the open ground in front was accessed up a steep rampart with cliffs on either side, leaving nowhere to retreat in the event of failure in any attack.

View of western end of rampart looking east with Manor House in right hand corner.

The southern side of this structure is now obscured in the hedge line, which runs back towards the Manor House site, with the eastern section almost completely obliterated by the gas substation which has been built there.

Chapter 50: THE SIGNIFICANCE OF CHAPEL FIELD

The Hastings Area Archaeological Research Group's study of Wilting[144] in 1987 concluded that '*Many aspects of the Manor of Wilting remain tantalising mysteries*'. However it does confirm:

'*Wilting Manor is also well documented because of its connection with Hastings Castle. The Foundation Charter of the Collegiate Church of St Mary in the Castle mentioned 'The Chapel of Wilting' before 1100.*'

Aerial photograph of Chapel Field Wilting showing fort perimeter and possible chapel site

The reference to the Chapel of Wilting suggests to me the chapel is situated in Chapel Field. This may seem an obvious conclusion, but no one has found it, despite a series of investigations by local archaeologists, including myself, who have spent most of their time looking in Chapel Wood. This is because there is absolutely no indication on the ground that there could be a chapel anywhere else. The reason it is situated in the top field (now called Chapel Field) is because on the night before the battle the Normans erected chapels in that field, where they camped on the night before the battle, and subsequently erected a permanent chapel[145].

William is reported to have given his pep talk in the same field on the top of the hill. If all the other elements of the story are correct it would seem most probable that after the battle a permanent chapel would be built there. The historical record goes back to approximately 1100, bringing the name of the field and the events of the Invasion almost together. I must therefore conclude that it is highly likely that the connection between Wilting and Hastings Castle, as mentioned in the HAARG report, is interconnected with the incorrect location of the castle at that time. This would mean that it could be possible that St Mary in the Castle is the actual name of the original church at Wilting, because it is known that the church was situated within the boundary of the castle in 1094[146]. If the castle was at Wilting before it was moved to the current position it must be within the original fort perimeter and would have been built after the battle. I have marked the site where I believe this to be on the photograph above. This is where the aerial photos show a large building enclosure and the shape of the land indicates a building to be located there. It also happens to be located on an east/west axis, which would be expected for a building of this kind. Close inspection also reveals what are probably large building stones located on various points on the perimeter.

A crucial piece of evidence to support this is found in 1446 when the King (Henry VI) made a grant of jurisdiction over the church to the Bishop of Chichester. The deed of grant states:

'a certain church of the Blessed Mary, within the Castle of Hastings, in the county of Sussex, since erected and established into a collegiate church by the former Count of Eu. . . '

This can be interpreted to mean that the Count of Eu (probably not the one who fought in the battle, but his son) re-erected the castle and or the church. The words *'since erected'* could apply to either or both buildings. Why would the bishop use the expression *'since erected'* unless it was known at that time that the buildings had been moved.

Whilst it could not be said that these observations are themselves evidence, it would explain why the manor house was built on the site, after the church and castle were removed. It would also explain why several huge man made sandstone blocks have been found on the Manor site, which have the appearance of weathered tombstones and why the manor house has a lot of sandstone construction in the lower and basement areas. It would explain the anomaly of the name of the field, with the apparent absence of any historical confirmation of a chapel and why the name goes back so far in the record. I would therefore propose that the site needs to be subject to thorough archaeological scrutiny, by a fully qualified investigation team.

This clearly illustrates the difficulty in dealing with documents from the distant past, since the use of the word to describe a castle can also be interpreted to mean fort. I have not sought to differentiate in any fine detail throughout this document, since it is clear to me that by any other name a fort was regarded as a castle in the time scale we are interested in. I conclude that Chapel Field, in the manor of Wilting, probably holds the ruins of one of the most exciting archaeological finds of the century, the original Norman wooden castle at Hastings.

Chapter 51: PLACE NAMES

Having covered most aspects of the site I believe it is important to address the issue of place names connected with the site. The connection between Chapel Field and the events of the Invasion remains to be seen. Any place name interpretation will be speculative in these circumstances. I shall briefly state that I do not think it possible for an event as momentous as the Norman Invasion to have passed without some record creeping into the place name registry. I would therefore propose that apart from Chapel Field the following fields are directly linked to the Invasion and thus explain their origin:

Monkham Wood

Monkham Wood is located half way between the lower and upper Norman forts on the landing site. It is reported by most chroniclers that William and Harold employed monks to parley on the night before the battle. Monkham Wood and Monkham Mead are named after the place where the monks camped and were employed as negotiator intermediaries.

Sandrock Field

This is the place where William's men first landed after they had climbed out of the Monkham inlet. The name of the field illustrates the nature of the ground at that time, more resembling a sandy beach than a field. The sandstone outcrop formed a small cliff along the southern and western sides of their lower fort, and the name Sandrock probably passed into use at that time, thus naming the site. The road from Wilting to the battle site also passes huge sandstone outcrops and is called Sandrock Hill(147). This may not seem remarkable, since the area is covered in such outcrops, but it is still a coincidence that the monk Orderic named the battle as the battle of Senlac. No-one has been able to identify where this name came from. There have been many different interpretations, but I propose that Senlac is a straight interpretation of the French words for Sand and Rock (sens roc). The written name Senroc was written Senlac, because of the difficulty translating foreign script. It is not uncommon for an *R* to be read as an *L* and equally likely that an *O* could become an *a* in script. Hence Senlac entered the vocabulary courtesy of Freeman's popularisation of the name in the nineteenth century. It was common for names to be mistranslated or copied in error by those unfamiliar with the tongue and this provides the first possible explanation of the name, which ties in directly with the proposed landing site.

Bulverhythe

A compelling indication that the name Bulver-hythe is linked to the Norman Invasion is contained in the translation of the place name to mean '*The landing place of the people*' in Old English. I propose that *the landing place of the people*, at the port of Hastings, links this site to the Norman Invasion. This translation links to the special events of that time, rather than the usual linking of a port name to the local town.

In the Place Names of Sussex(148) by A. Mawer and F. M. Stenton it is confirmed that *burhwara* is from the Old English meaning '*citizens*' with hyde and hythe directly linked to harbour of the port or town. This latter point was confirmed to me by Margaret Gelling, the foremost place name expert in England, as meaning a specific type of port – an inland port – exactly as I propose Hastings was pre1066.

Redgeland

Redgeland Wood is a totally insignificant wood situated in the northeast corner of the Combe Haven valley, where we now believe the old port was located. The written record(149) goes back to 1399, which is unusual. The translation of the name is given as '*Ridge land*' yet the site in question is at sea level and not even on the ridge, which so prominently surrounds Hastings. Hedgeland also is mentioned in the Chronicle of Battle Abbey, as the site where William the Conqueror camped, and names the site as being at the port of Hastings. This site was falsely named by the monks at Battle Abbey as being at the top of the ridge and translated from the Old English meaning '*hedge land*'.

In view of this obvious anomaly I decided to contact Christopher Whittick, Assistant Archivist at East Sussex County Council, to see if there is any record held in the Wilting collection of deeds held in Lewis. Unfortunately most of these have not yet been catalogued, but he was kind enough to point out that the Old English for RIDGE is *hrycg,* whilst the Old English for HEDGE was *hecg*. The similarity of both words being so great, if written in script, that making an error in the writing of the Battle Chronicle seems certain.

Whether this error was deliberate seems unlikely. If the scribe had deliberately intended to deceive his audience there would be no point is using a similar name. It appears to me that the name had passed on to the monks of Battle Abbey through word of mouth or written record, which has now been lost. Consequently the name Hedgeland came into existence because the Chronicler confirmed in writing what he believed to be true. Only later did the monks of future generations forge the charters to justify their position and at the same time invent Hedgeland on the ridge within the Battle Abbey lands.

I would propose that Hedgeland, as a name, confirms more than any other name the site at the port on the Combe Haven valley as the site of the camp of William the Conqueror. The document it is taken from is without doubt authentic in relation to its age. I propose therefore that the transcription error from Redgeland to Hedgeland explains the loss from the historic record.

Chapter 52: THE GRAVES

One of the great mysteries of the Battle of Hastings is where William took his men for burial and where he buried Harold? In Poitiers he states that he returned Harold's body to his own camp '*having arranged honourable internment of his own men*(150).' This might be presumed to mean that they were buried with honour at a religious site (possibly the Chapel at the camp or on the battlefield). The Carmen makes the same claim and so I decided to look for a mound that would fit the description of the burial site, on the headland at Wilting overlooking the shore and the sea.

Picture of initial excavation in second mound.

After searching for several months I located a mound that appeared to fit the description. I shall not put the location in print just in case it should be accidentally published prior to investigation. This could result in attracting treasure hunters who might believe that any remains could be removed. Those qualified to deal with such an investigation will be advised of the exact location.

The mound is close to the top fort and overlooks the shore and sea exactly as portrayed in the manuscripts we have looked at. An initial excavation revealed that it is not of the construction of the surrounding soil, which is sandy soil getting progressively more compact the lower you excavate. Having never excavated what might be a burial mound I investigated very slowly.

The picture above shows the construction. The top foot was relatively compact soil; below this was a pile of flat stones, covered with soil. Unlike any other excavations that I have completed the soil appeared to become looser the further down the hole I dug. The above excavation took several days as I was for ever in fear of damaging any remains that there might be. I decided to stop at approximately 80cm because this was the depth that I had found an image in the first mound at the lower fort. The following photograph shows a picture of the stones at the bottom of this 80cm excavation.

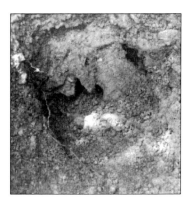

This shows the loose nature of the soil and the clear indication that the stones have been laid. The aperture beneath the main central stone was not caused by the excavation, but was already there when excavated. The site in question is completely devoid of the type of stones found in the mound.

History has taken the view that in the absence of positive identification of a grave William must have done the right thing. The proposal that he might have offered Harold a Viking funeral, under a pile of stones on a headland, was only questioned in retrospect after his death. Surely no great man would do such a thing to another king? This was of course the view of the victors, rather than the vanquished, with the benefit of hindsight. I therefore believe that it is quite logical for those nearest the actual events to have given a far better account of what really happened. This is the reason that I have only looked at evidence from manuscripts written in the first 150 years after the battle.

Wace appears to be offering an apology in this account and may have already heard the other stories about the burial and therefore sought to justify the story he had heard. In any event I consider the mound of paramount importance in respect of needing professional archaeological investigation. There is every reason to believe that if the other evidence provided here is correct then there is a case to be answered that this mound may be the burial site of the last Saxon King of England. If so there would also be a case for Harold to be given the Christian rights that William denied him. He should be buried in the church that was always his destiny to be buried. It was his right as King, albeit as such for only nine months, to be buried with his friend and confidant Edward the Confessor, in Westminster Abbey, with appropriate and due ceremony. The building was made for this purpose and I believe Harold was done a great injustice by denying him this right.

Harold was the strong man of England and the heir apparent. He fought his brother and the King of Norway at Stamford Bridge, defending York and England against invasion from the Norwegians. I believe that he has been falsely painted the villain or fool by History, because of lack of information. It is my belief that these matters will all be re-evaluated when all the information is made available.

In the meantime I would like to re-evaluate the evidence of the site requirements, according to the manuscript evidence. This will allow us to establish what level of credence to give to the information provided to date. You will recall that there were forty different aspects of the site which could be directly related to written evidence from the period concerned. It might be reasonable to expect at least fifty percent of these findings to correlate, since most appear to be fairly specific. With this in mind we will now re-examine the forty points concerned.

Picture of landing site taken from the centre of the port area

Chapter 53: ANALYSIS OF ALL REQUIREMENTS

In relation to the proposed site:

The issues raised in the chapter entitled Conclusion of Site Requirements, according to manuscript study(151) produced a list of observations directly linked to authentic manuscript documents from the period within 150 years of the landing. I decided to use 150 years as a completely arbitrary yardstick, upon the principal that as time progressed the likelihood of error creeping into the translations and recopying of the original works would reduce their reliability. All studies of the events concerned, as far as I am aware, have to date claimed that one or more of the documents we have studied is unreliable. This unreliability is due to the anomalies and inconsistencies, which we have discussed, as well as some which at this stage have not been covered.

The proposal that the Norman Invasion landing site was at Wilting Manor can not only be shown to be valid from the archaeological and geographical record, but more importantly the Wilting site fundamentally supports all the documents, which previously have been discredited as unsound.

It probably needs to be asked by someone like myself, who is not versed in an academic historical career, why such detailed accounts of the events by Poitiers, Wace or the Carmen should ever have been conceived to have been completely wrong. There is logic in dismissing all the evidence of a manuscript if it is believed to be unsound. However the proposal that you just take the parts that agree with current '*thinking*' is just as unsound. Hence those, who for one reason or another, prefer to believe that the Normans landed at Pevensey, should seriously question how they can use Poitiers to justify this position, when a number of the other authors' state Hastings was the landing site. As stated in the earlier text, the question of Poitiers actually making this claim is now seriously in doubt(152).

It could be argued that errors in transcription were common at the time these documents were written, and unless they were original copies, errors were almost certain to have occurred. This may be true, but it does not account for changing the landing place from one town to another. There must be a logical reason why these two towns featured in the writings and I believe the Wace account(153) provides a wholly logical explanation. Disregarding all the other sources that provide information to the contrary is not logical and in my view is unscientific. Especially when there is a document containing sixteen and a half thousand lines of text on the events of the landing, which to this day are completely acceptable as authentic in France, where the Normans came from. Has it never crossed anyone's mind why this may be?

The answer may be that it did not fit in with Victorian theories and therefore needed to be discarded, at a time when communication and cross checking the record was not that easy. Recent studies have shown that much of what was thought to be unreliable then, really is not in doubt, it is the interpretation placed upon them by the interpreters. Wace did not write all those words over many years just for fun. I believe it is fair to say that any scribe who dedicates his life to putting the record on paper for future generations does not undertake such a task lightly. Therefore this is a fundamental flaw in dismissing Wace or any of the documents we have looked at.

There can only be one wholly acceptable conclusion that satisfies all logic and leaves no room for doubt. This states that all the manuscripts were written by men who believed they were stating the truth as they knew it. In the course of time some of the items may have been changed in translation or error. Since many different sources of the same events have been committed to print, the summary of all the parts must paint a picture that will mostly show what really happened.

Taking these forty points, from the eight main manuscripts from the period, should thus provide us with a definitive conclusion as to the reliability of the proposal I put before you. Not all the elements are conclusive in relation to the Wilting site, but must be taken in the whole, with all the other details. Hence I am saying that it is not one point, taken on its own, that is important or conclusive. It is only the sum of all of them that can present the most persuasive argument; since this carries the implicit guarantee that none of the writers of the documents studied was inherently wrong about any of the information provided to us.

THE FORTY ISSUES:

1) Unopposed Landing. The landing was unopposed according to all sources and is probably due to the fact that the men of Hastings went on an annual fishing trip at this time of the year (October) to the east coast to catch herring. The Hastings town at Wilting would therefore have been undefended and so supports the agricultural community shown in the Bayeux Tapestry.

2) Town of Landing. It is proposed that Hastings town was situated at what became known as Wilting Manor, thus supporting the evidence that the landing happened at Hastings.

3) Camp By Or Near The Sea. The proposed camp is in such a location, an inland waterway and bay.

4) Camp At A Port. The camp was at the port of Hastings, which we propose is the inlet at Bulverhythe, below Wilting Manor.

5) Port Capable Of Holding At Least 696 Ships. The old port at the camp was capable of holding these ships and far more. As shown in the photograph at the end of the previous chapter and the aerial photographs.

6) Camp Site In A Calm Bay. The camp was next to a large inland expanse of water, protected from tides, but with access to the sea confirming the description as a calm bay.

7) Camp Adjacent To A Large Shore. The proposed camp at Wilting was adjacent to a large shore stretching several miles

8) The Ships Were Side By Side. The ships along the southern shore at Wilting could fit side by side in a continuous section of the shoreline, and evidence of their remains are, I believe, still there.

9) They Built A Wooden Fort. The fort at the landing site and the one at the top of the hill were both wooden, and resistivity surveys of the area highlight possible remains of such structures. Post holes confirm a wooden structure at the bottom and top of the hill at Wilting.

10) The Fort Had A Ditch. The fort shown in the resistivity survey at the landing site has a ditch on the front three sides.

11) There Were Previous Forts At The Site. I believe there is conclusive evidence that supports a number of different defences at the Wilting site, which account for this important observation.

12) The Fort Was On A Hill. Both The lower fort, on a headland and the upper fort, on the top of the hill can be found at Wilting as described.

13) The Ships Were Earthed Up. The inlet with the earthen bank confirms that the ships could have been earthed up

14) The Ships Were Dismantled. I believe that the Norman ships are still located along the shore and that this indicates that they could not be removed and thus comply with the concept of being dismantled, although this remains to be seen.

15) The Ships Were Burnt. The evidence in Monkham Inlet confirms that some, if not all the ships may have been burnt by the presence of charcoal at the old beach site.

16) The Ships Were Small. The evidence from the inlet confirms the size to be comparable with lifeboats, confirming them being small by modern day standards.

17) William's Ship Had A Figurine. Boat parts in Monkham Inlet; whether these include a figurine remain to be seen.

18) The Ships Had Viking Type Prows. This remains to be seen

19) The Prows Had Removable Heads. This remains to be seen but an item looking very much like one of those removable heads was found at the boat site.

20) The Camp Was Next To Or At A Manor Held By The King. Wilting Manor is next to Crowhurst Manor, which was held by King Harold at the time of the Invasion. Harold was the Lord of Crowhurst Manor as recorded in the Sussex Domesday Book.

21) The Initial Landing Site Was Small. This is confirmed by the inlet where they first landed.

22) There Was A Plain Near By The Landing Site. There are two huge plains immediately adjacent to the lower Norman camp at Wilting. Both have a copious supply of fresh water from the streams at either side.

23) The Neighbourhood Was Laid To Waste. The Domesday evidence confirms that Wilting and Crowhurst, the nearest other manor, suffered the greatest as a result of the Invasion, with both manors being laid waste, emphasising its validity as the landing site.

24) The Ground Was Uneven And Waterlogged. The site of the landing at the lower Norman fort is accurately described during the winter months.

25) One Camp Was At The Bottom Of An Agricultural Field. The lower Norman Camp is situated below a large agricultural field with no evidence that it has ever been other than this.

26) The Other Camp Was At The Top Of the Same Field. This describes the layout of the two camps at Wilting.

27) The Bottom Camp Was To The Right Of The Bottom Of The Hill. This describes the bottom camp exactly as shown in the Bayeux Tapestry.

28) The Fort At The Bottom Of The Hill Had Two Towers. At the bottom site evidence of post holes for two towers was found.

29) There Was A Mound Between The Two Towers. Confirmed at the lower Norman fort.

30) The Towers And Fort Walls Had A Terraced Bottom. The resistivity survey of the lower Norman fort highlighted this structure.

31) There Is A Circular Dining Room. The lower Norman fort has a raised circular area, which could be a dining area, however this remains to be seen.

32) The Exit Was To the Right Of The Fort Looking From The Sea. The lower Norman fort conforms to this layout.

33) The Duke's Quarters Were Elevated At the Site. The lower Norman fort has a raised area, but it remains to be seen if this is the Duke's quarters.

34) The Camp At The Top Of The Hill Had Two Towers And A Connecting Palisade. Two towers were located on the top fort connected by a palisade. Post holes have been dowsed at the site but not recorded in the previous text. (*Note: Wessex Archaeology confirmed two parallel ditches at this location, supporting the supposition that a defensive structure probably existed*).

35) The Camp Had Chapels In Adjacent Field Upon Departure. Chapel Field is located at this site and its origins explained.

36) The Landing Site Was Low Down Below Three Houses. The site at Wilting is below the main ridge at which Wilting Manor house was subsequently built. Three buildings probably sat prominently over the site, on the assumption that these buildings were later replaced by the ones that we know. These were Wilting Manor House, Mayfield Farm (at the adjacent cross-roads) and Adams farm (if one existed there at the time). By coincidence the site is surrounded by three unopposed landing areas and three manors.

37) There Is A Grave At The Site. There are probably at least two mounds at the site and possibly more that could qualify as graves.

38) The Grave Has A Marker Stone. I believe that I know the location of the marker stone for Harold's grave, which has been removed from the actual grave site. I shall reveal the location of this stone should it be appropriate after the other investigations have been initiated. The stone is in a place that is currently impossible to access through conventional methods, since it is under a building. In the meantime this item is not able to corroborate the other evidence.

39) The Camp Is In The manor Of Crowhurst or Wilting. The camp is in the manor of Wilting.

40) The Site Is Called Hedgeland. The site of the landing is at a place called Redgeland, which in Old English has been mistranslated in the Chronicle of Battle Abbey.

An inspection of all forty points reveals 34 items in agreement with the Wilting site (85%), with six which cannot at this time be revealed (15%)[154]. However these six are not dismissed on account that they fail the viability test, but more relevantly cannot be established as true or false, in relation to this site, until after further investigation.

Chapter 54: CONCLUSION OF LANDING SITE

(*Authors note: Revised 10th July 2007*)

The only conclusion that I believe can be drawn from this information included in this document is that the site at Wilting Manor exactly fits the requirements for the 1066 landing and Invasion site of William the Conqueror. The assumptions drawn from the Bayeux Tapestry are correct, even though historians have always claimed the pictures to be cartoon representations. Wace and the Carmen's descriptions all fit as if there were never any discrepancy. There is no contradiction in either the Chronicle of Battle Abbey or the Domesday information. The Saxon Chronicles support this site at Hastings, when you take on board new thinking as to the interpretation, whilst Poitiers and Jumieges also remain open to a new interpretation regarding Hastings as the Invasion site.

When this information is taken with the detailed archaeological record of growth of the inhabitation of the Combe Haven valley, it is impossible not to come to the conclusion that the ancient town of Hastings was situated on its northern shore, in Saxon times. Its subsequent destruction has been fully recorded in the Bayeux Tapestry and although rebuilt by the same conquerors, this record has been lost until now. Absolute proof of these events will only become possible when the earthworks have been properly investigated by excavation or other more tangible proof is removed from the soil.

Those who turn to this page without having read the evidence in the hope of obtaining a neat summary will be disappointed due to the nature of the task at hand. William the Conqueror spent in the region of six weeks in 1066 at this site with his army. Anyone seeking to prove occupation for six weeks nearly a thousand years ago should appreciate that this task is not easy. The important issues come from the detailed re-examination of the historical documents from the time. When applied to the previous site of Pevensey, named by Poitiers and prominently displayed in the Bayeux Tapestry, major anomalies come into play, which could never be explained by historians. As a result, the Victorians hypothesised that the conclusion must be that only one set of documents could be right and the rest were wrong, consigning highly detailed manuscripts such as Wace's Roman de Rou and the Carmen to the waste paper basket. This was a fatal flaw in the thinking of the age - since a neat answer was required. What the experts of that age failed to realise was that in the time of William and Harold, the French knew the south coast of England by the forts and castles that protected her. In consequence one simple rearrangement of our understanding that Pevensey meant the area controlled by that Castle, brings all the manuscripts into one clear focus, since the port and area of Hastings was within this district. At this time the archaeology is at its early stages, since funding is required to take this research forward. The primary documents, which support Wilting Farm as the landing site of the Norman Invasion, are difficult to argue against. These documents are the detailed analysis of the Domesday Book data, using the knowledge of the development of the road systems in the area, assisted by computerised analysis. No historian before me has been able to do this in such a conclusive way. I have yet to meet a historian who has the ability to argue against the results, even now many years after first publication - how can they, when the data comes from an impeccable source? In the meantime I believe I have made a satisfactory case for all these matters to be thoroughly investigated.

I am certain that those matters that have led me upon this path of discovery are fundamentally correct. I have placed the information into the public domain, upon the principle that others more qualified than I will complete the task involved. However, some of the issues raised here need to be expanded to complete the picture. It would have been impossible to do this without first destroying the myth of the Pevensey landing. Now that the camp and landing site have been rediscovered I shall turn my attention to the events of the battle. This battle was unique in English history and, like the Norman landing, raises many questions that have not yet been answered.

It is essential for those whose duty lies in protecting the English heritage not to underestimate the importance of the site at Wilting. It holds many secrets, a few of which have been exposed to public scrutiny on these pages. Full investigation and the preservation of the site from the road planners is not a matter that will wait. Even now new plans to build another road are under way, by those who place no value on English cultural heritage. This is the reason I need to file this document, even though I personally would consider it premature, given the spectacular possibilities presented by proper archaeological survey prior to public scrutiny.

This cannot unfortunately be the case, because the Bexhill to Hastings link road is now in the final stage of the line order, and this has been drawn right through the middle of the Norman Invasion site again. A copy of this documentation has therefore been sent to the Heritage Minister and the Secretary of State, to alert them to the inconceivable damage to the nation's heritage building this road will have. At the same time a copy has been sent to the National Monuments Commission seeking authentication of the material contained within these pages, with a view to securing a listing as a national monument, for all future generations to enjoy.

In the meantime I leave you with the words of Major General J. F. C. Fuller CB. CBE. DSO who wrote:

'For England, Hastings was not only the most decisive battle ever fought on her soil, but also the most decisive in her history, in fact, there is no other battle which compares with it in importance.'

Chapter 55: DOMESDAY VALUES

Annex Part One

MANOR NAME	(A) VALUE BEFORE 1066	VALUE AT 1066	VALUE AT DOMESDAY 1085/6	% OF (A) VALUE AT 1066
BEDDINGTON	£4	£2	£3. 10S	50. 0
LAUGHTON	£4	£2	£4	50. 0
BERWICK	£1. 10S	10S	£1. 15S	33. 3
EASTBOURNE	20S	10S	45S	50. 0
EASTHALL	£2. 1S	£1. 1S	£2	60. 0
BEVERINGTON	£2. 1S	£1. 1S	£2	60. 0
CHOLLINGTON	£2	18S. 8P	£1. 10	41. 0
YEVERINGTON	£1. 10S	15S	£1. 4S	50. 0
EASTHALL	15S	10S	10S	66. 6
CHARLSTON	£3	£2	£5	66. 6
SEDDLESCOMBE	£3	£1	£2	33. 3
WEST FIRLE	£60	£30	£44	50. 0
WILLINGDON	£60	£30	£47	50. 0
EXEAT	£4		£3	75. 0
CHARLSTON	£9		£4. 10S	50. 0
RATTON	£6		£1. 10S	75. 0
W. DEAN	£7	£3	£5	42. 0
RATTON	£5		£4	80. 0
RATTON	£3	£1	£2	33. 3
RATTON	£3		£2	66. 6
WANNOCK	£5. 10S	£2	£4. 10S	36. 0
FOLKINGTON	£5	£2	£3	40. 0
TARRING NEVILLE	£8	£6	£10	75. 0
SIDNOR	8S	6S	10S	75. 0
CHARLESTON	60S	40S	100S	66. 6
BOWLEY	22/4P	15S	30S	68. 0
HAILSHAM	£5. 10S		£1	18. 0
CHENONOLE	£2		15S	37. 5
HORNS	£1. 5S		10S	40. 0
HORNS	13S		63P	40. 0
BECHINGTON	100S	50S	60S	50. 0
RENCHING	16S		15S	93. 7
LANGLEY	16S 8P		10S	60*
HANKHAM	15S		8S	53. 0
ROTHERFIELD	£16	£14	£12	87. 5
WOOTON	£4	£2	£4	50. 0
BISHOPSTONE	£26	£11	£20	42. 3
ALCISTON	£48	£36	£40. 5S	75. 0
HOOE	£25	£6	£21	24. 0
CATSFIELD	£2. 10S	£1	£3	47. 6
MEDEHEI	£4	£1	£5. 10S	25. 0
NINFIELD	£6	£1	£5. 5S	16. 6
HERSTMONCEUX	£6	£1	£10	16. 6
ASHBURNHAM	£6	£1	£9	16. 6
FRANKWELL	£2	10S	£2. 6S	25. 0
BULLINGTON	£6	£2. 10S	£6. 3S	41. 6
MOUNTFIELD	£3	£1	£4	33. 3
BRIGHTLING	£5	10S	£2. 2S	10. 0
WARBLETON	£2		£1	50. 0
GOSSHAMS	£2	£1	£1. 1S	50. 0
EWEHURST	£10	£6	£9	60. 0
RIPE	£12		£8	66. 6
CLAVERHAM	£2		£1. 16S	55. 0
CLAVERHAM	£2. 5S		£2	88. 0
ECKINGTON	£5		£3	60. 0
HENDON	9S	4S	5S	44. 0
HAWKRIDGE	20S	10S	15S	50. 0
BODIUM	£10	£6	£9	60. 0
MAYFIELD	£4		£2	50. 0
BATTLE	£48	£30	£40. 5S	62. 0
CHALVINGTON	40S		30S	75. 0
RENCHINGS	16S		15S	93. 0
HASTINGS	£5	£2	£6	40. 0
HASTINGS	£34		£50	NEW BOROUGH
HASTINGS	£5	£2	£6	40. 0

MANOR NAME	(A) VALUE BEFORE 1066	VALUE AT 1066	VALUE AT DOMESDAY	% OF (A) VALUE BEFORE 1066
WILTING	£5	WASTED	£4	0
HOLLINGTON	30S	WASTED	58S	0
BEXHILL	£20	WASTED	£18. 10S	0
FILSHAM	£14	WASTED	£22	0
CROWHURST	£8	WASTED	£5	0
WHATLINGTON	£2. 10S	WASTED	£2. 10S	0
NETHERFIELD	£5	WASTED	£2. 10S	0
BROOMHAM	£1	WASTED	£1	0
HAZELHURST	£5. 14S	WASTED	£7	0
SALEHURST	£1	WASTED	£1. 10S	0
DRIGSELL	£3	WASTED	£4	0
GUESTLING	£5	WASTED	£5	0
HIGHAM	£5	WASTED	£6	0
LIDHAM	£1	WASTED	£1	0
HASTINGS	£20	WASTED	£18. 10	0

Chapter 56: SOURCES

PRIMARY SOURCES

William de Jumieges - Gesta Normannorum Ducum - English Historical Documents 1042 - 1189 edited by David C. Douglas and George W Greenaway 1953 (Eyre and Spottiswood)

William de Poitiers - Gesta Guillelmi - English Historical Documents 1042 - 1189 edited by David C. Douglas and George W Greenaway 1953 (Eyre and Spottiswood)

The Carmen of Hastingae Proelio - Guy Bishop of Amiens Edited by Catherine Morton and Hope Muntz 1972 (Oxford Medieval Texts)

The Chronicle of Battle Abbey, Edited and Translated by Eleanor Searle 1980 (Oxford University Press)

Master Wace his Chronicles of the Norman Conquest from the Roman de Rou translated by Edgar Taylor Esq F. S. A. 1837 (William Pickering London)

The Domesday Book text and translation by John Morris - Sussex edited from a draft translation prepared by Janet Mothersill 1976 (Phillimore)

The Bayeux Tapestry - Centre Guillaume le Conquerant Bayeux

The Anglo-Saxon Chronicles - English Historical Documents 1042 - 1189 edited by David C. Douglas and George W Greenaway 1953 (Eyre and Spottiswood)

SECONDARY SOURCES

A Palaeoenvironmental Investigation of Flandrian Valley Deposits from the Combe Haven Valley East Sussex, C. T. Smyth Quarterly Review Vol2 1986

The America Ground, Barry Funnell HAARG 1989

Anglo-Saxon England, Martin Welch 1992 (English Heritage)

Battle Abbey and Exemption: The forged Charters 1968 (English Historical Review)

The Bayeux Tapestry Norman Denny and Josephine Filmer-Sankey 1966 (Collins)

Calendar of Patent Rolls 1494 - 1509, p214

Castles of the Conquest, J. H. Round (Archaeologica Vol. 58)

Combe Haven Valley Environmental Study. Sussex River Authority 1979 (SRWD)

Crowhurst a Village in History J. F. C. Springford 1990 (Springford)

Ferns Mosses and Lichens of Britain and Northern and Central Europe, Hans Martin Jahns 1983 (Collins)

Feudal England - Historical Studies on the Eleventh and Twelfth Centuries. J. R. Round 1895 (George Allen and Unwin Ltd)

The Genealogists Magazine, September 1944 **Companions of the Conqueror** G. H. White p417 - 424

Geomorphology, B. W. Sparks 1972 (Longman)

Holocene Evolution of the Gravel Coastline of East Sussex, S. Jennings and C. Smyth 1988 (Dept of Geography London University)

Hastings,The Story of the English Towns L. F. Salzman 1921 (SFPCK)

Historic Hastings, A Tapestry of Life. J. Manwaring Baines 1986 (Cinque Port Press)

History of Hastings Castle Vol. 1 & 2, Charles Dawson 1909 (Constable and Co Ltd)

History of the Combe Haven Valley, E. McCall 1991 (C. A. C.)

History of the Norman Conquest of England: its causes and its results E. A. Freeman 1867 - 79

Julius Caesar Man Soldier Tyrant Major-General J. F. C. Fuller (Eyre and Spottiswoode)

Late Roman Fortifications, Stephen Johnson 1983 (B. T. Batsford Ltd)

Latin Poetry and the Anglo-Norman Court 1066-1135 Elisabeth M. C. van Houts

Journal of Medieval History 15 (1989) 39-62 Lichens Jack R. Laundon 1986 (Shire Natural History)

Medieval Reckonings of Time R. L. Poole 1921 (London)

Mid to Late-Holocene Forest Composition and the Effects of Clearance in the Combe Haven Valley, East Sussex. Christine Smyth and Simon Jennings 1988 (Sussex Archaeological Collections 126)

Parish of Crowhurst Tithe Map 1842 East Sussex County Archive Lewes

Parish of Hollington Tithe Map 1844 with field names edited by David Padgham 1990 Hastings Public Reference Library

Pevensey Castle, Sir Charles Peers CBE 1985 (English Heritage)

Place Names of Sussex. Judith Glover 1975 (B. T. Batsford Ltd)

Report on the Assessment of Archaeological Deposits at the Central Cricket and Recreation Ground Redevelopment Site, Mark Gardiner 1988 (Field Archaeology Unit Institute of Archaeology) for Hastings Borough Council.

Roman Britain 55BC - AD400, Malcolm Todd 1981 (Fontana Press)

Roman Britain (Map of),Ordnance Survey 1978

Romano British Bloomeries in East Sussex. Straker and Lewis 1938 (Sussex Archaeological Collections 79) p224 - 229

Roman Ways in the Weald, Ivan D. Margary 1965 (Phoenix House)

Senlac - More about the Battle Col. C. H. Lemmon D. S. O. 1956 (Battle and District Historical Society)

Some Notes on the Church and Manor of Crowhurst, M. E. Newman 1971 (Crowhurst Church)

South East England - The Channel Coastlands. Millward and Robinson 1973 (Macmillan)

The Bayeux Tapestry and the Battle of Hastings 1066. Mogens Rud 1988 (Christian Eilers, Copenhagen)
The Decisive Battles of the Western World 480 B. C. - 1757, J. F. C. Fuller 1972 (Paladin)
The English Channel. J. A. Williamson 1959 (London)
The Evolution of England. J. A. Williamson 1944 (Oxford)
The Evolution of the Hastings Coastline. E. M. Ward 1920 (Geographical Journal)
The Field of Hastings Lt. Col. C. H. Lemmon 1970 (London)
The Foundations of England. Sir J. Ramsay 1892 (London)
The Gesta Normannorum Ducum of William of Jumieges Orderic Vitalis and Robert of Torigni Vol1 Edited and Translated by Elisabeth M. C. can Houts 1992 (Oxford Medieval Texts)
The History of the Southern Railway, Michael R. Bonavia 1987 (Unwin Hyman)
The Iron Industry of the Weald, Henry Cleere and David Crossley 1985 (Leicester University Press)
The Nature of History, Arthur Marwick 1970 (Macmillan)
The Norman Achievement, Richard F. Cassady 1986 (Sidgwick and Jackson)
The Norman Conquest - Documents of Medieval History, R. Allen Brown 1984 (Edward Arnold)
The Place Names of Sussex, A Mawer and F. M. Stenton with J. E. B. Gover 1969 (Cambridge University Press)
The Prophesies of Nostradamus, Erika Cheetham 1981 (Corgi)
The Puzzles of the Bayeux Tapestry, Roger S. Porter 1986 (Ferndale Press)
The Sussex Landscape. Peter Brandon 1974 (Hodder and Stoughton)
William the Conqueror, David Walker 1968 (Clarendon Biographies)

Chapter 57: PHOTOGRAPHS

Annex Part Three

Picture of Sandrock Field looking south over marsh showing summer crop markings (ref page 74/1)

Terrace crossing field above Sandrock field (Ref page 75/4) see image below

This is the Roman track that connects the '*cobbles*' to the lower field by the port

Roman track terrace across field at Upper Wilting (Ref page 75/18)

End of original manuscript (23rd December 1994)

It is now 1999 and you will recall that some six years earlier I laid out the proposal that the inlet immediately adjacent to the landing site, at Monkham Inlet, was enclosed by an earthen bank and this bank formed part of the necessary supporting evidence that the Normans landed at this site. This is detailed in the chapter on the Inlet.

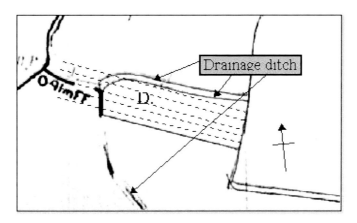

One of the main claims in the Carmen (now re-established as probably authentic, due to the work of Dr. Van Houts of Cambridge) is that William earthed up his ships in order to avoid desertion by his men - a prudent move given the circumstances. If this is the true site of the Norman Invasion then evidence of that event should still exist. Hence the interest at that time in seeking to establish whether this earthen bank were man made in recent times, or whether the unusual aspects of the construction could be attributed to a hitherto unknown distant link with the Invasion.

A drainage ditch was hidden in what now is a deep reed bed. This cuts through the left hand side of the inlet (looking north), along the inside of the bank. This is something that is illogical, since a stream runs into the inlet from the north. The effect of building an earthen dam across this is to keep water inside the earthen structure. The cut through the bank is also on the shallow side of the inlet. This is not logical since engineers who knew the structure of the valley floor should have known that the eastern side of the inlet was twice as deep as the side which they put the cut through. If they were the ones to form the earthen bank they would have placed the excavation on the marsh side of the earthen dam, since the object of the irrigation ditch was to drain the marsh. Yet in this case the decision was made to cut the ditch along the inside of the bank. My proposal is that this decision was made because the earthen structure was already there. Now as a result of recent developments I am convinced this is the case.

These photos were taken much earlier in 1993/4 when the water levels were high on the marsh to the south. The work was done in early summer and on the picture below the grey fleck flowers that are in the foreground at marsh level are in fact yellow buttercup type flowers indicating the marsh level.

Looking north into Monkham inlet mid summer.

View of earth bank at Monkham inlet from marsh side looking northeast

Steve, the farmer at Wilting, had been using major earth moving equipment to clear out the ditch to keep the water flowing. I therefore found myself back at the inlet and decided to investigate.

It was interesting to see how much the valley floor had changed in the previous four or five years. This is the view looking south out into the inlet in 1993.

Here is a similar view in 1997 showing the reed beds have been completely decimated.

The green grass area in the foreground runs up to where the earthen bank is located. The bank has retained the slurry from the stream that runs south into the marsh and formed a level plain, which was at one time deep water on the east side and shallow on the west side. Over time the level inside the inlet has risen higher than the main marsh in the background (by in the region of 30cm). In the recent photo (above) it is now just about possible to see the level differences, because the reeds are no longer there.

Further work was completed in this inlet between 1997 and 1999 dealing with a huge timber log with an axe cut in it., found in the drainage ditch. The detail is held upon the web site for those who are interested in the archaeology. Carbon dating of that log showed it was dated between 1890BC and 1520BC making it one of the oldest man made objects ever found in Sussex. Whilst it acted as a diversion from the Norman Invasion investigation it confirmed the thesis that Wilting marsh at Monkham Inlet is a special site rich in real archaeology consistent with the recorded Norman Invasion story.

Chapter 59: INTERREGNUM 2001-2009

Those who read my web site and this book may be forgiven for believing that my whole life revolves around searching for the Norman Invasion site. That could not be further from the truth. My life is dedicated towards a much larger concept of bringing a greater truth into existence of which the Norman Invasion evidence is the starting point. Those who read my books will also follow the same path that I did.

My life revolved around my family, living in the Crowhurst valley, and the decision to develop a satellite television channel called the Landscape Channel. Landscape is a television channel that broadcasts music without language and has the ability to reach into every country without cultural or ethnic barriers. It shows the beauty of the natural world accompanied by classical and instrumental music. It can touch people in a special way and so my life was divided between my family, my work and my inner drive to make my channel happen on the global stage.

The years between 2001 and 2009 had little impact upon the search for the Norman landing and camp site. My work on Norman research effectively ceased, as I realised that I had done all the work that needed to be done. I became convinced that someone else would find that special something that would one day show that my thesis was correct and was happy to leave it at that. I knew more than I was letting on, but had no inclination to move further.

Fate was to intervene when having effectively won the round with the Highways Agency in 1996, through default, local politicians in East Sussex decided to resurrect the road through Wilting again in 2009. It was my view that the people who proposed this road were guilty of supreme arrogance, because they must have known that the historical claim existed against the Wilting site. Despite a huge amount of public money having been spent at the last public inquiry in 1996, they chose a route that crossed the main area of archaeological interest far worse than the original route. The inspector at the last inquiry reported that he had not seen proof of the Norman Invasion taking place there, and therefore those who proposed the new road must have assumed that the heritage claim for Wilting was and could never be supported.

Technically the inspector's decision was correct; in the same way an inspector could rightly say that he has not seen proof that Druids used Stonehenge. A trick issue, since people believe the Druids used Stonehenge, because like the Norman Invasion, they were told that at school. In fact the Druids are very unlikely ever to have used Stonehenge, and like the Norman Invasion site, there is no archaeology that will provide definitive proof. That does not remove Stonehenge or Woodhenge down the road, from a list of monuments that need protection - just because Woodhenge is a circle of holes in the ground where posts once stood.

My original claim, as I previously stated, was not that the Normans landed at Wilting, but like all people who study history seriously, that the Normans *probably* landed at Wilting on the balance of historical proof. The archaeology that will prove this site is authentic is extremely difficult to obtain, but undoubtedly is there. It is a specialist field that neither of the teams who have visited the site have asked for or used, and is of course also dependant upon funding that has not been provided either.

I therefore declined the invitation to attend the new inquiry which took place in 2009 after due consideration. I decided that having endured three months in 1996, where the evidence I had submitted was dismissed, because it was historical evidence, there was no point in trying to persuade another inspector upon the same basis. I attended the first day and was told in no short terms by the inspector that if my evidence was historical he was unlikely to accept it. He didn't actually say that in so many words, but I got the drift of being put in a position where he was setting me up for a fall. I therefore politely declined the invitation to attend and decided to publish my final report instead, because that would be received into the public domain where it would not be hidden after the event.

I had originally decided that I would not publish, because I live in the area concerned. I could see no value at that time in publishing this information, whilst the Wilting site was secure and available for further investigation. However now that the sword has again been removed from the sheath, clearly there is going to be an attempt to cover Wilting in concrete. I felt that now I had no choice. I therefore decided I should publish my final conclusions and time will be my judge as to who is right and who is wrong.

PART TWO
THE NEW BATTLE OF HASTINGS SITE
Chapter 60: THE FINGER OF SUPICION

Readers may be surprised at this stage in my book to discover the search for the Battle of Hastings site started in the spring of 1986, when I went to Cambridge to see one of the leading British experts on the Norman Invasion. I told her that I believed that there was evidence that the Normans had not fought the battle at the traditional battle site located at Battle Abbey in Sussex. That Abbey is located 5. 5miles from where the port of Hastings was at the time believed to have been; below the castle, where the shopping centre is now built.

It is not appropriate to say at this stage why I was looking for the Battle of Hastings site, since this is a document concerned with historical truth. My reasons have been published elsewhere and all it is necessary to know is that there were compelling reasons to understand whether this were true.

At the time I knew nothing about Norman history or the Norman Invasion, because my life did not involve academic study. I had not studied History at school as a specialist subject and had no special interest in it. I was the owner of a fairly successful UK record label. My world did not connect with the past in any way, but I felt compelled to investigate.

My first stop was Battle Abbey and the Battle of Hastings battlefield, to have a look around. At the time there was no English Heritage shop to speak of or heritage center - more of an entrance with some books on the wall. I did my due diligence and walked around the path, which was unmarked. I came away thinking what a miserable show our country had put on for tourists in those days, visiting what I had always thought was an important world history site.

I asked the receptionist if there was anything to show from the battle. She said that they didn't have anything there, but if I went to the museum across the road I could probably find something of interest. So, like a good tourist on a day out, I went over the road into a musty old hall. It looked like it was some sort of scout hut posing as a village hall, with wooden and glass cases, just out of an old Hollywood movie.

There was no-one there, so I waited around and eventually found the curator, who was exceedingly knowledgeable and helpful. The long and the short of it was that there weren't any battlefield relics at the museum and he didn't know of any. He told me the much quoted adage that the reason for this was that the soil in the Weald of Sussex was slightly acidic and therefore anything that went into the ground simply disappeared over the period of 1,000 years. It turns to iron oxide and is lost for ever. That struck me as strange, as I had seen relics from a number of Roman bloomeries in the area and my suspicions were aroused that this might be a simplification of the truth.

He did say that they had a Norman sword I could look at. It came from Waltham Abbey, where King Harold was supposed to be buried. He recommended that I go to the museum in Hastings, as they were sure to have some Norman things from the area to look at. How strange I thought, that when people who go to the site of the most important battle in English history, and ask to see the relics of the battle, they are shown a sword from Waltham Abbey.

Far from being put off, I felt like a challenge had been thrown down, in that maybe my search for the site of the Battle of Hastings was not such a strange concept. After all if there were no known relics of the battle at the site, which claimed to be where the battle took place, perhaps it really was located somewhere else. I could have come away from that first visit with a flea in my ear, after witnessing a glass case or two of the sort of things you would expect to find.

The finger of suspicion was tapping me on the shoulder and saying that it was rather strange that there was nothing found at the abbey site. This Abbey had been there since the time of the battle. Surely someone would have found something. In battles you don't expect people to clean the site of every item. Buckles and rings are lost, swords are broken, and horses are killed and no-one takes the shoes off a dead horse after battle. Rings are made with gold, people carry coins into battle - yes some will be taken, but always there will be things that are lost for the archaeologist to recover a thousand years later.

It had been reported that the Normans also lost a lot of men in an incident at the end of the battle called the incident of the Malfosse - bad ditch (in French) - but there was no bad ditch on the site at Battle Abbey or adjacent to it. At that site there was nothing much except a quite gentle slope leading up to the Abbey. I therefore resolved to go to the Museum in Hastings and ask some questions there.

Chapter 61: THE MUSEUMS

Hastings Museum was at the time of the start of my search located in a building in the old town of Hastings. In many respects it had the same air of ancient decay as the one in the town of Battle. The ground floor had a dusty manikin of a Norman soldier in battle dress and there were the same glass cases, with the feel of a bygone era. The main displays were upstairs in glass cases and again there were no Norman period exhibits.

This time it was explained to me that like Battle Abbey there were no Norman exhibits, because there were surprisingly none in the town. It was supposed that coastal erosion had taken place, where the castle is located, resulting in any Norman artefacts having been lost to the sea. It was also pointed out that the castle came into existence after the battle, so perhaps the Normans had removed Hastings from the map.

In any event there was an apology and it was suggested that because the Battle Abbey site was in a different borough, the borough of Rother, perhaps if I went to the Bexhill museum they would have something of interest there. In the meantime perhaps I should go up to the remains of the castle on the cliff and ask there, as that was certainly Norman, and they would know where I could find artefacts to confirm the presence of Normans.

I found this extremely confusing. I was relatively new to the area, having moved there the previous year (1985). I had young children and foolishly I thought that going to Hastings there would be some sort of tourist bonanza, like they operate in places like Bayeux in France, which has hundreds of thousands of visitors a year. They have a tapestry and a cathedral but no invasion or battle site.

What I found in the Hastings museum, and also the one in Bexhill, which didn't even have a stuffed Norman soldier, is a total lack of any credible evidence of a Norman presence in the archaeological record. The tourist industry was dead and the town was close to death - probably as a result. The sole evidence appeared to be based upon historical documents, which historians accept as valid. That weight of evidence is supported by the fact that the Count of Eu, one of William the Conqueror's right hand men, built Hastings Castle just before 1100 according to the records of stone purchase.

Battle Abbey on the other hand was built immediately after the battle and so these two buildings are the lynch pins that hold the whole Norman Invasion story together. The visits to the museums were important, because they were at the start of this quest and they showed me that something was wrong with recorded history. I could see what others failed to see - a silver thread of truth in my search.

What concerned me most of all was the unexpected discovery of no archaeological record in Hastings before the castle was built in 1100. I knew enough about logic to tell me that something wasn't right there. If there was no archaeological record of pottery, or anything else prior to 1100, it meant only one conclusion - Hastings - the town of Hastings was not there before 1100. This meant that if Hastings wasn't at the traditional site, because there is no evidence, then the place called the port of Hastings, where Hastings was supposed to be must also be somewhere else pre 1100.

At the public inquires that followed over the years, this simple truth was ignored by the road builders. It isn't considered their problem to explain these issues. It was however important in my search for truth, because the Normans are reported to have landed at the port of Hastings. We have covered that thoroughly in the earlier chapters.

Having found nothing to support the case for the battle site to be located at Battle, or anywhere else for that matter, I started to think this was a rather mad idea. Everyone I spoke to told me that finding nothing on a battle site was quite normal. I was quoted Bosworth Field as a good example of a similar situation. I should not concern myself with such issues, because history was written in history books, and it isn't that important to worry about. If all the historians agreed then surely that is enough for us mere mortals, who do not spend all our lives studying such a specialist subject as the Norman Invasion, we should accept their word.

It seemed to make sense and so my passion for this subject dropped for about half a year. Life got back to normal and took its usual path. Then I went to Cannes in the South of France for a trade show connected to my music business.

Chapter 62: CAMBRIDGE

Everything had returned to normal in my life, apart from a desire to own a metal detector, which the family found amusing. Then as I sat on the bus returning from Cannes to the airport on business, on an early spring day, I found myself reading the Daily Telegraph over the shoulder of the person in front of me in the transfer bus.

There as the lead article, on page two, was a big picture of what were obviously Normans, with a big headline along the lines of new thinking about the Battle of Hastings. I could hardly believe it and had to wait till I got home before being able to locate a copy.

The story was less about the Battle of Hastings, but more about a remarkable young lady by the name of Dr. E. M. C. van Houts who worked in Cambridge on ancient texts. She had studied one of the manuscripts that had not fitted the traditional thinking of the Victorian era. Like others it had been trashed as unreliable. The article was effectively about the rediscovery of this manuscript called the Carmen of Hastingae Proelio, by Guy Bishop of Amiens.

This manuscript had a lot of new information in it and was written before 11th May 1068 - less than two years after the battle. It was therefore a landmark rediscovery - as sometimes happens in the study of History. I therefore resolved to go to Cambridge to meet the author of the study of the Carmen, to discuss my theory that perhaps the Battle of Hastings took place somewhere other than the Battle Abbey site.

I eventually met Dr. van Houts in her rooms at college and I realised from the first words how inadequate I was in comparison to her knowledge. I explained that I would like to read her paper and that my theory concerning the Battle of Hastings was based upon my observations, because I lived close to the battle site. She was very accommodating and told me where I would be able to get her work. She also encouraged me not to simply accept what I had been told at school, because the story was far more complicated than people generally think.

She told me to go away and read up on the subject, naming a few books that would get me started. It was the best advice I could have been given, because she was indirectly telling me that there may be something worth looking at. It appeared that there were inconsistencies between the various events of the landing and battle. She said to me that I should concentrate on the Norman Invasion side of the story, because there was a general consensus amongst historians that the Battle of Hastings took place where the Abbey was built. She did not know of any evidence to the contrary, but believed the Norman landing site was of interest to historians.

She agreed that the failure to find relics was not an indicator that the battle did not take place there, but also qualified that by saying that she wasn't an archaeologist. I left that meeting and in some ways it changed my life, because I discovered History in books. It was of course a very specialist area of History. I was only interested in documents written within 150 years of the battle; because this was the time scale I was told to look at. Dr. van Houts said that I could only rely upon these and so I took her at her word. I wasn't interested in the theories that people offered to accommodate the discrepancies between one text and another - just the actual source material related only to those six week of the Norman occupation of Hastings.

I did what I was told to do by Dr. van Houts, who was an expert, and I don't expect that the lady from Cambridge University probably ever expected to hear from me again. I did get a huge compliment from her when I delivered a first draft of the original thesis. She contributed towards the fight to keep the road out of Wilting by writing the following:

'I would certainly be happy to accept the site of Wilting Manor as the most likely place of William's landing. The fact that William of Jumieges refers to Pevensey does not particularly bother me. As I argue in my first volume of my edition of the chronicle. I do not think he was very well informed about the crossing and the subsequent events in England. He may well have mentioned Pevensey because it was better known and roughly in the same area as the one you have pinpointed. I particularly liked your work you have done on the Domesday Book and the archaeological and geographical studies which you initiated. ' (3rd April 1995)

Clearly not every word of a thesis so complicated as this can be right and I understand that History can never be delivered in a manner that is without differences of opinion. It is the consensus of your peers that deliver historical proof of evidence and only then does the archaeology make sense.

The experience of the public inquiry produced correspondence with a number of Norman history experts, the most eminent in my mind being Dr Marjorie Chibnall of Clare Hall Cambridge. She too contributed in supporting my work on the Norman Invasion site at the time of the first inquiry. A number of letters were submitted to the inspector to support my thesis. Whilst neither of these experts were involved in the later work that ties the evidence to the battle site it is important to understand that by the time the first part of this thesis was published the evidence was starting to be accepted by those who specialise in the specific study of Norman history.

Dr Chibnall summed up my work at that time in a letter to me dated 30th January 1996 in which she wrote:

'To sum up I believe your evidence does support:

Landing along the coast, some of which probably took place at Bulverhythe from Pevensey to Hastings.

The existence of William's base camp for the fortnight between the landings and the battle in the neighbourhood of Wilting Farm.

If you concentrate on these points I think you have a case of substance and hope you will succeed'

It was after these events that I immersed myself in the reading and studying of the books necessary for me to research my subject. I confined myself to publishing the issues related to the Norman Invasion site, because that was the advice given to me. In my first part of the thesis I only dealt with the period of the Invasion before the battle. I now needed to revisit those manuscripts to look at what happened once the Normans left the Invasion camp site on morning of 14th October 1066.

Chapter 63: THE CARMEN REVISITED

The rediscovery of the Carmen was an important work by Ms Van Houts, because it re-established the authority of the poem, or prose, as a valid means of passing on history in a spoken form. It was originally discovered only in 1826 and not published until 1840 - some 200 years after the accounts by William de Jumieges and William de Poitiers were published in the 17th century. This in part explains the reason it was not universally accepted at the time it first came under scrutiny. As a result it was considered inferior by critics of the time and had less authority attached to it. Ms Houts re-established that authority and so what we find adds value to our understanding of what happened on the day that the Battle of Hastings took place, as well as the events pre-battle.

The poem is translated as *'The Song of the Battle of Hastings'*. It is 835 lines long of which 600 of those lines relate to the Invasion and the battle. In many respects it can be seen to be an early version of events, because there are sections of text that in a later period might have been considered disrespectful to the all conquering King, by referring to Harold as an able general, with personal abilities, at least as great as William's. Such prose suggests a source that is not close to William.

The section of text that interested me was the reported discussion between the Duke (William) and his envoy, who had been sent by William to talk with Harold on the night before the battle. We know that this took place, because the same discussion is reported in Wace and Poitiers. In this manuscript we are told in this paragraph:

'Harold, his face distorted, throwing back his head said to the envoy; 'Give place fool! Tomorrow, with the Lord as arbiter of the kingdom, the rightful claimant will appear. '

The Duke then sees the envoy and says:

'Where is the King? 'Not far off' answered the monk. He said to him in his ear: 'You can see the standards!'

We know that this was the night before the battle and one of the inconsistencies that those who have studied this subject cannot avoid is this: How could this be correct? The so called accepted version of events claims Harold was camped where the Battle Abbey ground now stand. The port of Hastings, where the Norman camp was supposed to be located is 5. 5 miles away over a huge ridge that surrounds the whole of Hastings town, being part of an extension of the South Downs. See the map I have drawn at the front of this book showing the topography of the Hastings Ridge.

Due to the difficulty in traversing this major obstacle horses and carriages needed a route that they could actually use. The incline out of Hastings directly north was too great. There was no London road over the ridge, as there is now. To assume that this is perfectly feasible is not sustainable. The only road that we know existed pre 1800 was the one from the Priory in the same valley as Hastings Castle, along the coast over two small valleys to the Manor of Wilting, and from there over two more steep valleys to the Manor of Crowhurst. From Crowhurst the road went directly north to the town of Battle, over two more steep valleys. These roads still exist in part as tracks and footpaths, with the old houses along that route showing the historical development of the route. There was no ridge road until the early 1800's when the Victorians built it.

The Carmen now confirms what Wace tells us in his manuscript, that the two camps were within view of each other on the night before the battle. Something that confirms the wrong location of the camp at the port, or the other alternative is that the location of the battle site is incorrect, because there is no line of sight from Battle Abbey to the sea. A third alternative which might at first seem unlikely is that both these sites have been misplaced. Anyone who has visited the Battle Abbey site will know that there is no way that you can see any port or anything outside of the immediate area of the battlefield, even if every tree were removed. This is because the Battle Abbey site is located on the other side from ridge that surrounds Hastings, making any view towards the sea impossible.

The Carmen states there is line of sight from the battlefield to the port. If the Carmen is correct, which is now believed to be the case, the Carmen confirms that the battlefield cannot be where Battle Abbey was built.

Those who study logistics also know that it was impossible for armies to do what is written in the school books. The distance from the port to Harold's camp and the location of the correct battle site needed to be shorter than five and a half miles. We can travel this distance in a few minutes now, but an army travelling with men, arms, horses and the paraphernalia of battle require considerable time to get ready. To do so travelling over the route proposed would be a formula for disaster. William's men would have been exhausted before they even started fighting.

This issue of the two camps seeing each other before the battle was actually a major fundamental issue in the Victoria era, when this matter was last examined. So much so it destroyed careers and resulted in the need to adopt either one view that the manuscripts were wrong, or the other that the site at Battle Abbey was wrong. The Victorians simply accepted that the Abbey was built on the site where William made his battlefield oath. This is an oath that experts now accept as unsubstantiated.

Here we are again looking at this issue now with the benefit of knowing where the Normans landed and camped - Wilting Manor Farm. That site is adjacent to Redgeland where evidence is found of the ancient pre 1100 port of Hastings. From that site it is possible to see the London Road, about one hour's walk from there, as it leads up to the top of the Ridge at Telham. The Victorian experts didn't know that and were faced with either accepting or dismissing the evidence of the manuscripts before them.

Wace's manuscript suffered the same fate in Victorian times as the Carmen. His manuscript the Roman de Rou was trashed in the academic press of the day. The reason was because everyone who had ever visited Battle Abbey would know that it was not possible for the two armies to see one and other the night before the battle. This is to me one of the greatest of ironies, because here we are nearly two hundred years later realising that the argument that removed Wace from the bookshelves, is the same argument that now removes the authority of the Battle Abbey site, as the true site of the Battle of Hastings from the history books.

This evidence damned Wace and the Carmen to several hundred years of oblivion on the top shelf of specialist libraries. Now I can confidently predict that this same set of verses will not only identify the site of the Battle of Hastings, but also by reverse logic also confirm the Norman Invasion camp site - since the same rules must be applied to both.

The site at Battle Abbey may have no archaeology to support it, but the site of the correct site of the Battle of Hastings does. We shall come to that later.

Both the site of the Norman Camp and the site of the battle must by virtue of the authority in these manuscripts, as authentic documents, identify both the Norman camps site at Wilting and the battle site. The two sites are inherently linked in history and inherently linked by visual identification. I now know that the battle did not take place at Battle and that the actual site is visible from the Norman camp at Wilting. This makes it possible to identify the site almost immediately on any winters day, when the leaves are off the trees, standing in the middle of the upper field at Wilting, where the Norman camp was located.

Later on in the Carmen text we are told that whilst preparing to meet the enemy:

'The King (Harold) mounted the hill and strengthened both his wings with noble men. On the highest point of the summit he planted his banner, and ordered his other standards to be set up.'

This clearly identifies Harold being positioned on the very top of a hill. The Carmen continues:

'The humble and God-fearing duke led a more measured advance and courageously approached the steeps of the hill. The foot soldiers ran ahead to engage the enemy with arrows (against crossbow bolts shields are of no avail).'

At this point the battle starts and the first death is recorded in several accounts as the jester Taillefer. But the point of interest to me was the confirmation that this was a steep hill. The expression *'steeps of the hill'* simply did not fit the concept of the hill at Battle Abbey. The Carmen uses the same expression again later when referring to the Duke sighting Harold.

Work at Battle Abbey by archaeologists confirms that the Abbey hill was partly created at the time the Abbey foundations were built. It doesn't have the concept of steeps - meaning rises of the land that lead to the top of the hill.

Those who know this area where I live will know exactly where the steeps of the hill at Hastings are located. They are located on what was the old Hastings to London road at Crowhurst. The place where the Domesday evidence located Crowhurst, as the most devastated manor in Sussex, at the time of the Norman Invasion - along with Wilting.

This Domesday evidence has been accepted now by those experts in Cambridge, who study this subject, as probably the most significant part of my work. This is because it is based upon evidence of the time and analysis that cannot be faulted, once the location of the network of old roads is factored into that analysis. It explains in a logical and scientific way exactly why the manor values changed before and after the Norman Invasion, providing an answer to what otherwise appears to be a complete and until now unsolved mystery.

On the other hand the element in my research that had mystified me was why the resulting conclusion showed that Crowhurst was more devastated than Wilting (graph3). It should have been less devastated. The answer now became apparent - because it was where the battle took place. That manor took the longest to recover, because it was totally destroyed by the Normans, like no other.

It was clear to me that the Norman Landing site and camp of William the Conqueror were both pointing me directly to this one place where the battle must have taken place, by virtue of the historical documents. Before investigating those suspicions I needed to do more research. It was winter at the time and winter was the time to be in libraries and not out in the fields. I therefore moved on to the Chronicle of Battle Abbey. This was a document I had read before in relation to the Invasion site. The significance of what I read now, with the benefit of the knowledge gained over twenty years is impossible to express. Since I, like many before me, had failed to recognise what the monks had recorded the first time I read the work.

Chapter 64: THE CHRONICLE OF BATTLE ABBEY REVISITED

The Chronicle of Battle Abbey is strictly speaking two manuscripts, which were bound together by the monks of Battle Abbey. Apart from the Domesday Book it is the most important source evidence I have looked at, because it is the only document to support Battle Abbey as the battle site. It tells how the Abbey was founded by William the Conqueror on the site of the Battle of Hastings. It also claimed special privileges, which allowed it to enjoy a degree of autonomy, free from the prying eyes of the taxman and other institutions. The first 22 folios that deal with the Norman Invasion and the battle are in one person's handwriting, followed by a different section in a different hand.

We know the Chronicle was written after 1155, nearly 100 years after the battle. It contains information that is not available anywhere else. With the benefit of knowledge of exactly where the Normans landed and camped, it throws light upon the events of the day, confirming matters that might otherwise just be supposition.

First it is necessary to understand that the document came into existence as a justification for the Abbey. No sooner was the Abbey built than the politics of the day sought to interfere in its activities. Church and State didn't like the idea of monks existing in Sussex in an autonomous fashion. As a consequence of work reported by Eleanor Searle (Oxford Medieval Texts, The Chronicle of Battle Abbey 1980 p2.) we know now that the Charter was forged and the Chronicle of Battle Abbey followed about thirty years later. This was mainly as support for the Charter, but also in order to instruct those who followed in the legal administration of the Abbey estate.

What I found is a document packed with information that could only have come from the time. Much of that information was later used by the monks to seek to justify their own position. They dared not change the names of the places passed down to them, for fear of undermining their own authority. Understanding what it tells us requires an understanding of the thinking of the time.

The Chronicle was a simple thing to understand in the real world, when sitting in Battle Abbey in 1180, some thirty years after it was first written. Those who were familiar with its content would ask themselves where the places that are named in the Chronicle were actually located. It is a natural thing to do, especially if the Chronicle and Charter came under the scrutiny of the crown, who would like to reinstate their authority and charge appropriate taxes upon those who sought to use it to justify their exemption.

The answer is to name every place that appeared in the early pages of the Chronicle within the Abbey lands. This supported what was written, without the need to address those who lived outside the Abbey's control. In many respects this was probably not a deliberate deception, but simply an observation. If the Chronicle stated that the Normans could be seen on the night of the battle, then that must be where Hedgeland was located. This is because the Chronicle names Hedgeland as the Norman camp site at the time of the Invasion. Hedgeland was consequently located adjacent to Telham –at the place that was the very furthest visible point, as seen from the Abbey buildings.

This worked in terms of satisfying local curiosity, but at the same time created some serious flaws in the thesis that was being created. That thesis was that the Abbey was built on the site where William made what was called his *'battlefield oath'*. It forms the basis of the authority of the Abbey. It states William addressed his men before the battle thus:

'And to strengthen the hands and hearts of you who are about to fight for me, I make a vow that on this very battlefield I shall found a monastery for the salvation of all, and especially for those who fall here, to the honour of God and of his saints, where servants of God may be supported: a fitting monastery, with a worthy liberty. Let it be an atonement: a haven for all, as free as the one I conquer for myself.'

The problem with this oath is that it isn't mentioned in any other document of the time detailing the events of the Battle of Hastings. The Bayeux Tapestry did not mention the oath, even though it might be expected to, because the Tapestry was planned to be hung in Bayeux Cathedral where William would definitely see it. The Chronicle states the oath was sworn on the battlefield after William left his camp at a hill called Hedgeland, at a site *'near Hastings'*.

The monks could not drop the name Hedgeland from the first part of the manuscript, without undermining their own authority. This was because Wace and the Carmen identify that this place Hedgeland, where William camped, must be visible from the Abbey. It is further known that a copy of Wace's Roman de Rou was also held in the same library at Battle Abbey, and so any contradiction would immediately have become obvious.

In order to create the justification for Hedgeland, it was created on the boundary of the Abbey around 1180, shortly after the Chronicle was written. This was of course the logical thing to do. Not necessarily as a deliberate deception, but by virtue of the authority of the Chronicle. After all, if the Chronicle says that the Normans can be seen on the night of the battle from where they sat, then they knew exactly where that place must be located, simply by looking out of their window.

The monks did not know where the Normans camped, and they certainly did not appear to know that the camp was located at '*the port of Hastings*' according to their own Chronicle. This is probably because the manuscript was in two parts. Those who wrote the second part may well not have known what was in the first. When the two were put together only then would the issue come to light, and only then if you have knowledge of the actual original events, which had taken place several generations before. The original document could not be altered or destroyed, so the result was the creation of all the elements necessary to support the story within their own land. Eleanor Searle in her book The Chronicle of Battle Abbey concludes, in relation to the Charter:

'*It had become the 'natural' commencement of their own story, and a tradition that even the fastidious main chronicler was willing to foist upon his successors as truth: a lie, as he must have known, but one that would be harmless to their interests in the years to come.* '

This lie eventually has become a fraud that was continued by the church, in order to obtain funds and authority.

The creation of the forged Charter showed that the reason for doing these things was not in the interests of creating a false story, but in order to justify their own existence. This is the reason the correct names were left in the documents and bound into the second manuscript as one. It was probably considered right to include the original document, because it gave credibility to the second.

We have the benefit of understanding the circumstances of the origination of the Charter and Chronicle. We can read what is written there and now see a story emerge that firstly confirms that the Abbey created this Charter to justify what could not be justified any other way. Secondly it tells us with the benefit of hindsight that the Abbey was not built in the place that William had ordered it to be built.

This comes as a massive surprise to a historical researcher. You may suspect the truth for twenty odd years, but the last place you expect to find it is in the 12th century document that was used to support the authority the Abbey claimed.

On folio twelve the monks have invented a reason to explain why the Abbey was not built straight away. This needed to be explained, if the battlefield oath really took place. Historians understand the device of the battlefield oath to be something employed on many occasions to justify ecclesiastical enterprises. Few if any had any basis in fact. Once the person who is supposed to have made the oath is dead, it suited the church to confirm such practice as authentic, but there is no evidence to support any such oaths being taken.

In this instance the Abbey was not built straight after the battle. The monks came from Marmoutier in France several years later. The Abbey was not finished until 1094, meaning William never saw it, leaving the question in people's minds - why such a gap? In order to address this issue the scribe states, according to the expert Eleanor Searle, in one paragraph on folio 12:

'*The illustrious King (William) was fully occupied, as we have mentioned, and although he never actually forgot his vow, yet because of his preoccupations of this period, he put off its fulfilment (amongst other things) for a long time. However his conscience was urging him from within, while from without the monk William 'the smith' kept reminding him assiduously, no easy thing to do. At last, since the monk was nearby, the king committed the building of the abbey to him as he had wished, commanding him to fetch some brothers from his own church and set speedily in hand the establishment of a suitable monastery on the battlefield. Accepting the alacrity, the monk went quickly to Marmoutier and brought with him into England four monks from there; Theobald, nicknamed 'the old', William Coche, Robert of Boulogne, and Robert Blancard, men outstanding in character and piety. They studied the battlefield and decided that it seemed hardly suitable for so outstanding a building. They therefore chose a fit place for settling, a site located not far off, but somewhat lower down, towards the western slope of the ridge. There lest they seem to be doing nothing, they built themselves some little huts. This place, still called Herste has a low wall as a mark of this.* '

The Latin original text is important because the sentences above written in bold type are written with these words:

'Qui memoratum belli locum considerantes cum ad tam insignem fabricum minus idoneum, ut uidebatur, arbitrarentur in humiliori non procul loco, uersus eiusdem collis occidentalem plagam, aptus habitandi locum eligentes ibidem ne nil operis agere uiderentur mansiunculas quasdam fabricauerunt. '

Followed by:

'Qui locus, hucusque Herste cognominatus, quandam habet spinam in huius rei monimentum. '

Translated as 'This *place, still called Herste has a low wall as a mark of this.'*

The key to understanding these sentences is the Searle translation of '*Qui*' (Latin '*who*' or '*which*') - meaning **They studied the battlefield,** is also understanding the '*Qui*' (Latin – '*who/which*'), as used in '*Qui locus*', whom Searle has then translated as ***'This place'***. I do not believe it can possibly be the intention of the writer to apply this meaning. The scribe who wrote this was referring to '*Qui*' at the start of both sentences, identifying the common subject under discussion - the battlefield. The naming of the original site, from where it was moved, was intentional as a means of explaining the move. There is no other possible explanation for its inclusion that can make any sense.

The way it reads there is an assumption that ***'This place'*** is the place lower down on the ridge where the huts are located. This meaning does not make sense, because the Abbey was not built at Herste, but to the east of that location. In order to be sure about the interpretation of the Latin I contacted Dr Martin Brett, an expert in Medieval Latin, at Cambridge University and asked him to provide a translation.

Dr Brett was familiar with the Searle translation and agreed that the meaning given by Searle was in essence correct if not the exact words, since translation is an art. He confirmed that the original translation had been vetted by the most eminent living Latinist in England Michael Winterbottom.

The important point is the second singular verb and use of the word '*locum*' as '*site*', or as Searle chooses '*place*', because it supports a completely different understanding of the paragraph. A more precise understanding would be to understand this translation of this paragraph to read as follows:

'They studied the battlefield and decided that it seemed hardly suitable for so outstanding a building. They therefore chose a fit place for settling, a site located not far off, but somewhat lower down, towards the western slope of the ridge. There lest they seem to be doing nothing, they built themselves some little huts. The site (i.e. the battlefield), still called Herste, has a low wall as a mark of this. '

'*Qui*' at the start of both sentences is the common reference, because they each refer to the same place '*Qui locus*' and that site is the battle site and battlefield.

This is something that academics can mull over for the next ten years. It could be argued that I am being pedantic to home in on the difference between the understanding of the word '*place*' or '*site*'. It was however important to me, because when I had read this the first time I had failed to recognise that the text was identifying the site of the battle. Like many who read those words they would have thought the document was referring to the place where the huts were.

The important issue is that Searle recognises the problem in her translation. She adds a footnote attempting to explain why her translation states that the Chronicle of Battle Abbey says the Abbey was moved from the battlefield and the reference is to Herste - when it is apparent to everyone that it has not been reported as moved from the battlefield at all. It is well known the place the monks named Herste was supposed to be within their boundary to the north-west of the Abbey. That place, like the others included in the Chronicle, was invented at the time the Charter was forged. Her footnote identifies the location of Herste, but cannot explain the anomaly, so ignores it. If the translation were correct it would tell us that the Abbey was moved from Herste and not to it. If this translation provided by Searle were correct we would have to assume that everything in the Chronicle was fabricated, because it would be shown to be completely unreliable in the most basic information, if the rules of Victorian England were applied today.

When discussing this with Dr Brett I believe it is fair to say he, like Searle and others, sees the position as one that can only be explained in relation to the understanding that the monk wished to create. I do not think any academic is going to disagree with Searle that the monk reports the Abbey being moved from the battlefield. It is more a matter of seeking to explain this in terms of what is written later.

Dr Brett says in his correspondence with me:

'For what it's worth I am entirely happy to accept the outline of the story as the Searle translation (which was vetted by one of the most eminent living Latinists in England, Michael Winterbottom) represents it. It may not be true, but I'm confident it is what he meant' (referring to the scribe who wrote the original text).

I would simply make the point that the text identifies the original battle site at Herste and that is an absolute truth. Even if like Searle we seek to ignore this we cannot escape confirmation, in the document written to justify the Abbey, that the Abbey was moved FROM the battlefield and not to it, since Searle acknowledges this fact. That truth is now exposed and provides a logical understanding of the Latin, which is an absolute confirmation of the location of the correct battle site. It also removes the authority of Battle Abbey to make the claim that it was a tradition that the Abbey was built on the battle site. It never was a tradition; it was always a confirmed lie, perpetrated by the church. This is a claim that stands in the way of discovery of the true site of the Battle of Hastings. There cannot be two sites

Shortly after the battle the monks started to build the Abbey at the place they called Herste, but as Searle shows, it was moved. Then, 100years later, when the monks needed to justify their presence to the king, they created a new Herste within their own lands, this time to the North and West of the Abbey. The problem with this place, like the one the monks named Hedgeland, was it was not as described *'low down on the western side of the ridge'*. It is no-where near the ridge, as defined by the understanding of those who live in the area. Those who study this in a desktop exercise will never see this or understand the expression *'the ridge'*. That expression is a specific place in the Hastings area. It is the place that encompasses the population of most of Hastings and still today retains that name - it is not a simplistic description of any land mass.

Understanding the text as identifying the correct battle site at Herste could in some respect explain why it was necessary to create Herste within the Abbey's control. It could be described as *'not far off'*, but does not escape the deception of later seeking to claim it was where the Abbey was built and is where the Abbey is today. As Searle comments the whole document was *'a lie. . harmless to their interests in the years to come'*. It is impossible for any thorough historian to disagree with this assessment.

Unknown to the monks who wrote this document, who were probably French, there is a place low down on the western side of the Ridge, which is identified by a low stone wall built into the churchyard for the last 1,000 years, it is called Crowhurst. We know that the low wall has been there 1,000 years, because that same churchyard has a yew tree that is approaching 2000 years old growing next to it. The yew and wall have been co-habiting that churchyard since long before the time of the Invasion. The roots of the tree have been confined by that wall, which is under it's bough at the far end of the wall in this photograph:

A further photograph shows the size of the girth of the trunk of the tree, with the low stone wall out of shot down to the left.

It could of course be argued that this is not the same wall as referred to in the Chronicle. I would answer that by stating that this comment regarding the wall is not in any way conclusive. It is another part of the jigsaw that needs to be taken into account. It should be remembered that the time that this event is referred to (1066), stone was not a common building material. All castles and buildings (including churches) were normally made from wood. The existence of the stone wall warranted its inclusion in the original manuscript as a landmark, which would allow its identification by the reader of the day. The wall at Crowhurst was and has been a landmark since its creation, because it was an 'enclosure' where a number of yews were planted in a circle – a place where men met to do business, long before the church was built there. No such wall exists in the place that was subsequently named

148

Herste by the monks north and west of the Abbey. This stone wall is probably the oldest feature in Crowhurst and it is located next to ruins, which we shall deal with later. It is my contention that this low stone wall is identified in the Bayeux Tapestry, which we shall also address later.

The Sussex Crowhurst yew should not be left to an unscientific investigation, since the Battle of Hastings was first named after an old tree (the '*Battle of the Hoary Apple Tree*', Saxon Chronicles). I was therefore exceedingly grateful to Alan Meredith, the world's greatest authority on the age of yews to contact me. His work can be found on the ancient-yew.org web site. That site contains reliable data that supports the dating methods used.

The study of the growth of yews shows that yew growth is not a straight line. Its age is determined by trunk girth, but also a complicated equation related to the years of growth, as the rate varies according to age. Fortunately the Crowhurst yew has been studied in detail since 1680, thanks to Alan Meredith and those who came before him, who care about such trees. Consequently an accurate estimate of age can be obtained.

Alan tells me that The Crowhurst Yew was 27ft in girth in 1680. When he last measured it in 1982 it was 28ft at a height of 4ft from the ground. This makes the Sussex Crowhurst yew one of the slowest growing in the world and probably much older than first thought. I believe the reason for this slow growth is probably in part due to the restriction of its roots, determined by its position confined between the church and the stone wall.

The measurements confirm previous data gathered in 1835, 1879, 1894 and 1954. As a result Alan confirmed to me that contrary to what a casual observer may feel the tree is nearer 2,000 years old than 1,000 and may be even older. Some have estimated it might be as much as 3,000 years.

Alan's observations therefore have the effect of actually verifying that the wall must have been there much longer than we might expect. The wall could not have been built when the yew was already 1,000 years old, because the roots would have been too well established and the wall would have had to have been built further from the tree. Yews, like most old trees have extensive root systems at least as wide as their height. What we therefore have is a record in the landscape that confirms that at the time of the Battle of Hastings this yew was almost certainly near 1,000 years old, and the oldest tree in the landscape then, as it is now.

It would be strange if it were not noticed by the Normans, being next to the then London Road. Even stranger if it were not recorded in the Bayeux Tapestry, if that yew was in the valley where the Battle of Hastings took place. We shall look at that later.

I would like to think the monks of Battle Abbey wrote down what they knew to be true and recorded it in the Chronicle of Battle Abbey. They worked for God and therefore sought to record for their own benefit and the benefit of God's work what was necessary. That Chronicle confirms that the monks started to build the Abbey in a place they knew as *Herste*, unaware that this is the local dialect for the name Crowhurst. I know this to be true, not because of what I have read in any book, but because Mary Oliver, God bless her soul now deceased, told me that when she was a child the people of Crowhurst never used the Crow part of the word. They only ever called it *Crurst*. I believe that information to be true and can be confirmed by those who study the local Sussex dialect.

The monk's version confirms the Abbey site being moved from the battlefield at the very start of the Chronicle - this is really the only point that we have to concentrate upon. It is a really significant point. The rest of the text is all diversion aimed at justifying the events that took place later. The Chronicle then goes on to explain why the Abbey wasn't built to the north and west of the Abbey in the place where the monks named *Herste*. This needed to be done in order to explain why the Abbey wasn't where they said it should have been:

'Accordingly, when the solicitous King inquired meanwhile about the progress of the building, it was intimated to him by these brethren that the place where he had decided to have the church built was on a hill, and so dry of soil, and quite without springs, and that for so great a construction a more likely place nearby should be substituted, if it pleased him. When the king heard this he refused angrily and ordered them to lay the foundations of the church speedily and on the very spot where his enemy had fallen and the victory been won.'

The story as detailed in the Chronicle confirms the one important decision: to build the Abbey in *Herste* before the monks from Marmoutier came from France and moved the location. The fact that this new location is referred to as the one where Harold's banner fell has little relevance, because we know that the basis of the whole Charter was also a deception. Those words can no more be relied upon than those of the Charter. In a court of law a judge would see through this presentation of evidence straight away. It is remarkable that historians have swallowed this misinformation until now. I can only assume that few, if any, have actually examined this particular document. Like so many internet documents the old story is simply repeated without anyone actually looking at the source documents concerned - especially if they challenge conventional thinking.

The reasons for moving the Abbey from the slopes of the Ridge are as outlined in the Chronicle. Not only is there no water where Harold fell, but the site of the real battle is a logistical nightmare for anyone who had the job of levelling the intense slope. The gradient is probably approaching 1 in 10 in places, with no easy road access. Almost every document referring to the Battle of Hastings calls the ground steep and it truly is on the correct site - unlike the position chosen by the monks from France, who chose the convenient and relatively level access point to the peninsular, near the bottom of the rear of the Ridge.

Fortunately for this research the monks, who probably never travelled beyond the edges of the land they controlled, effectively identify *Herste* as the original actual battle site. This site is not identified in any other document. It is truly inconceivable that anyone would start to build the Abbey anywhere other than the actual battle site, given William's reported reaction to being told it was in the wrong place – also reported in this Chronicle. If Battle truly were the battle site, then it would have featured in the data held in the Domesday Book, as the most wasted manor. There would have been no need to include the story of its movement, or any of the authentication elements that are added to the text to justify the move. The fact is, the Abbey building site was moved and that is the reason this information was included in the Chronicle of Battle Abbey. The Domesday data confirms the deception. (Graph 3).

The Domesday data undermines the claim of authenticity, because Battle suffered little damage from Norman involvement, because it is off the peninsular and out of range of the Norman's activities - which were spread along the coast and peninsular roads. The value of Battle in Domesday was reduced from £48 to £30 at the time of the conquest. If the Battle of Hastings took place where it was believed, then Battle is the manor that should have a zero value recorded in Domesday - it does not, because the monks built the Abbey in its current location, for the reasons given in the Chronicle. Who in their right mind would build a new Abbey in a manor with no resources to sustain the work force?

The Chronicle of Battle Abbey is therefore an important document, because within its pages we do not find the detail that supports the Abbey battlefield, but one that provides the true story. Having forged the Charter, upon which the Abbey relied, it could not change the history upon which it was believed to be built. As a result of naming the lands that were written into the early folios, within their own Abbey boundary at the time of the creation of the forged Charter, they inadvertently identified the true story, because they retained the names passed to them.

The identification of the Norman camp by this chronicle at Hedgeland, at the port of Hastings, in conjunction with other documents, confirms that the battle site was moved from the correct battlefield. The Battle Abbey site cannot see any port and never could. The monks created a site they could see in about 1180, but could do nothing about the port reference, and so it was left unaltered.

This same discussion was run in the 1800s to discredit Wace in the eyes of the Historical Society, incorrectly as it turns out. It is an inevitable conclusion that this chronicle confirms that the Abbey movement took place and then sought to justify it. The justification employed confirms that it happened; otherwise it would not need to be recorded there. In effect the Chronicle of Battle Abbey, no matter how you look at it, confirms the record of the battle site was moved, because the building was moved and condemns itself through its own words.

At the time it was written it was never suspected that anyone else would ever see the documents that concern us. As Eleanor Searle says it was '*a simple lie that would never harm anyone*' - now the truth is out, because we have identified the site that fulfils the requirements and the archaeology. The name of that site is the one that the Chronicle of Battle Abbey confirms as the place where the Abbey was started. They wrote the name down as they heard it, applying their French thinking to the word. The Norman French understanding of the word Herste meaning a clearing in a wood. The Anglo-Saxon Olde English word Hurst meaning a wood or thicket. Words in those days had no correct format and were written in phonetic terms – especially surnames and places, which could have various spellings, depending upon the education of the person writing. The Normans assumed it to mean a clearing and named their Herste accordingly, where a clearing was located to the north-west of the Abbey site. This was an easy mistake for a Norman to make, since the English language was even then difficult to understand, by those who were not born here.

Those who believe Herste is not the same Hurst low down on the west side of the ridge at Hastings, have not understood the topography or language of the area. This is an easy mistake to make if you have never been here. I have identified the connection and have drawn together all the other threads that confirm a major deceit by the monks who sought to justify their position at any cost. That deceit was never uncovered, because William never returned to the site and the church confirmed the lie. In the past that concept was not something that was open to challenge. Now we know that even the church in those distant times could make up the story if it had a financial benefit to the organisation.

The monks are now gone from the Abbey, the building is not even in ruins, not a standing stone exists above ground from the original 11th century Abbey. The silver thread of truth can now be seen and those who question the conclusions I draw must ask themselves this simple question. If the Chronicle of Battle Abbey states that the Normans camped at Hedgeland at the port of Hastings, how can you reconcile the Abbey being positioned 5. 5miles from the port of Hastings, out of sight low down on the northern side of the Ridge, where no line of sight is possible?

If the Chronicle of Battle Abbey, the only document that supports the building of the Abbey states the Abbey was moved from the battlefield to where it is today - as translated by the world's leading expert on that text - how can you deny this evidence?

It is impossible to see the Norman camp at the port from the Battle Abbey site. It is not possible to argue that they might have moved the day before, because it is confirmed in a number of other documents that they were in the camp at the port on the night before the battle. This is an irreconcilable issue that can remain hidden no longer. The discovery of the correct site of the Battle of Hastings, together with the correct site of the Norman camp at the port of Hastings, confirms that Battle Abbey cannot be the battle site. At the same time it confirms that it was not only the Charter that was forged, but the Abbey was also built upon a written deception designed to enforce the forged Charter. The location of the Abbey, which has never produced any battlefield relics or archaeology of any kind relating to the battle in the last 943 years, was also a lie and can now be confirmed as such.

I shall now move on to the other important document that is by far the most detailed account of the actual battle, known as the Roman de Rou by Wace.

Chapter 65: MR WACE

Wace lived and wrote some time around 1173, according to current thinking, quite late in the day for my 150 years from the battle rule. His manuscript the Roman de Rou claims to be an account of the Invasion of England and the Battle of Hastings, which was passed to him by his father. It just fits the time scale possible and has that ring of truth. He tells us that he was born in Jersey, probably soon after 1100 and was taken to Caen to be educated.

Wace's patron was Henry II, who gave him the prebend of the Cathedral at Bayeux. This is according to the archives of the church, where he held the office for nineteen years. He says in the main text that he wrote the majority of it in 1160. English Historians will argue for ever as to whether this is right or wrong, when it comes to this particular author. I have studied all the texts from the time and I conclude that Wace is the most reliable source. I take this view, because information is recorded in Wace that confirms the correct locations of the Battle of Hastings and the Invasion camp. This information cannot be correct and his manuscript to be fundamentally at fault.

The reason for current disquiet by many historians is that they are haunted by the past episodes of ego inflation, by eminent historians from the Victorian period, who all thought they were right, and are now seen to be hopelessly wrong. As stated previously it all goes back to the Victorian era when Wace's work was discredited, because of the argument about who could see whom on the night of the battle. No-one ever considered that the cause of this difficulty could be because the battle site might be in the wrong place, because the church did not lie. The only conclusion possible at that time was the belief that one or more of a number of authors from the time must have made the whole story up. The impossibility of the port being visible from the Abbey site meant that Wace was the one at fault, and consequently his supporters were discredited in a very public humiliation in the pages of the Historical Society papers. It is therefore some surprise to find that the claim that Wace is not reliable is based upon nothing more than inadequate Victorian research. As if to emphasise this point, no such discrimination process took place in France, where Wace is and always has been a pre-eminent source for Norman history. You will find his writings accompanying the text of the Bayeux Tapestry in Bayeux, as it rightly should.

Having read Wace in full I conclude that the 16,000 lines of battle poem have a legitimacy that defies logic to criticise. Many of those who attended the Invasion and Battle of Hastings were included in the text by name and family. This was at a time when the close ancestors of those who died and fought were still alive. These were the very same people who inherited lands in England, as a result of their deeds at the Battle of Hastings. It would simply be madness to invent the pedigree for those who attended.

Clearly, like all historical texts of the time, certain names may have been embroidered into the narrative for political or other reasons without the knowledge of the author at a later date. That does not undermine the validity of the record. I do not think Wace would have known this, but simply reported what he believed to be true, like Poitiers and Jumieges before him. There was no intended deception and therefore the bulk of the information is probably reliable. It is an extremely foolish historian who believes he has the authority to dismiss works written 1,000 years ago, when the same work is the leading authority in the home of those who created the story in the first place - the French.

Wace unlike any other scribe of the time tells the whole story of the Invasion, how Harold was captured by William and held hostage. How William cheated Harold at Bayeux Cathedral, by hiding the relics under the cloth and obtaining an oath of allegiance. The chapter that covers these events isn't painted with the political thinking of the likes of Poitiers, who was part of William's court. It tells the truth of the occasion and doesn't pander to being politically correct, because sufficient time had elapsed for the truth to be told, as it was known to the storytellers of the day:

'To receive the oath, he (William) caused parliament to be called. It is commonly said that it was at Bayeux that he had called his great council assembled. He sent for all the holy bodies thither, and put

so many of them together as to fill a whole chest, and then covered them with a pall; but Harold neither saw them, nor knew of their being there; for nought was shewn or told to him about it; and over all was a phylactery(158), the best he could select; I have heard it called. When Harold placed his hand upon it, the hand trembled, and the flesh quivered; but he swore, and to deliver up England to the Duke; and thereunto to do all in his power, according to his might and wit, after the death of Edward, if he should live, so help him God and the holy relics there! Many cried 'God grant it, and when Harold had kissed the saints, and had risen upon his feet, the duke led him up to the chest, and made him stand near it; and took of the chest the pall that had covered it; and shewed Harold upon what holy relics he had sworn; and he was sorely alarmed at the sight'.

At this point Harold is released to go home to England.

What this manuscript tells us is that William is now dead and the deception imparted upon Harold can be told. The fact that Harold has not been informed of the relics does not undermine the oath, which has major significance, because an oath before God upon the relics of saints cannot be disputed in the eyes of the church at that time. It also explains why Harold never accepted it as a legitimate oath, because it was obtained by deception and whilst he was held captive. The principle of an oath obtained under duress or deception has never been valid in an English court since.

Wace's manuscript is packed with details that suggest authenticity and knowledge of events, which were known at the time to the general population. Wace tells the story of William's boat having a brass child on the prow, the Invasion arriving near or at Hastings, building a prefabricated fort and the story of the death of the soothsayer. William falls as he gets out of his boat and tells his men he has *'England with my two hands'* turning what would have been interpreted as a bad omen into one that gets reported as good. Harold's men dig a fosse (ditch) across the battlefield and the exchanges with Harold's spokesman take place over many pages. Harold comes to the Norman camp with his brother Gurth the night before the battle to spy on the Normans. It is clear from the description that the Norman and Saxon camps are very close.

On the day before the battle Wace records Harold creating some form of ditch on the battlefield with a defence at his camp:

'He (Harold) had the place well examined, and surrounded it by a good fosse, leaving an entrance in each of three sides, which were ordered to be well guarded.'

It is reported that each side fears the other will attack at night and both sides make ready for battle. The names of many French families are embroidered into the tale and as a consequence of this it has become the major source in France for the Norman Invasion story. It was never discredited in France, because there was never any reason for French history experts not to believe its authenticity, as a historical report of the events of the Battle of Hastings.

Wace tells us it was 14th October the day of the battle. The text we have read up to this point is almost a script for the Bayeux Tapestry. All the events shown in the Bayeux Tapestry are recorded in Wace with details. The conclusion must be drawn that Wace had access to the Bayeux Tapestry and that formed the basis for his story. There is much more detail in Wace than shown on the Tapestry. There is no reason to believe the Bayeux Tapestry to be correct, but Wace to be wrong - something that would be highly illogical, given that the two texts follow the same narrative.

Wace tells us that the Normans attacked in three divisions, with a full transcript of William's pep-talk to his men in the Norman camp before the battle. It includes the story of the armour being held up the wrong way round, which is also reported in the Chronicle of Battle Abbey, and the choice of horse given to him as a present from the King of Spain.

Twice Wace reports in the same section that Harold has enclosed the field, where he expects the battle to take place. This appears to be an important issue, since other issues of the battle are not repeated:

'Harold knew that the Normans would come and attack him hand to hand; so he had early enclosed the field in which he placed his men.'

There is more in this statement than meets the untrained eye, once the true battle site is known. We are being told that Harold had certain knowledge that the Normans would not only have to come to him, but that they would have to fight hand to hand. This was not the way that the Normans fought - it was the way that the Saxons fought. It must be remembered that Harold had fought with William in France, as one of William's men whilst he was held captive. He had earned a position of favour, as a result of his rank and acts of valour in battle with William. Most important of all Harold knew that these were people who fought on horseback and he had seen how they fought. It was a style of engaging the enemy that was completely different from the style employed by the Saxons.

The normal style for the Saxons was to fight on foot and to lock shields, creating a shield wall, through which no man could normally pass. Battle was engaged by using the free arm to wield the battle-axe against any opponent within range. Yet Harold knew, according to Wace, that not only would the Normans need to come to him, but they would also be forced to fight on foot.

This is because Harold knew the land and made preparations that made the Norman horsemen impotent. He had dug a ditch, enclosed the defence, and as shown in the Bayeux Tapestry put stakes across the field next to the stream. He knew what the Norman horsemen could do. This was an invading army, who unlike any other army in England before, or since, brought with them their secret weapons - heavy horses. Harold knew how these horsemen worked and he knew that stakes driven across the field would force the horsemen to fight on foot. If they wished to escape the trap he had sprung, as a result of force marching his men to Crowhurst, the Normans would need to fight on foot.

The Bayeux Tapestry shows the horses tied in the ships and William expected to use them with devastating effect. These horses were not runners in the Grand National, but were devastatingly fearless man killers in battle. They were what are now known affectionately as cart horses - but trained for battle. Approaching a ton of horse meat, moving at thirty miles an hour, Harold's shield wall would be blown away by the first charge. William knew that, but so did Harold. That is why the battle lasted all day. Harold was prepared and took the initiative.

Wace confirms that the field of battle was not an open field, but was in a confined place. One of the Saxon Chronicles confirms this too. Wace goes into some detail about the tactics employed by the English in creating a fence on the battlefield. This of course makes a lot of sense if the Normans had to pass through the area of the battlefield to exit the land on which Harold had them contained. It makes no sense at all on the Battle Abbey site, because that site has unrestricted side approaches.

'They had built up a fence before them with their shields, and with ash and other wood; and had well joined and wattled in the whole work, so as not to leave a crevice; and thus they had a barricade in their front, through which any Norman who would attack them must first pass.'

and

'The English stood in close ranks, ready and eager for the fight; and they had moreover made a fosse(ditch), which went across the field, guarding one side of their army.'

The problem is that the Battle Abbey site is not confined by the geography of the site, because it is possible to bypass any defence that might be made there. It is also confirmed by Wace to be the wrong location, because there is and never has been a ditch that has been created as a defence across that field. A man made ditch would be detectable by archaeologists. Both of these requirements are necessary to satisfy the due diligence of the correct battle site, which can be found at Crowhurst.

I realised as I read Wace that once you have seen the correct location of the Saxon defence and the Norman camp the text in Wace and the Bayeux Tapestry springs to life, as an actual true description of the day. You can see where Harold was standing when the descriptions of the Normans arriving is made. You can see the area of land which is called *'the plain'* in Wace, where the first division arrives, because it truly is a plain in all the senses of the word. You can also imagine the Normans arrive over the rising land in the distance:

'Meanwhile the Normans appeared, advancing over the ridge of a rising ground; and the first division of their troops moved along the hill across a valley.'

You know where the valley is - missing from the Battle Abbey site, along with the *'plain'* and the *'hill'*. Wace continues to describe the events just before the battle commences:

'The youths and common herd of the camp, whose business was not to join in the battle, but to take care of the harness and stores, moved off towards a rising ground. The priests and the clerks also ascend a hill, there to offer up prayers to God, and watch the event of the Battle. '

This is an unexpected confirmation that this was the first recorded entertainment event in history. We often forget that battles are not just won and lost by those who fight. A large number of non-fighters are required to support an invading army. There was a hill that had to be behind the Norman lines and yet still provide a view of the battle site. That hill is the Hye House hill in Crowhurst, which looks out over the valley in one direction providing a grandstand view of the events of that day. In the other direction, as we shall see when looking at the 1841 Tithe Map, the same hill provides a view of the Invasion port.

Every knight had his manservant and they all needed feeding and looking after. Wace confirms that there is a nearby hill that requires the priests and clerks to ascend - exactly as detailed at the Crowhurst site and completely missing from the Battle Abbey field.

Wace tells us that the ingredients of the most important battle in English history, are a confined battlefield, steep hills, valleys, a plain, at least one and possibly two ditches, one of which is man made across the site and the other within the battlefield with viewpoints. This is not the Battle Abbey site. It is too far from the Norman camp by the sea and topographically wrong for the descriptions that are available. The only evidence to support the site at Battle Abbey is the discredited Chronicle of Battle Abbey. Once that is understood to confirm the battlefield to be somewhere else, the only alternative is the Crowhurst site - which fulfils all the descriptions. Instinctively you know you are in the right place when you read the texts, because like William's camp at Wilting, there is nothing out of place.

The account of the battle now follows with Wace detailing those who attended and their valour. Wace refers to an incident which may be interpreted to be a confirmation of the *Malfosse* incident:

'In the plain was a fosse, which the Normans had now behind them, having passed it in the fight without regarding it. But the English charged and drove the Normans back before them, till they made them fall back upon this fosse, overthrowing into it horses and men. Many were to be seen falling therein, with their faces to the earth and unable to rise. Many of the English also, whom the Normans drew down along with them, died there. At no time during the day's battle did so many Normans die, as perished in that fosse. So said those who saw the dead. '

It is not known whether this is the so called Malfosse incident or not, but appears to be an event that caused Bishop Odo to take up arms to rally his men, as he orders the fleeing Frenchmen to *'Stand fast, Stand Fast'*. It is however more likely to be the incident shown in the Bayeux Tapestry, because the story follows the same format. The Chronicle of Battle Abbey tells us that that the Malfosse incident is at the end of the battle after Harold has died. The image in the Bayeux Tapestry shows this incident at the bottom of the main hill next to the plain - exactly where it is on the battlefield in Crowhurst during the battle.

155

The important element from the point of view of looking for the right site for the Battle of Hastings is that the battle site and the Malfosse can be validated by the lay of the land. One is located next to Harold's final stand near the top of the hill and one next to *'the plain'* at the bottom of the same hill. I shall deal with that in the next chapter.

Wace tells us that the battle starts at 9am in the morning and continues through till 3pm, when the Normans start shooting arrows up into the air and down onto their enemy. This is important information, because dawn was at 6.30am in October 1066. The time taken to get the men into position and the time battle commences is a key element in authenticating Crowhurst. Moving up to 5,000 men from Wilting Manor to Crowhurst in that time is possible; moving them further in the time allowed was not. Wace acts as a further authority to undermine the Battle Abbey site by virtue of the logistics involved.

I shall write here what Wace reports about the death of Harold. Not because it adds anything to the investigation into the correct battle site, but because it offers an insight into a truthful understanding of the events of that day. For the last two hundred years, since the Victorians synthesised their definitive, and selective, understanding of historical truth, it has been believed by people who have not studied the original source documents that Harold died with an arrow in the eye. That is what we all learnt at school. In the same way many historians still believe that Pevensey refers to the town in Poitier's manuscript, when he was referring to the area under the control of Pevensey Castle.

The Chronicle of Battle Abbey tells us that Harold was laid low by a chance blow. The Carmen on the other hand says that four knights killed Harold. Poitiers and Jumieges omit the story completely - which infers they did not know how Harold died. Wace's description satisfies all accounts, by offering a comprehensive understanding of the events of the day.

Wace states that first Harold is hit above the eye and wounded - his eye is put out:

'The arrows now flew thicker than rain before the wind; fast sped the shafts that the English call 'wibetes'(159)*. Then it was that an arrow, that had been shot upwards, struck Harold above the eye, and put it out. In his agony he drew the arrow and threw it away, breaking it with his hands; and the pain in his head was so great, that he leaned upon his shield. '*

This is not the end of the battle. There are still many lines of verse describing the heroic events of French knights. The Battle is by no means easily won by the Normans. It is clear from the text that there were times the Normans were in danger of losing the day.

Wace fails to mention any battlefield oath, but recounts specific events involving those who were subsequently to enjoy great privileges, after winning the battle. The English are said to *'fall back upon a rising ground, and (the Normans) follow them across a valley, attacking them on foot and horseback'.* Only at this time near the end of the details of the battle are we told that Harold is killed:

'And now the Normans had pressed on so far, that at last they reached the standard. There Harold had remained, defending himself to the utmost; but he was sorely wounded in the eye by the arrow; and suffered grievous pain from the blow. An armed man came in the throng of battle, and struck him on the ventaille of his helmet, and beat him to the ground; and as he sought to recover himself, a knight beat him down again, striking him on the thigh, down to the bone. . . . . . The standard was beaten down, the golden gonfanon was taken, and Harold and the best of his friends were slain; but there was so much eagerness, and the throng of so many around, seeking to kill him, that I know not who it was that slew him.'

As a result of the dismissal of the Wace text in England in Victorian times it was necessary for the academic fraternity to unite under one version of how Harold died. This consensus eventually settled for the Bayeux Tapestry version of events, which is open to interpretation. The image with the picture of Harold with an arrow in the eye is the one we all know and to some extent is due to the marketing power of Bayeux, in selling their heritage to the world.

In conclusion Wace is a vibrant source of information which endorses the new battle site at Crowhurst. Wace is also confirmed by the editing of the Bayeux Tapestry to contain authentic information about the battle that is not confirmed in any other text. The distance between the authentic battlefield in the Crowhurst valley, and the Norman camp site at Wilting, is less than 2 miles; the sort of distance that would allow 5,000+ troops to be organised to move the distance involved in the time scales recorded.

The Chronicle of Battle Abbey is as good a document as we can probably get that points to Crowhurst as the original site of the Battle of Hastings. However there is more. Identifying the site as somewhere in that manor is narrowed down by the inclusion of the event known as the *'Malfosse'* incident.

Chapter 66: THE MALFOSSE

The Malfosse incident is recorded in the Chronicle of Battle Abbey and also alluded to in Wace. It records where at the end of the battle the English desert the field. They are pursued by a number of Norman knights on horseback, who die in a huge ditch adjacent to the battlefield. This is another unsolved issues relating to the battle site located at the Abbey, since no such place exists where it should be located. The Chronicle describes the events thus:

'Lamentably, just where the fighting was going on, and stretching for some considerable distance, an immense ditch yawned. It may have been a natural cleft in the earth or perhaps it had been hollowed out by storms. But in this waste ground it was overgrown with brambles and thistles, and could scarcely be seen in time; and it engulfed great numbers, especially the Normans in pursuit of the English. For, when all unknowing, they came galloping on, their terrific impetus carried them headlong down into it, and they died tragically, pounded to pieces. This deep pit has been named for the accident, and today it is called the Malfosse. '

No Malfosse exists at the Battle Abbey site, although like the other names taken from the Chronicle one was created at a much later date about a mile north-west of the Abbey, in a crude attempt to justify all elements within the lands of the Abbey. It was like the other places within the Abbey lands, which were named after events detailed in the Chronicle. The real battle site, which we shall deal with shortly, has all the identification marks including the path leading from the battlefield to the Malfosse, where so many Norman knights died. None of the important identifying features are missing, because it is I believe the correct location.

The description in the Battle Abbey Chronicle makes it clear this is not just a ditch, but a significant cleft in the landscape, probably caused by storms. It needs to be a place, which was *'just where the fighting was going on'*. It is described as an area of land that was *'waste land'*, concealing the drop, where brambles and thistles grow. That land is still today as it was on the day of the battle. It is adjacent to, as well as the boundary of, the correct battle site.

The English had formed their main defence behind their shield wall and also behind the main defensive stakes across the battlefield. This was the last line of the Saxon defence, where Harold was located with his standards. If the Normans broke through here the game was up for the Saxons, requiring them to retreat in order to reform or fight another day.

It is therefore relevant to note that a footpath leads from the correct battlefield site in Crowhurst to the Malfosse. It does so from a position which would allow the Saxons to flee the field, without allowing the Normans to follow. This path was another trap set by those who planned the battle. It demonstrates that considerable care was taken in choosing exactly where to place the last Saxon defensive line. If the defensive line were 50 meters further up the hill this exit would not have been available to the Saxons.

Unlike the Battle Abbey site the correct battle site is laid out on a steep hill at the entrance to the Crowhurst valley. Those who had been camped at the Norman camp, at Upper Wilting at the port of Hastings, were forced by the terrain into a narrow corridor along the then London Road if they wished to escape. That corridor had the Malfosse on one side of the battlefield and another cleft on the opposite side of the field, with the dense thicket of the wood called the Forewood to the west - making another exit route impossible. As Wace comments; *the Normans were forced to come to Harold.*

Crowhurst was Harold's manor - he owned it, his father owned it before him, and Harold almost certainly had personal knowledge of the lie of the land. The decision to stop at this particular place was a tactical move, which forced the Norman's hand. It was a decision that those who study warfare will give Harold great credit for, because Harold then reinforced his defence with a ditch with stakes across the battlefield. This was not the normal way that the Saxons of the day fought. Harold was creating a new form of defence and it explains why the Normans, with their war-horses were unable to penetrate the Saxon line.

Historians have criticised Harold for his rashness in marching from Stamford Bridge straight to the site of the Battle of Hastings. They did not know there was a good reason to do that. Harold knew the land, as he was it's Lord - a title that is confirmed by the person who delivers the message to him at Stamford Bridge - where it is reported in the Carmen with the words '*Harold his Lord*' were recorded.

Harold realised, as I did, that if William was camped at Wilting Manor, by the port of Hastings, the Normans were in serious trouble if a defence were mounted on the Crowhurst side of the Ridge south of Telham. The land did not allow the Normans to exit the peninsular without passing through one particular place where the road was confined on both sides by impassable clefts in the landscape. This is local knowledge that I have, and so it appears did Harold. Those who held the land to the north could build a defence and starve the invaders to death, because they could not get provisions once their supply ran out.

William had no choice. If he did not engage the English early on the morning after the Saxons arrived, then the Normans would never have got off the peninsular alive. A battle would probably never take place if Harold was allowed to fortify that defence with major structures. Harold sought to exploit his local knowledge of the land to provide him with a tactical edge that would win him the battle. The lay of the land as it has been reported is shown as follows:

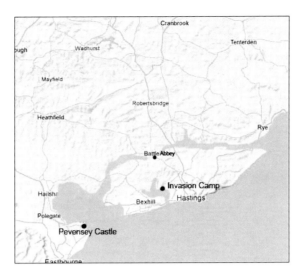

The Hastings peninsular as it was believed to be in 1066 with Norman campsite at the port of Hastings.

The roads marked on this map and place names are those used today, with the sea coloured blue. Since 1066 the sea was believed to have retreated leaving marsh and now some farm land close to Battle Abbey. Historians have long understood the significance of the Abbey marking the entrance to the peninsular and have assumed that this was why the Battle of Hastings was fought there. Most historians have never visited the area and few if any have ever gone beyond Battle along the old London road, as opposed to the post 1840 ridge road. They have read the theory, but not understood Harold's mind. He knew the significance of the road from Battle to Crowhurst, because he was Lord of that manor and I am absolutely certain from his actions he knew that land well.

If Harold had fought this battle at the Abbey site he would have had a very small chance of success against the Normans, because they could destroy the Saxons with their horse in open country. Harold had seen and fought with them in France. He knew their leader and he knew their fighting strategy. William's men fought with war horses. These horses where massive compared to a man on foot and Harold knew his men were used to fighting on foot. These horses were the equivalent of today's tanks against infantry. Standing men in a field had little chance against a ton of horse in full gallop with an armoured knight on its back.

Every year the Saxons reform for the Battle Abbey re-enactments, where men line up on each side of the slope to fight each other on foot. That is not what William had planned. If the battle had been allowed to happen at the Battle Abbey site Harold and his men would have been wiped from the face of the earth by 500 battle hardened horses at the first charge. That site has no confinement for the horses and no ability to stop circumvention of the defensive line.

Those who attend these re-enactments must know this. They must know that regardless of how well you can hold a shield wall together it is no match for a charge by 500 armoured heavy horsemen. That failure was because Harold had enclosed his field with stakes, with the ditch on the hill in Crowhurst, which is missing from the Abbey site.

Only at the end of the battle were the Normans able to engage their heavy horses to attack the fleeing English. That should have been with devastating effect, except a contingency plan appeared to exist for that too. The path to the Malfosse was strategically positioned to allow fast exit directly from the Saxon line over the deep ravine on foot. Those on horseback unfamiliar with the territory would find themselves running down a narrow path through undulating thicket that is a not unduly steep. Those on horseback who strayed from the path would find themselves in a headlong dash towards a fifteen to twenty foot drop to certain death - *'the pit'* of the place named *'The Malfosse'* in the Chronicle of Battle Abbey. Not enough drop to necessarily kill a man on his own, but on a horse with nowhere to go, and others behind *'pounded to pieces'*, it was a formula for the disaster, exactly as it happened to the Normans.

159

Even today it is possible to see this path in the thicket that has since grown, as it forms part of the old track network that connected the Crowhurst Roman bloomery system. Those old tracks are still marked on the Ordnance Survey maps as hedgerows that align to the bloomeries at Forewood, Bynes Farm and Crowhurst Park. They may appear today as hedgerows, but they were made by men long ago and now form the boundaries of land, which have long since been sold or broken into small parcels.

These tracks were created during the Roman period, when the Crowhurst valley went through a major period of occupation. Little remains today, but we know that the main bloomery at Beauport Park produced most of the iron needed for Caesars legions. An extensive track system developed to move the iron ore to the ancient port of Hastings on the Bulverhythe using carts. These carts left their mark in the landscape. Whilst those who pass them every day may not observe them, the trained eye can still see them, as they pass through or remain part of the boundaries of land.

The issue of the Roman tracks has been dealt with in some detail in the Roman Development Chapter. That chapter dealt with the infrastructure connections between Beauport Park bloomery and the port of Hastings. It showed that there was a reason for the Romans to use that port and argued that this network was part of a major iron production process. The discovery of major industrialisation deposits at the port area by Smyth and Jennings is also documented on my web site in the correspondence section.

The track network that developed in the Crowhurst valley was not my invention to somehow persuade the inquiry in 1996 that the site at Wilting was in some special need of preservation. I simply reported the evidence that exists and drew conclusions, which were logical and persuasive. The Wilting and Norman Camp site are not historical sites that exist in isolation, as road developers may wish to believe. They are all connected, because the Romans were there first, quite a long time before the Normans considered Hastings a good port to secure.

The bloomery at Beauport Park was by far the largest in the southeast of England, but the garrison that looked after it also had a number of lesser bloomeries within their control. This required Roman road connections to enable the industrious extraction in an efficient manner. It also needed roads able to take substantial loads, which could be used all year. Those roads had to enable passage of carts pulled by oxen or horses in summer and winter.

The design therefore of the track system between the main bloomery at Beauport Park on the southeast side of the Ridge was designed to run down hill from each of the sub-bloomeries. This was not possible on all sections, because of the nature of the land. The sections between the actual bloomeries themselves, as opposed to the tracks that connected the bloomeries to each other, did that, as much as was humanly possible.

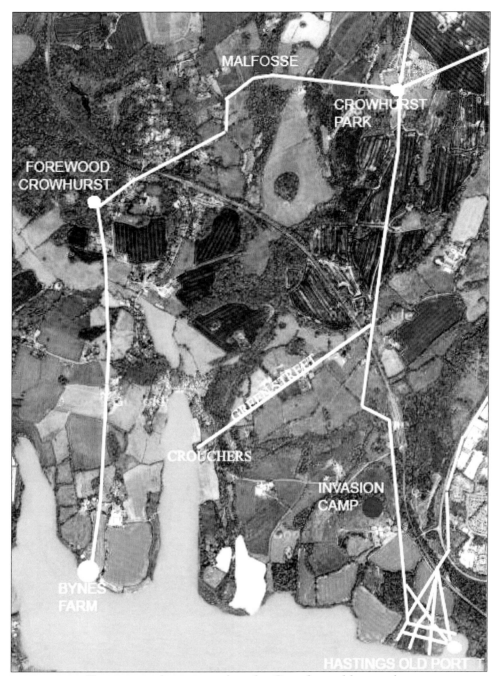

Roman tracks connecting the Crowhurst bloomeries

This map shows where the three sub-bloomeries of Beauport Park were located and the tracks that connected them. Each ended in a system for loading barges in the inland lake at the old port of Hastings. The bridge at the Malfosse is identified at the top of the aerial photo, with the red dot. It was a necessary construction to cross the ravine by cart. The evidence for this unreported bridge exists in physical form today in the traces left behind

View from battlefield heading east down track to Malfosse

This view, shown in the photo above, cannot be seen from the battlefield, as it is obscured by trees. Once into the wood there is low vegetation, including a lot of briars making it difficult to run through. The land is moderately open, although undulating in a downwards direction, making it easier to gallop through on a large horse. Those who came off of the battlefield on horse at speed would see this view in front of them and assume it was safe to continue at speed. There is a strong illusion that the open field in front of you connects to rising ground in the next fifty yards.

In fact looking north along the same Malfosse the drop is quite apparent in the following photograph:

View north up Malfosse, logs show bridge

A bridge was necessary here (B) because the drop in the land was too great for carts to cross without it. The original position of that bridge was higher than the replacement, which we can see the remains of today. The earthen platform position (A), where the higher connection was located, can still be seen in the photograph above, about half way up the photograph on the left hand side of the ravine.

This photo (1994)shows the detail of the remains of the current Malfosse bridge, which is now almost gone.

Those who took the path on foot escaped to higher ground over the ravine bridge, whereas those who followed by horse never got that far. Perhaps Harold had planned this as an exit for the nobility, should that be needed. As we know fate was not with him that day. His planning undoubtedly cost the Normans dearly and saved many who would otherwise have perished at the end of the battle. This is the Malfosse of which so much has been written by historians in the past. Today it is very much the same as it must have been then. This was a place of death in 1066, but today a place of serene beauty, where the only visitors are the animals of the forest.

Chapter 67: THE CROWHURST TITHE MAP 1841

The Crowhurst Parish Tithe Map of 1841 is an invaluable document in terms of understanding the site of the Battle of Hastings. This is because it was created at a time when only the old properties were in existence in Crowhurst. The tell tale signs of boundaries and ancient pathways had not at that time been diverted to take account of the railway, which went right through the centre of the Crowhurst valley in the mid 1800s. In fact the Crowhurst railway station was built two thirds of the way up the hill upon which the Battle of Hastings was fought. It is an excellent place to meet for those who have to come by public transport, as the station is on the main line service from Charing Cross. The best assembly point for those who come by road is the Plough pub, by the Crowhurst recreation ground.

The effect of the railway was to divert the original road and paths, many of which dated back to the Roman times. The 1841 Tithe Map shows those pathways that have been lost by field boundaries changes, as well as land that has been bought and sold over the last two centuries. Using this map it can still be established where roads that once existed must have connected. Many of these are now in hedgerows and remain until this day, but are only revealed by actual physical examination.

The other element that is available to a historical researcher today, which was not available even a few short years ago, when I started this project, is the world satellite mapping system in Google. In consequence it is possible to take the 1841 Tithe Map and compare it side by side with a full colour aerial photograph of the same area.

It is notable that it is not possible to superimpose one map upon the other, because of anomalies in the perspective of the photos, because they are not taken from directly over the site, but pointing from the south towards the main area. It is possible to clearly see where the woodland used to be located prior to the development of the last two hundred years. Those mature trees and tree lines leaving little doubt as to where the ancient woodlands extended around the Crowhurst valley.

Simon Jennings and Christine Smyth, from the University of London, are probably the only expert sedimentologists who have done any serious study of the Crowhurst and Wilting valley. Their 30 years of work is a tribute to their dedication to understanding the importance of this valley in terms of its development. Simon told me that his work with pollen in auger samples confirmed that deforestation had taken place in this valley very early and indicated a thriving community along the foreshore long before the Romans. This appears to have been born out by the discovery of the Bronze Age log on the edge of Wilting and the host of early finds found by Wessex Archaeology, when the first road was threatened to be built through the Wilting Invasion site. Simon suspected that this sheltered inlet was far more important than the Shinewater site further down the coast, because of its special inland waterway and protected habitat.

At the same time we know that by the time the Normans arrived in 1066 there were 22 ploughs in the parish of Crowhurst. This is because the number of ploughs is recorded in the Sussex part of the Domesday Book. In conclusion we know that enough deforestation had occurred by 1066 to sustain the Lord of the manor and at least 22 families and their fields using oxen to plough.

The manors of Crowhurst and Wilting are connected by a common wooded ridge that separates the two parts of the parish, running east/west about 800 meters north of the Norman Invasion site at Wilting. This ridge had a Roman track running its length and was named Green Street. The hamlet of Green Street is still situated at the west end of that ridge. The name indicates a disused Roman road in Old English. It connected the largest iron bloomery in the south-east with the harbour at Wilting through one branch of a network of tracks through to the Crowhurst inlet at Crouchers Farm. That ridge road was reduced to a track by the time the Normans arrived and as a result obtained that name. It is also reported in the Carmen that there were dismantled forts at the site of the Invasion - indicating the presence of a disused encampment of some kind.

The Roman track has since been diverted around the quarry at the top of the Crowhurst road, leading out of the village, as you head south towards Hastings. The road that follows the old Roman track is now called Swainham Lane. It leads from Crowhurst up to the main Ridge. The original track connected to the hedge line of the entrance road to Crouchers Farm, at the Crowhurst sea inlet, with moorings where the high tide reached, at the point where the marsh and pasture can now be seen to start. A footpath leads out from the Crowhurst recreation ground, along the edge of the inlet past Crouchers on the left as you walk to the sea. That walk down the Combe Haven Valley goes through a Site of Special Scientific Interest ('SSSI'). This same pasture and marsh floods every winter as the land is still reclaimed by waters. If the entrance to this valley had not been lost in the 13th century by a great storm sealing the entrance with a shingle bar, it would still be a tidal plain. This is because it was confirmed to me that the Crowhurst valley is at least 1 meter below sea level, by Simon Jennings and Christine Smyth, who took GPS accurate readings in order to get the sedimentary spot levels correct.

This is what the Crowhurst Valley looks like in winter, looking south from Hye House near the centre of the old village towards the sea, which can be seen beyond the far ridge on a clear day. That ridge separates the sea from the inland waterway called the Combe Haven. It is one of the rare wetlands along the south coast and of particular importance to many migrating birds from all over England, heading south in the autumn:

This sea inlet to the west of Wilting effectively provides an impenetrable barrier to any army camped at the Wilting Farm site, where it enters the sea further along the coast to the left in this picture. It stops anyone from being able to march along the coast. It is the main reason why those who live in this area understand that the traditional story that the Normans landed at Pevensey and marched down the coast to Hastings is clearly incorrect. Wilting, where the Normans camped to the south was an excellent defence, occupying a very steep hill of 40 meters. It was also surrounded on two sides by the sea inlet, through which the Normans had sailed to get there, with good moorings to hold many small craft.

Here is a picture of the same valley in early autumn, before the valley is completely flooded, looking west, and parallel to the coast over the left hand ridge. It shows the view of the main inland waterway. In Norman times the whole of this flat area was tidal and could accommodate well over 1,000 vessels of the day along the shore. This view is taken from the Norman Invasion site at Wilting.

Undoubtedly Wilting was an excellent choice of landing site, because it guaranteed an unopposed landing. The Carmen reports that *'they left the sea behind them at the third hour'* - an unfathomable expression, since it was before the actual landing - unless you understand exactly where they had chosen to land, in this inland waterway.

The tide was with them on that day and so there would have been a force of water travelling through the narrow confines of what is now the constriction where the holiday camp at the Bulverhythe entrance stands. Any opposition would have been completely ineffective if it had been there. The arriving boats would have sped right past any defensive positions, where they would have arrived in a calm and extensive inshore estuary out of range of any long bow.

That estuary was, as we have discussed at some length earlier, called the Port of Hastings. It was the largest Cinque Port on the south coast. Having sailed into that port unopposed the Normans then had a choice of three possible landing sites; Wilting being the prime site, where I strongly believe the original town of Hastings stood pre 1066. This is because of the pottery found on the Wilting Manor site, where there is none of that age found anywhere else associated with the Norman Invasion or even Hastings town. Should Wilting have been occupied by a defending force, then there were two alternate sites which could have taken the force of the landing. They were either Bynes Farm to the west of the Crowhurst inlet, or in the area to the west of the second arm of the inlet now known as Bexhill.

In many ways it shows William's expertise as a military strategist. The choice of sailing into Hastings port guaranteed that Harold could not mount a defence on three sides at the same time. It guaranteed the Normans a successful landing, even if Harold was waiting at the port with 10,000 men. This was because the area of the port was too great an area to defend. It was not possible to defend three separate shores at once. William has never been given the credit for this and now we can see that landing at Hastings was not luck - but must have been a well researched plan.

The Tithe Map shows a number of roads in existence in 1841. The copy of the map has been recreated using photocopies of the original from East Sussex County library. This was done twenty years ago, before computers, but is still valid. This is what the Tithe Map looks like:

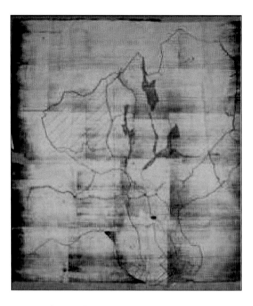

You can see old fashioned marker pens have been used. It covers just the parish of Crowhurst, with the parish of Battle off the map at the top. None the less the markers do the trick and even though rather elementary by modern standards it will suffice. I have marked the roads in existence at that time (1841) in red. These roads were not there in 1066. We know that because the properties that developed in the valley developed along the old coaching route.

The coach road from Battle to Crowhurst and on to Hastings followed the route of the old properties. It did not run along what is locally called the Ridge, now the A2100 west of Crowhurst. The Ridge is 140 meters high and until 1820 was covered in ancient oak forest. Some of which can still be seen to the east of the A2100 at Crowhurst Park. There is public access by footpaths to the old Roman bloomery at Beauport Park - I recommend a visit to Ring Wood and Alder Wood at the same time. There you can still see truly ancient trees in excess of 500 years old, in places resembling the ancient English woodlands that surrounded the Crowhurst Valley, undisturbed by man. (Note: take boots and a map, you can still - believe it or not - get lost).

There is a general assumption by the population at large that because you travel by car from the town of Battle to Hastings, along the A2100 (the Ridge road), that this is how the Normans came to the battlefield. That is because it is difficult for people today to understand the logistics of moving iron ore, and a world where the horse or cart was the way normal people travelled, until the last two hundred years. The Romans knew that carts with oxen can only carry heavy goods up and down certain gradients. Consequently roads developed according to the requirements of the transport and people who lived there. Very few people travelled any great distance, unless you were nobility or appointed by the court.

The Ridge, shown on the topography map at the front of the book, was a major obstacle to the early development of Hastings. This next picture is taken from the Wilting Norman Invasion site, near the coast looking north, towards Battle town, showing the main field where the Normans camped (in the foreground) on the night before the battle. Wace recorded that camp fires were lit and the Normans said prayers preparing for battle. You can see in the distance the line of what locals call *'the Ridge'*.

A closer look at that view into the distance shows that there is line of site between that field and Telham on the Ridge.

In the very centre of this photograph is a difficult to distinguish white building, right on the ridge line. That building is located on the Hastings side of the road on the Crowhurst parish boundary to the north. The field to the left of it is the field that is to the east of the Malfosse and the site of the Saxon camp is in the field to the west (left) of that. That field shows as a dip in the trees. It is difficult to identify from Wilting, because the area is still well wooded either side of the real battle site.

The land between this position and the Ridge rises steeply, as we are looking up the hill. Between us and the Ridge there are two deep wooded valleys, making approach from that direction impossible.

Looking the other way, from the Saxon's perspective at the top of the Ridge, looking down upon the Norman camp at Wilting we see this view, with the sea in the distance. We are looking down on the Norman camp from a height of 100meters (14 meters higher than the Battle Abbey site approximately 2km. behind us):

A better view can be obtained from the higher resolution web based image. You will see that we are looking towards the coast in a south-east direction. The town of St Leonards on the edge of Hastings occupies most of the view along the coast. Again in the centre of this picture is a green field, just below the horizon, with a ridge line that runs left to right across our view. The green field is located on that lower ridge line that is just below the line of the coast. If you follow the lower ridge line to the right (west), you will see what looks like another white building. It is in fact a greenhouse type building, located at the entrance to the Combe Haven and Bulverhythe site of the old port of Hastings.

Wilting Farm house and the Norman Invasion camp field is located in the middle of the point between the greenhouse building and the green field on that ridge line. It too is partly obscured by trees and not easily identifiable from this photograph. Wilting farm house has an elevated chimney stack and that can just about be made out on the photograph. That farm house is located in the field that the Normans camped in.

The photograph does show the perspective of how the Saxons dominated the landscape, because it was this field, in the foreground, that Wace identified as the Saxon Camp, on the night of the battle. It is the highest ground on the old London road and now private land.

Hastings was on an effective peninsular with no direct coastal access from east or west. Until 1820, quite recently in terms of history as a whole, the old London road at Battle Abbey went directly south, via what is currently the Tesco site, at Senlac Hill, at the entrance to Battle railway station, and from there to Crowhurst. The old track can be found on the Ordnance Survey map, as a field boundary footpath running past the back of Telham Court School to Malthouse Wood.

It is still a public footpath (next to the Tesco petrol station) and can be travelled on foot - I recommend walking it if you really want to understand how the people who fought this battle, on the side of the Saxons, felt when they arrived in 1066 from Stamford Bridge.

If you are brave enough to take this journey you can travel the same way that Harold's army came to the battle site. There are some minor recent diversions, but it is quite clear to anyone with any knowledge of map reading where the early road went. It was travelled by cart and so the signs remain in the hedgerows and field boundaries even today. It takes about an hour from Battle to Crowhurst on foot.

This is not an easy footpath, as it has sections that are very steep, but it does not go through the ancient woodland known as Great Wood, which ran from the marsh of the Wilting inlet to the north, through to the bloomery at Beauport Park. The old London road was therefore probably relatively safe, because of the open pasture of most of the journey. Travelling along this ancient way you pass through two steep valleys from Battle, before ascending the main ridge at Telham Hill, into the Crowhurst valley where the battle took place.

Telham is the name of the hill where the Crowhurst parish meets the Battle parish at the north of the Crowhurst Tithe Map. It is not where the Ordnance Survey map shows Telham Post Office on the A2100 road. A post office that I believe has now been closed.

The name Telham Hill features in the history of the Abbey, because it was the name of the hill where the battle took place. The crossroads at Telham Hill is not in existence today, but is easy to find where Forewood Lane in Crowhurst joins the Crowhurst to Battle road, next to the Old Forewood Lane signpost. This is found as you enter Crowhurst village from the north, along the main road, in a section that was also the original old road to Battle and London. It is just after the Crowhurst sign.

Three of the roads are in existence, but the fourth going east is the parish boundary and is now only a footpath. That footpath shows the original road with cart tracks, where it enters the tree line to the east, at the property known as Telham Place. It is likely that the land to the north of this footpath, which is now in the Battle parish, was included in the Battle Abbey lands (the Leuga) around the time that Battle Abbey decided to support their claim to the battle site in 1180. It is of particular interest that they also purchased one large site in the Crowhurst parish on the south side of the ridge.

That site is now called Telham Place and is the property that runs down from the Ridge on the opposite side of the Malfosse from the Crowhurst battle site. I find this an intriguing coincidence. It suggests to my suspicious mind that the Abbott knew what they were doing and wanted to make sure no element was left to come out later. In order to eliminate any possible discovery of deception he ordered the land where he thought the battle had really been fought to be included in the Abbey's lands.

The Abbey protected its lands and only those within its control farmed there. At the same time the Church diverted the road in Crowhurst away from the what was called the Great Field to avoid prying eyes. It purchased the land for the Rectory right in the middle of the battle site - not next to the Church of St George's at the bottom of the hill, which would have been the normal practice.

I do understand that some considerable time elapsed between the building of those properties you see today, however there were properties on the same sites under the ownership of the Church. It does seem likely that those who faked the Charter, upon which the Abbey was founded, did their due diligence in order to make sure that later nothing came out of the ground to haunt them.

It must also be remembered that not one Norman or Saxon body has ever been found relating to the Battle of Hastings. Not a buckle, belt, horse shoe from the relevant period, axe head, ring or trace of any kind. Harold was reported to be buried overlooking the shore and the sea, which can be seen from that ridge. It is in my view more than probable that evidence exists on that ridge somewhere, which will confirm the battle site. Too many men died on that day to be buried and the earth holds memories that today can be recovered using modern technology.

Those who look on the Ordnance Survey map will see that Telham is marked at the top of the Ridge, at the entrance to Crowhurst Caravan Park. This is the place people in the area know Telham to be today. However it is not Telham Hill and the difference is probably an important difference that accounted for the mistake in locating the original battle site 100 years after the battle took place.

The crossroads at Telham Hill is an important place, because next to it is Apple Tree Field. It is my contention that this is because it is the place where the hoary apple tree was located. Names in farming communities stick and there are many names on the Tithe Map which are still known today.

It is one of the most ancient English traditions to mark parish boundaries with trees. In particular the yew, because of its ability to live longer than any man, and its use to mark circles at religious sites, prior to the arrival of Christianity. The hoar apple also played its part as I have seen a report in the authoritative 800 page Hastings Castle study, by Charles Dawson, confirming 19 separate examples of 'hoar trees' marking parish boundaries. Now with the benefit of the internet it is possible to confirm that this was a very common practice, as the records still exist of many more than that online.

I think this is significant information, because it has always been assumed that the 'hoar apple tree', was simply a marker tree of unknown significance, known only to the Normans. At the site at Battle Abbey it could not have been a boundary marker, because it was not on any boundary. Its absence from being a boundary marker is an important clue to where the battle really took place. It acts as a really good colloquial confirmation of the real battle site, once the significance of the name is known.

In the Saxon Chronicle (Manuscript D) there is reference to the fact that the Battle of Hastings was at first known as 'the Battle of the Hoar Apple Tree'. A hoar apple tree is one that is old (probably hollow) and with gnarled witch like features. If the Battle of Hastings first attained that name to the population at large, without any explanation of the location, the name must have had a meaning to the common man of the area. It suggests the battle took place where there was no other name for the location. It looks highly likely that it meant the parish boundary marker, because of its use throughout the country in such a manner. As a consequence of that you would ask 'which parish was it in?' - and the answer is of course Hastings - and so you have another confirmation that this was the Battle of Hastings location. It isn't rocket science to come to this conclusion on how a name comes into existence, especially when the battle isn't in the place it is meant to be.

It cannot be proven that this field adjacent to the cross-roads at Crowhurst is the site of the hoary apple tree, from a field name alone, but it is a remarkable coincidence if it isn't. There is no evidence of a hoary apple tree in any of the abbey documents and of course there is none on that site today. But most telling of all there are no parish boundaries anywhere near the abbey site. The monks probably chose the site in question at Battle Abbey specifically because it was not near any boundaries. They could not however change the name by which the population at large knew the battle. Having made the decision to move the Abbey it would only have been moved in order to locate a better site, where they could exert their control over as much land as possible. The fact that they chose the field that straddled the London road, at the entrance to the peninsular, confirms a motive for that move.

I do not think it is a coincidence that the lady who built the new property at Pye's Farm, immediately adjacent to Apple Tree Field, found a spear head in the property foundations when the new extension was built. It is a shame she did not know the significance at the time, so she threw it away. None the less it is a true story and it will not be the only one from this site, because of the large numbers of properties that have been built within the boundary of what was then the Great Field.

As you come into Crowhurst from the north using the old London road from Battle, which is now a track, you eventually reach the top of the lower part of the Ridge at Telham Hill. This is below the summit of the Ridge, by at least 40 meters and to the east of the main ridge line that surrounds

Hastings. Telham Hill is about 100m (330ft) above sea level. That ridge is a defining barrier in the landscape, rising to over 140 meters (450ft) further to the east. Those who lived to the north of this Ridge were in a different landscape from those who lived south of it.

This is best demonstrated by going there yourself. Today we live in a world where private land has removed our ability to see what Harold saw when he arrived at this crossroads in 1066. In consequence you need to take the old London road from Battle, until you come to the *'hoary apple tree crossroads'*. There you must take the footpath over the style to the east and follow the path up to the top of the first field and look south under the pylon wires. When you get to the top of that path you will see what Harold saw - the whole of the Hastings coast, port and Invasion site at your feet.

As we have seen without detailed knowledge it is difficult to identify the Norman camp site during the day, but with camp fires burning at Wilting at night, it was easy for the two sides to see one and other. This is at the head of the Crowhurst Valley and the place where Harold camped on the night of the battle. It provides a stunning view of the landscape, where you can see in front of you much of the south coast, as far as Eastbourne and Beachy Head to the west on a clear day. Behind you, less than two steep valleys away, on a winter's day you can see where the Abbey was eventually built – *'not far off'*.

The next chapter is probably one of the most important, because it is about Crowhurst Manor House and its secrets. Possibly the most important manor house ever built, because of its hidden secret place in the history of England and at this time ignored by the world at large.

Chapter 68: THE MANOR HOUSE

The Manor House at Crowhurst is an ancient ruin located at the bottom of the Great Field overlooking the Crowhurst plain. It appears to be at the centre of the village, from a modern perspective, and is located immediately adjacent to the Church of St George - the Crowhurst parish church. This is a church that has a recorded history dating back to well before the Norman Invasion. It was first recorded in a charter of 771 in which King Offa of Mercia gave the Bishop of Selsey a parcel of land in the village. In return the Bishop built the first church. After the conquest the manor was given to Robert, Count of Eu, by William the Conqueror in gratitude for his part played in the Invasion and battle.

Robert was an important man in the events after the Invasion, because he was given Hastings and the manor of Wilting, where the Sheriffs of Hastings lived, as well as the manor of Crowhurst. Robert was a builder and the man who organised and built the stone castle on its present site at Hastings. The castle at Hastings was finished around 1095. We know this because the records of the purchase of the stone were found by Charles Dawson, who wrote the definitive 800 page treatise on the history of Hastings Castle in the 1800s. Almost every single web page that I can find on the internet is completely wrong in regards to Hastings Castle history. Not because it has anything whatsoever to do with the research I have been doing, but because those who write web pages on history, such as this, never bother to check the sources, or do any serious research themselves. They take the information from armchair historians, who populate Wikipedia and rewrite history based upon the popular press. It is a sad indictment of the modern evolution of the internet. Dawson on the other hand received a bad press in his time, but actually carried out extensive and accurate research into almost every aspect of Hastings Castle and the surrounding area.

Most of the nobility of France and England attended the ceremony when the Abbey at Battle was consecrated in 1094, but it is also important to understand that those who attended that consecration were not those who fought in the battle. William never returned to Hastings and neither did any of his retinue that we know of. An earlier consecration had taken place in 1076 - ten years after the battle. It is probable that the first consecration was to confirm the new site, indicating that the first site may have been under construction for up to ten years before the monk Smith moved it to the site at Battle.

All that is known for certain about the Crowhurst manor is that the church was where it is today, because the records show that the church was built on the site of the old one around 776AD, when the charter records it. There is a huge gap in the records between 776AD and 1259 when the next recorded event occurs. This is 300 years when nothing is known other than the manor passing from Harold, upon his death, to the Norman Count of Eu. He gave it to Walter Fitz Lambert according to the Domesday Book (1086) after which it is then passed to Walter De Scotney (descendant of Walter Fitz Lambert through Lambert de Scotney).

The next thing we know about the Manor House is it came into the possession of the Scotney family. We know this because Walter de Scotney came to grief in 1259, accused of poisoning his master the Earl of Gloucester, who was his brother. Walter De Scotney was the Lord of Crowhurst Manor and his brother died as a result of the poisoning. Consequently Walter was executed upon the orders of the King. Later in the early fifteenth century the Pelham family took possession of the Manor, of which there is an extensive recorded history. Even today the sign of the Pelham Buckle can be found on the church, rebuilt by the Pelham's, as well as other places around the parish.

Crowhurst Manor House is therefore an enigma in many respects, because the evidence of the Chronicle of Battle Abbey points directly at that manor house as being the landmark for the field where the Battle of Hastings took place. The ruin that is located just south of the church, next to a low stone wall, should have a recorded history of when it was built. It is big enough to be a seat of government, in a place that is completely out of character to its potential importance.

There is no record of such a building project. The building just materialises as a very large property, of unknown origin, which became a ruin. That in itself is a good clue, because if the De Scotneys had been responsible for building that manor house, you can be almost certain that records would have existed. John Springford, the gifted Crowhurst historian, painstakingly went through the parish records - a huge task involving deciphering what to many would be incomprehensible Latin script, some of which were still on vellum. No records of the building of Manor House exist, or even the purchase of stone for that building, despite a lot of alterations taking place. Bearing in mind we can find the records of the stone for the purchase of Hastings Castle, this simply adds to my conviction that the Manor House was built upon the site that the monks started in 1067, and was already there when the De Scotneys took possession.

Walter Fitz Lambert, who is recorded in the Domesday Book, was an important person. As well as being the lord of Crowhurst (Crohest) he held Hazelhurst (Haslesse) and Sedlescombe (Selescome) for the Earl. He was based in Crowhurst, most probably because the manor house was exceptionally large and for this reason it is quite likely that he was the first occupier of the building that was already there.

Crowhurst Manor House is therefore a building that needs to be investigated, because it is more than likely that its origins are part of the story of the Norman Invasion. I come to this conclusion because the Manor House is real and datable archaeology. Unlike the intangible elements of battlefields, the written record obtained from the Chronicle of Battle Abbey confirms that the Abbey was started low down on the west side of the Ridge, at a place called Herste, *'where a low wall now stands,'* -exactly where the Crowhurst manor house was built.

The Victorian County History, Sussex edition, confirms that Crowhurst was in the Baldslow Hundred area. It also confirms that Crowhurst was written as *Croghyrste* in the 8th century and *Crowherst* in the 11th century. During that time the Normans had taken over the record keeping process, resulting in names being written in the way that Norman thinking would have them recorded - Hurst the English name, changing to Herste, the French version. Local dialect did not pronounce the Crog or Crow in the spoken tradition of the area. The village was always known as *'Crurst'* in the Sussex dialect even up to the mid 1900s. It is not too much of a giant leap to conclude that the *'Herste'*, recorded by a Norman in the Chronicle of Battle Abbey, was the same *'Crurst'* which the scribe wrote down as Herste when recording those events of the first 12 folios - the ones they could not alter to fit their version of events. This to me looks very much like the silver thread of truth appearing again to tempt us to look closer at this very interesting building.

If that assumption is correct, datable archaeology will confirm that the foundations of the Crowhurst manor site are actually the foundations of what was intended to be the Abbey, which was to be built upon the true battle site. The monk Smith, from Marmoutier, intervened in that process, resulting in the Abbey being moved to where it is today. Despite the removal of the Abbey to that site, the building process had been under construction for at least three years according to the records and could possibly be as long as ten. During that time substantial work would have been completed and as a result the record will exist in the archaeology. It is unlikely they would have removed every stone block, especially if it the building was on the Abbots land. Studying the archaeology of that building will open the door to confirming the story of the Norman Invasion - that is why the Crowhurst Manor House site is important.

Most old stone buildings of antiquity, which are large by the standards of the day, have had thorough investigations in the past. Crowhurst Manor House for some reason has slipped through the net. It is after all now only a ruin and has been recorded as a ruin since people started to take an interest in such things. In many respects it stands next to the Crowhurst church, ignored by the world that passes by, more like a scene out of a Hogarth landscape painting. It is hard to believe anyone ever lived in it, let alone understand its size and significance in the past. The new version of the Manor House (called Court Lodge) is built on the adjacent building plot and may well cover the site of the original building. It would be surprising if it did not.

W. S. Walford was the first recent historian to record the Manor House ruin in detail as recorded in the Sussex Victorian History in 1854. This engraving shows the ruin as it was in the 1787:

Ruins at Crowherst, Sussex.

173

Walford has a lot to answer for because he attributed the building to Walter de Scotney, without any written record to substantiate his claim. It was based upon the fact that the building was apparently rebuilt and enlarged by John, Earl of Richmond, between 1357 and 1360. His view was that the only owner prior to that must have been the De Scotneys, since it was only the De Scotneys who could have afforded such a major building project.

According to Walford the remains were the north cross wing and east porch of a building with a great hall attached to the south, with probably another wing. Walford believed that the plan that he drew up showed that of the complete structure. He concluded if a hall existed then it must have been of wood. The Victorian County History record for Sussex also records a question mark at this point in the text. It makes the comment:

'But it seems incredible that a porch of such excellent architecture and very solid masonry could have been the adjunct of a timber framed building, or led merely to an open space '

Clearly something is most definitely wrong with that assumption. The size of the building was large enough to be a palace by the standards of the day, but shows all the hallmarks of an ecclesiastical building. It is located upon an earthwork; similar is style to the one where Battle Abbey was built, requiring a monumental amount of work, even before the first stone was laid. Whilst I have no problem with attributing the building, as it stands today, as probably 13th century, it is clearly built upon something that was there before that. Adaptations exist in almost every part of the structure making dating highly speculative.

Walford did not know what he was looking at, because he had no reason to suspect that it might have been there a lot longer than he thought. The thickness of the exterior walls, the inclusion of buttresses, and most importantly the issue of the re-arrangement of the land upon which it is built, should have rung bells. He could not have stood back and looked at the land the building was located upon. It can clearly be seen that the Church is sitting on an odd piece of land that does not fit the natural geography of the valley. Men have been at work there moving the earth around over some considerable period of time.

Apart from the churchyard, which is elevated above the levels of the surrounding fields by over a meter, with no natural process to account for it, the lower half of the site where the Manor House is built has distinct terracing. There is no reason to do this work, except that the Manor House is there. The question is what lies beneath the terraces and how did they get there?

This is the floor plan showing the rectangular length of the part that Walford looked at. It is 40ft long by 23ft wide:

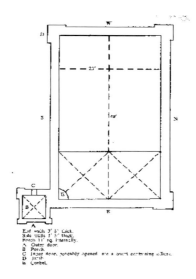

174

This is a visualisation of what it was believed it might have looked like:

Image taken from Crowhurst a Village in History by John Springford.

In some documents the Manor House property has been listed as *'Crowhurst Castle'* and is defined as a defensive manor house, because of the size of the walls. I suspect this is because the building was originally much older that 13th century and designed to hold a monastic order. The size of the walls simply reflects the style of buildings at that earlier time in history. Walford recorded at least one buttress and assumes it must have been for a chimney fireplace, but it was no longer there. The presence of buttresses confirms to me that this was planned to be a substantial building, of at least two storeys. The presence and size of the buttress confirms this. The fact there are no other visible ones does not mean they are not there, or were not started. Walford assumed that he was looking at a building that had been built as a manor house. What he could not understand he found reason to make supposition of elements that were not there.

When I look at the remains of this ruin I see the remains of a very small part of what must have been a much larger building. I see a building that is completely wrong as a manor house. The fact that the De Scotneys used the site, along with those who lived there before them is simply a testament to the fact that men who own large buildings use them. Either that or they build upon the foundations that have been left there.

Let us first look at the main view as you walk along the path towards the Manor House, going east. The church and the low stone wall that marks the place is out of sight immediately on the right of the photo below:

This shows the exterior of the building as detailed in the Walford plans. There is an obvious 13th century window by which the property has been dated. The size of the building is clear and also the depth of the walls making this a substantial structure. However as clear as day we can see the regular sockets for the wooden beams that show this could not under any circumstances have been the exterior. Those sockets confirm that this was an interior wall - making the previous visualisations that have been discussed at length over the centuries meaningless. It is clearly a mystery to me how learned gentlemen can look at the window, assume 13th century and also assume this is an exterior wall.

Yes we can see that the windows indicate their construction pointing in this direction - indicating that the interior was on the other side. Yes they appear 13th century windows, but clearly they are alterations of the original wall, because the different stone building elements can be seen. Look carefully at the facing stones and you can see that they are just that - facing stones. There are two arches where the two lower windows are located, much larger, occupying most of the width of the building. The lower sockets for the beams are about 150cm from the floor indicating a wooden floor construction, because the beams that held the floor run across the face of the stonework on both walls.

The positioning of the socket holes on the wall that runs parallel to the path, in positions half way between the walls, running at right angles to it, indicates cross beams running in the opposite direction. To me this appears to confirm this wall was part of a tower construction, most probably with a central staircase rising around an open centre, because the risers between the beams are too low for a man to stand. The buttress is clearly visible on the right, but it is located on the corner of the building, which is not normal, and the bottom facing stones from the buttress are missing, indicating that some sort of adaptation work may have taken place in the past.

If we now go around the other side of the wall and look at this wall from the east looking west. This is what we see:

The two original arches provide a walk way between the rooms we are in and the area of the tower construction, where the car can be seen through the window, are obvious. Yes the construction of these windows and also the main window unseen above are almost certainly 13th century, but the original building is to my mind much older. The fact that these appear upon a cursory inspection to be 13th century windows, however it is quite clear to see that they have been adapted into this wall, meaning the wall must be much older. This side we can see the additions and structure of the work required to install those windows, in what was previously two 11th century arches.

If we compare these to the 13th century undercroft at Battle Abbey we see an identical construction method, where the side walls have been built as support for the later designed decorated arch with coving.

The difference between 13th century and the 11th century construction is the stonework since it is less refined, as the stone masons were learning the art of how to hold large stone blocks in place. The detail in the stonework came later and in fine facing stonework. The rough stonework in the foundations suggests this manor house is much earlier than 13th century.

In the image of the manor house windows we can see that sockets for beams also exist, but on this side of the wall they are in the newer window masonry, appearing to confirm that they could not have existed in the original building. It is also notable that the ones that would support a wooden floor are also missing at the lower level.

Staying inside the main area of the above floor plan, if we look at the part of the right hand wall that still exists we can see this:

What is interesting about this plan is that buildings of this age do not normally have internal windows. Therefore the most westerly above ground wall remnant - with window, must have been an external wall. A most recent dig, detailed later in the chapter, found another parallel wall to the west of that window. It is understood that it is exceedingly rare to modify a house to make it smaller. This anomalous layout reinforces the conclusion that the visible wall remnant, with the window utilised existing foundations, was originally intended for a different bigger building.

Look carefully at this image and you can see that two arches have been built in this wall, one within the other. The outer one is large and rough, like the construction on the adjoining wall running at 90 degrees to it, suggesting that it too is 11th century. It is as if this is the original rough stone construction. Inside, slightly smaller, is the finished arch that has been added later and then eventually bricked up.

If we go on the other side of this wall we see the original finished construction of what looks to me like a very distinct Norman arch, which has been dated as 13th century.

Again we can see the adaptations of the old building in the left hand corner where another decorative feature has been added inside the original building in lighter coloured stone. The lighter coloured stone which has been used in the carved features strongly resembling the soft pale stone that came from Caen in France, which William used on his most important buildings. The corner stone appearing to confirm that we are standing in an area that originally had been intended to be a stone vaulted ceiling, showing the base of the return arch footing. Here is the detail together with some decorative edging.

Manor House detail

It isn't the detail in the foreground that I find interesting, because it too must be an adaptation, because of the stone differences between the coving and the base construction. It is the base of the column that catches my eye, because it uses different stone from a different quarry from the top stones. Those earlier footings suggest to me that this property is much older than previously has been given credit.

I am not convinced that the detail and skills required to create these mouldings would in any way be appropriate for a manor house in the wilds of 13th century Sussex. In many ways they are far too grand and expensive to be funded by the De Scotneys. Everything that we can see suggests expensive embellishment suitable for a large ecclesiastical building funded by the king. An example of the style of ceiling and layout that we can see here is mimicked as the undercroft of the 13th century building at the Battle Abbey site, which still exists today.

Of course the original abbey was taken down at the dissolution of the monasteries in the 1500s. All we have now is the floor plan for the 11th century part, as recorded by the Victorian excavations. This style of roof was common to both the 11th and 13th century. The reported layout of the abbey site can be seen here:

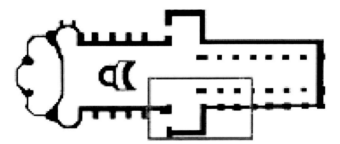

That floor plan appears to confirm that the main abbey building at Battle Abbey was constructed around two towers with a central nave. The construction of the property that we now know as Crowhurst Manor House (blue line), would fit quite neatly into that construction, since the scale and size of the property is similar. It even has the semi-circular end where the altar was positioned at the eastern end. It does not at first appear identical, but close enough to indicate that the Manor House may have been the original plan. The abbey site at Battle appears to be a larger version - which is what you would expect if the monk by the name of Smith decided it was too small for the ambitions of the monks who inherited it.

I look at this building in Crowhurst and it tells me that it may well hold the definitive archaeological clues as to whether this was or was not the site of the Battle of Hastings. There is no reason in the world that the Normans would have built the abbey to commemorate the battle in the wrong place, unless ordered to by the monks from Marmoutier, who acted upon the authority of the king. If the Chronicle is correct, they would have been forced to start the construction process again.

It was probably not practical to take the building that had been completed in Crowhurst in those first few years apart. It probably suited everyone to leave the building as it was, for the occupier of that manor to build upon, because the land was owned by the Count of Eu - the most powerful land owner in the area and a close confidant of the new king. If this manor house holds the hallmarks of Norman construction, or Norman period pottery, this will confirm the thesis. A non intrusive resistivity survey will allow us to establish where the foundations on the site exist and further exploratory work will enable experts to assess both the age and origins of that building. These are archaeological finds that will not be lost through the processes of chemical disintegration.

The ground floor of what is left of the stone ruin looks to me remarkably like what we would expect the undercroft of the Abbey to have looked like. The main site where this building is located is really quite substantial. If we look at the ruin from a short distance we can see that the ruin is only a very small part of a much larger set of buildings. The site merits proper archaeological investigation and I am very pleased to report that the current owner is agreeable for that to take place.

These buildings cover a large proportion of the manor site. The earthworks extend at least 20 meters south of the existing ruin, as well as east and west of it. Given that the ruin element is furthest from the road, it would seem logical for anyone who wanted to use the existing foundations to have built the main manor house upon those foundations. If that is the case the total size of the original building would have been massive by the standards of the day. It was in many respects far too large to be a simple manor house.

The present owners of the Manor House tell me that there is rubble wherever you care to dig in the garden and perimeter of the site. They were intrigued to have found masses of oyster shells, which might seem odd to the casual observer. This too is the hallmark of an ecclesiastical work force, who would be employed to serve God and king in such a massive building venture. Unlike today the cheapest food for such a large number of people was seafood, with oysters being the local supply through the port of Hastings, about than an hour by cart away.

In conclusion I believe the case can be made that the Manor House at Crowhurst should now come under the spotlight of those who have a responsibility to preserve our national heritage. It is very difficult to go against the view of someone who is considered an expert - which Walford definitely was in his time. I think there is now sufficient new information for Walford's previous assessments to be understood as wrong. If he had the knowledge relating to the additional walls and buttresses, I am sure he would have come to a different conclusion. For that reason I think Walford's report needs to be understood as based upon incomplete information and needs detailed re-assessment based upon new work being undertaken.

Currently the manor house is protected by English Heritage, who has the duty of protecting any property that is considered of historical importance. There has until now been no reason to look too closely at this ruin, because no-one has suspected its historical heritage. This is not surprising, because the country is full of ruins of little significance. However this site has unique potential to further our knowledge of English history. I believe it now deserves the attention of those who study history and archaeology, or intend to study archaeology for a living. I am therefore hopeful that English Heritage may be able to play their part in assisting in any investigation.

Whilst the current owners have been living in Court Lodge, they have been required in 2005 to produce an archaeological watching brief, in order to be allowed to place a surface swimming pool for their children close to the ruin on the lawn. That report can be found on my web site (Watching Brief by Samantha Worrall Bsc PGCE).

That report in my view raises more questions than it answers. It certainly confirms that previous beliefs in regards to how big the building was, and its purpose. The foundation of another structure believed to be another buttress was found on the remains of a new wall. The wall runs at right angles to the main ruin in a north/south direction. That discovery undermines Walford's assertions that the building was limited to the existing ruin and that a great hall existed of wooden construction.

This all adds up to confirming suspicions that the Crowhurst Manor site holds the key to confirming it as being the marker for the site of the Battle of Hastings, as confirmed by the first twelve folios of the Chronicle of Battle Abbey - the part that was not altered to support the forged charter - an authority that few, if any, modern day historians would challenge.

I have taken the view that the evidence gathered over twenty-four years, justifies the involvement of expertise that is outside of my capacity, in regards to taking the study of this building forward. I say that not because I am unwilling, but because I have not been trained in the disciplines necessary to document and record an investigation in the way that for instance is shown in Ms Worrall's excellent watching brief.

My web site is currently receiving between 10 and 20,000 visitors a month. I am confident that some of those who will read about this will have the backing of their archaeology departments, in a number of eminent Universities. I am pleased to report that many University History and Archaeology departments read my site regularly. Hopefully one of those Universities will now contact me, if they would be able to undertake an investigation, as a project for their students. It is not my intention to be involved personally in that, but have the ability to put the right people together and obtain the necessary permissions, as this is on private land where permission of the owners is required. I am pleased to say that the County Archaeologist has indicated that he would be prepared to meet me at the site to discuss the way forward with the owners if necessary.

Unfortunately, like most County Councils, there is no money to invest in archaeology issues that concern history, unless you happen to be building a road. There is considerable expertise that can be called upon to oversee any work, with the involvement of the local elements of English Heritage who would like to know more about this building. This all of course requires the consent of the owners, who have indicated they will provide access to those who have the necessary qualifications to undertake the necessary assessment. I am therefore confident that progress can be made if those with the suitable skills are prepared to do the work - initially a non intrusive resistivity survey requiring a day's work - and then later some trial trenching based upon what that shows - and take it from there. To start with it would be little more than a brief investigation from an organisation such as the television Time Team.

Chapter 69: THE BATTLE SITE

As we have noted, looking at the Tithe Map and putting the woodland back where it can be seen to have been, is not too difficult (courtesy of Google Maps). We cannot be 100% accurate, but we can see from the aerial photographs, which areas are still wooded. We can also make a good estimate based upon local knowledge as to which fields were wooded in the past, based upon the road and property development. Using that information it is possible to have a reasonably good estimate of what Crowhurst would have looked like in 1066.

I have drawn a map of how the land would probably have looked like in 1066. This shows the road to Wilting in the south (the Invasion Site where the Normans camped). It shows where Harold camped on the night before the battle with a red cross. I have marked the Saxon defence with a row of black crosses across the Great Field. I have marked the clefts in the landscape dark green where the Malfosse was located, with the woodland lighter green. I have marked what was probably pasture or arable land light brown, with the main road from Wilting to Battle red. Some of this road is still in use today, with some of it marked on the Ordnance Survey map as footpath. I have also marked buildings that act as landmarks.

We see that the arrival of Harold at his camp site, on the day of 13th October 1066, caused William a great deal of difficulty. This is because the road from Wilting was the only way off of what was then a peninsular. To the east, from the Norman camp, the road led to a dead end. The Crowhurst road to Catsfield, to the west, was a later development around the time that Hye House was built in Georgian times. Hye House and the road between the church and the Plough pub were developments associated with the 1840 coach road to Bexhill. That road came from Telham Hamlet at the top of the ridge and cut through from the top right of the Tithe Map to the bottom left, going around Hye House. It split at that point and went across the marsh to Bexhill via Bynes Farm and back down the twitten to the pub. It then crossed the inlet, before following the existing road out to Hastings following the old road to Wilting.

The Field at Hye House is called the Tye Field and it has always been difficult to understand why it held that name. The Tye Field was always the centre of a village, whereas Crowhurst didn't have an obvious centre, being strung out along the roads that went into it. When seen in the context of Crowhurst in 1066, with the agricultural land mainly to the south towards Bynes Farm, the centre point by ox cart was exactly where the Tye Field is located.

The crossroad at the hoary apple tree next to the Saxon camp was the way to exit the peninsular, and not as many historians have assumed, much further north at Battle. Initially I had made that mistake when I had started my search for the site of the Battle of Hastings. I had assumed that Battle was the only exit, because this is what I had read and assumed it to be true. However, anyone who does feet on the ground research can find out that you can get to Pevensey from Crowhurst without going to Battle, and without crossing what was the sea inlet in 1066.

This therefore is a map of the correct battle site for the Battle of Hastings, showing the crossroads where the road out of Hastings divided (red dots):

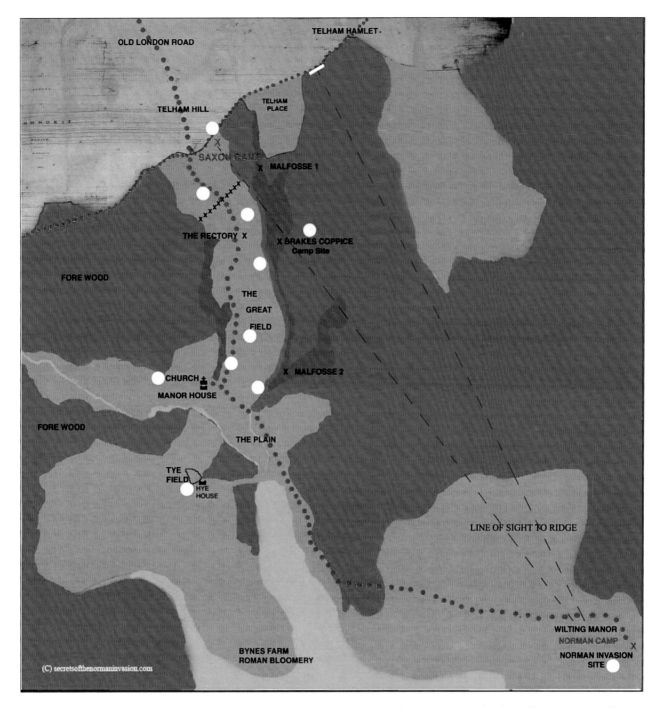

The map drawn earlier in my research in Chapter 66 (the Malfosse chapter) is therefore a simplification of the peninsular concept. The correct map of the coast as it actually was in 1066 is shown at the front of this book. This slight difference explains why the Domesday data is correct. Even now the road along the ridge between Telham and the Powdermills Hotel exists. In those days this road was a small track further south, through the edge of Fore Wood, connecting to the hoary apple tree crossroad. This was the dividing track that became the parish boundary. The parish boundary identified the fastest and most direct way from the crossroads off of the peninsular, without going anywhere near where Battle town is today. Parish boundaries came into existence because they were easily identifiable - not just a random choice.

The exit point from the Hastings peninsular was on the main road at Saw Mill, close to the Squirrel public house. It can be seen that the parish boundary turns sharp left at this point, joining what is now the coast road to Pevensey, from Battle via Boreham Bridge.

The important aspect of the terrain of the Crowhurst valley is that the road from Wilting Manor through Crowhurst had no usable exit points. The woodland was dense, as it still is today in places. There were no side roads to make a detour to avoid the enemy. It was a single track road heading north/south. To the west the ancient Forewood occupied most of the land. To the east the road was confined by a deep cleft in the land, less than 100 meters from the road in most places. To the west of the road there was also another cleft, starting half way down the slope, whilst to the south of the main battlefield a third deep trench confined anyone hoping to bypass the only road that lead from Hastings town.

In short; if you are camped at Wilting you have no-where to escape. You have to take the road to London and confront your enemy in battle at Crowhurst. When Harold arrived on the day before the battle he must have thought there could only be one possible outcome. He would have known that he had superior numbers, because he had the whole of the English army rapidly approaching along the road from London. He would also have known that even though the Normans may have as many as 5,000 men he would probably have double that. All he had to do was build a defence at Crowhurst and wait.

The main feature of the map is the location of the Crowhurst church and the Manor site, which I shall deal with in the next chapter. This is located at the bottom of the hill, more or less at the centre of the parish. That hill to the north rises all the way from there to the top of the ridge, where Harold camped. The Tithe Map clearly shows that there were a continuous series of fields that mark their way up this ascent. It is called the Great Field in the section below where the railway is now located.

It is my contention that this great field was so called because it was one great field in 1066, upon which the Battle of Hastings was fought. One of the Saxon Chronicles also states that the battle was fought in *'a great field'.*

Having read all the accounts of the battle, especially Wace, I am not convinced this battle took place in a small section of field, but was spread between the plain at the bottom of this valley and the top where Harold had built his defence. That defence is still visible on Google maps, now as a tree line.

In all respects this great field fits all the battlefield descriptions, with nothing missing. In particular it fits the descriptions of the battle, as described by Wace with the Malfosse incident, also described by Poitiers. A stream also crosses the bottom section of the plain, as shown in the Bayeux Tapestry, at the foot of the main hill - exactly as found on this site.

Unlike the battle site, which was previously thought to be at Battle Abbey, this land upon which this battle was fought was hard upon the Normans. They had to fight up a very steep and arduous 100 meter hill. The site at Battle Abbey is a mild slope by comparison rising only 15 meters.

Since publishing this information it has been brought to my attention, by archers who have attended the re-enactments, that they consider the site at Battle Abbey to be wrong, because the Normans could not pull their bows with sufficient poundage to attack the Saxons. This is because those who occupy the higher ground have a major advantage in being able to use their bows over greater distance. It is therefore illogical, and some say impossible on the Battle Abbey site, for the Norman archers to have done what is reported.

In the case of the Crowhurst site that would also apply to a greater degree, except it is probable that Harold's initial activity was to harass the Normans with his archers to his advantage keeping the horses at bay. This partly explains why the battle took much longer than normal to take place. It lasted all day and was only concluded at dusk. As the battle progressed up the hill, there is level ground where the Saxon line was positioned in Crowhurst. This is an unreported anomaly of the battle site, where the Normans could respond on an equal basis. The heavy horse cavalry, William's secret weapon, proved useless, because Harold had as Wace described built a defence of stakes across the field. This defence was erected on the night before the battle and went right across the field - there was no way out and it rendered the cavalry impotent.

The Normans would be forced to come to Harold on foot, as Wace had confirmed. All Harold had to do was sit and wait while his men arrived. Every hour that William waited was an hour that would mean certain death to the Normans, if battle did not commence immediately.

The Normans arrived on the plain, as described in detail by Wace, where the church and manor house now stand. At that stage battle commenced and the long fight up the hill took all day. I have marked on the earlier plan the exact spot where I believe the Saxon defence was located. There is a ditch that can be seen on Google maps as darker green vegetation close by. Historians have denied that a defence was dug, because archaeologists have not looked in the right place. The bank and ditch located near the top of this site, where the image can be seen on the aerial photographs, is also the place where the crossbow was located. We shall deal with that in a later chapter.

Having lived in Crowhurst for nearly thirty years I shall also recount the story of the spears found at Blacksmiths Field, because it may be true. When I arrived in the village I was told that the village policeman had found three ancient spears under the old barn at Blacksmiths Field, when it was demolished.

A number of people in the village, including parish councillors, told me that prior to my arrival in the village these spear heads had been mounted in a glass display case in the village hall. The research into trying to locate these objects lasted many months and the policeman in question had unfortunately moved from the village to Bexhill. I was therefore unable to confirm whether this story was true. Being a small village I wondered if the people concerned were pulling my leg, because no-one at that time ever believed the research I was doing would ever prove anything.

Now, knowing what I do, I realise that Blacksmiths Field, and the reported find under the barn was exactly where the blacksmith would have been located when this battle took place. It was at the rear of the battlefield, ready to support those who needed their armour reworked, and where those who organised the supplies would be located. This story and the spear find at Pyes Farm appears to contradict the belief that all iron from the period would be lost in the soil.

It is another colloquial story that indicates this site probably has archaeology present and should therefore be thoroughly surveyed by a proper team of archaeologists.

The Malfosse incident is I believe clearly identified by the fact that there is a hidden path that runs from the battlefield position of the Saxon defence. This particular cleft in the landscape is not the only one. It separates the whole of the eastern side of the battle site from any exit, and is impassable even today. Part of that ditch becomes marsh, around the point where the old coach road went. There is a bridge built there with the Pelham Buckle carved into the side, confirming its construction at the time the coach road was built in the 1700s.

This is a photograph of the Malfosse at the point where the old coach road crosses about two thirds down from the top of the ridge. The image was taken from the coach road bridge, which is now south of the mainline railway.

At this point the Malfosse is marsh and quite impassable on foot or horse.

The Malfosse stream cuts south, through the landscape and meets a second tributary at the bottom of the Great Field, forming another hidden trap for anyone who should think it might be an escape route. I have called this Malfosse 2 on the battlefield site map.

There is another ditch running through the landscape to the east of the Great Field. This is now the approach road to Crowhurst Station. This is to the left (west) as you look at the map. It performs the function of funnelling any enemy into what Harold must have believed would be his killing field. The ability to go around or avoid the Saxon archers on the higher ground was impossible. It was in many respects a brilliant strategy for Harold. Unfortunately for the Saxons he made one fatal flaw.

That flaw was not the issue of arriving at the battle site too quickly, because he knew what he was doing. He was the Lord of this manor and he knew the site. I am convinced of that, by the decision to build a defence in the place he chose. The fatal flaw in Harold's plan was the decision to allow flat ground to sit in front of his main defence, half way up the battlefield hill.

I should mention that very recently a Saxon battle axe has been reported to have been found on the site at Battle Abbey. This information raising hopes that everything in this book is no more than supposition. I know the circumstances of this find and to the dismay of the support Battle Abbey brigade, who are aligned against the evidence, the Saxon battle axe was within what is described as the battlefield site. This area, defined by English Heritage, is much larger than the battlefield site that people know. This is hard archaeological evidence that the Saxon battle-axe was either discarded after the battle or placed there later. It is not proof of the battle taking place at Battle Abbey, but more likely proof the battle site was further south. If it is evidence it can only be evidence that supports the other evidence in this book. One battle axe does not constitute evidence of the Battle of Hastings, as any archaeologist or historian knows.

This is a picture of the battlefield plain - you are looking south-east towards the sea with the Saxon hill climbing 100 meters behind you.

The hill behind us in the photograph was a hard fight for the Normans, who were able to use the land half way towards the top of that climb to regroup and create their main attack. That second section of level ground meant the Saxon archers lost the advantage of bow pull, whilst the Norman crossbows played their part in destroying the Saxon shield wall. The Normans had a lucky break when Harold was hit above the eye. Once that happened, in the absence of most of his force, which had still not arrived from London, the Normans were able to obtain a win through luck alone. In my view the Normans should have lost - this is the story of history - the tide on that day flowed with William and his men, not with Harold.

The Normans would have known this field well, because they needed to exit the peninsular through this field on raiding parties to provide provisions for the army stationed there. Having been located at Wilting Manor for two weeks there would have been many raiding parties needed to sustain a large force of men and their support troops. In consequence they would all have known the tree well that marked the crossroads. This is almost certainly the reason the battle was called the battle of '*the hoary apple tree*' - because it was the landmark that the raiding parties used to establish where to turn left, right or go straight on. They did not know the name of the place. Only later did it become known as the Battle of Hastings.

There is a compulsive logic in the fact that the battle became known as the Battle of Hastings later, because those who knew where the battle really had taken place identified the land south of the Ridge as Hastings. Crowhurst was the manor between the port of Hastings and the Ridge. In consequence the battle was known by the name of the land in which the locals recognised it as having been fought. Even school children ask the obvious question *'Why wasn't the Battle of Hastings in Hastings?'* The answer is - it was. It was in the Hastings area and so the name stuck, even if the monks moved the abbey after the event.

This is a picture of Brakes Coppice battlefield picture of the Saxon last defence line (oak tree) where the higher '*plain*' is located

I remain optimistic that the force of truth that brings the information to you regarding this site is more powerful than those who are supposed to represent our people at this time. This is the second time greedy politicians have tried to destroy the Norman Invasion site by selling land next to the proposed road. I am confident they will all be gone soon. The economic factors have made a few suddenly realise that central government is not there to bail them out. Hopefully the site will remain intact, but it is currently still under threat and I must not underestimate their ability to cause difficulties. It is not in their interests for the academic fraternity to suddenly look again at these issues. It is however important for our country's heritage that they do.

The next chapter concerns the discovery, of another element of cross-referencing evidence, pointing to the Great Field at Crowhurst as the site of the Battle of Hastings. I have called it '*the crossbow.*'

Chapter 70: THE CROSSBOW

This chapter concerns the discovery of an artefact which I believe may be the earliest crossbow ever found in this country. To be fair to those who will probably object to this claim, I cannot make the claim myself, but am prepared to accept what I was told. It is probably incorrect technically to call it a crossbow, since it is the Carmen that tells us that *'balisters'* were used at the Battle of Hastings. Historians have argued till they are blue in the face that Hastings was too early for such a weapon. But it is true that the Carmen details their use. According to the translation by Catherine Morton and Hope Muntz it states:

'He (William) dispatched the foot in advance to open the battle with arrows, and set the crossbowmen in their midst so that their speeding shafts might pierce the faces of the English.'

Morton and Muntz devote four pages of the appendix to a discussion of the subject, noting that the version of the Carmen, written by Guy Bishop of Amiens, refers to *balistantes* three times in the text and there can be no mistake that these are crossbow men. This is because later in line 376 he describes the effect of the crossbow bolts on the English shields stating:

'against crossbow-bolts shields are to no avail'

In this case I believe the Saxon last defensive line was located two thirds of the way up the Great Field at Crowhurst. There I looked for *'Norman armour.'* I was looking for definitive evidence of the Battle of Hastings and decided to use dowsing to see if I could obtain a result. Foolishly I thought that looking for Norman armour, using dowsing, would produce something definitive and therefore reduce the need to find other evidence in order to obtain assistance from experts.

Dowsing did however identify the site of the Saxon line and I found several places that responded to my search. However no metallic response was obtained from the metal detector employed to obtain a quick confirmation. I had obtained permission from the land owner and realised that what I was looking for would require very careful uncovering.

I had read about the archaeological recovery work at Sutton Hoo and realised that the sandy top soil, with considerable lower slope wash, finishing on clay was going to require a slow painstaking recovery process. Dowsing is not a scientific art, but one which involves engaging the mind in a process that is similar in many respects to meditation. To allow the intellect to turn off, to allow those thought processes which might normally guide you, to be put out of your mind. The art appears to be to concentrate upon the subject matter and to allow the rods to guide you.

In that state of mind I am able to obtain simple guidance when you might pass over a hidden wall for instance, or an object upon which your mind is concentrated. In this way I found myself in the middle of an open field, 50 meters from the road in the Great Field, with rods crossed over a spot that responded to *'Norman armour.'* I was not looking for or expecting a crossbow. A crossbow would be expected to be made from wood and so it could not under normal circumstances be what you would possibly expect to be able to find.

The reason you would not expect to find small iron objects is because the mechanics of chemical decomposition of iron and almost everything else, except the most precious metals, such as gold and silver. Those items that are likely to get lost in a battle are usually made from iron and wood in the period of the Normans. Iron objects fall into the ground and rapidly get covered by the undergrowth. The custom at that time was to leave the dead of your enemy on the battlefield to *'be eaten by the dogs'* - not a very good end for the vanquished. Anything of value would have been taken as a prize by the winners.

Looters would strip the bodies of anything of value and that process is even confirmed in the fringes of the Bayeux Tapestry.

Almost anything that a man owned in those days was of value to someone, but those things that were broken would stay where they fell. Those items too small to be found, such as buttons, belts, keepsakes and small personal effect, not kept in clothing, might well find its way into the battlefield soil. Whilst arrows would be unlikely to survive any length of time in this wet terrain, broken axes and spears would still probably be found by expert excavation. Items such as brass, silver and gold would most definitely be recoverable.

It is my view and most professional battlefield experts, that even if the equivalent of a complete cleanup had taken place down to the last button, the horses that fell in that battle would not have had their shoes removed - and horseshoes are very datable. They should be found on this site, because of their ability to withstand corrosion. To find nothing at all after two hundred years looking at the Battle Abbey site tells us with some degree of certainty that the Battle Abbey site is not where five thousand men - the might of England - fell in 1066.

The hole that I was excavating in the Great Field at Crowhurst was not a professional archaeological excavation. It had started out as a quick attempt to locate something, which would shortcut the research process. It was born out of frustration and intended initially to be completed quickly. It was less than eighteen inches square and in a part of the field that appears to have a well defined ridge running across it from east to west. A part of the field that has a hedge line on one side of the main road and none on the other - indicating that at some earlier time the tree line may have extended right across the field, before the modern road was put in place.

The structure of the ground at this position is interesting, because when standing on that ground there is a natural assumption that the slope of the land reflects the slope of the substructure of the hill. This is not the case. The slope of the hill is an even gradient. The position where the tree line is located has soil almost a meter deep on the upside of the line and less than half a meter on the downside.

This indicates that the tree line was formed against some earlier structure, which acted as a break on the slope wash. This has caused the soil on the upside of the line to bank up where the trees still exist. On the side of the road where the tree line no longer exists, a drop in depth is still seen today, long after the structure has gone.

If the Saxons had built a wooden defence out of stakes across the battlefield at this point, as reported by Wace, and it had been abandoned after the battle, as it would have been, this is exactly the structure of development that you would expect to see. The stakes would act as a refuge where trees saplings would be protected from grazing. Those saplings would become trees and so create a barrier to the natural wash of the soil. A bank would build where soil levels on each side of the tree would be different. Later, if those trees were removed by farming and the agricultural process, the bank would be created exactly as we see on the line in Crowhurst, where the Saxons would have stood.

Having spent a week slowly moving down the hole I had reached a level that was 80 centimetres down. At that depth I can only just operate, because the arm reach is almost too great. If anything was there it was very deep and I had not anticipated that when I started. I knew the soil depths in the area and the soil should have been no more than a foot at the most on the slope. At the time I was worried, because the general accepted norm is an inch of soil depth for every hundred years. I was not aware at that time of the story of the defence by Wace, or had any knowledge of the issues relating to the build up of the slope.

I had almost reached the stage when I was ready to abandon the site, because I thought that I had dug through what I might be looking for, when this was revealed over the course of a day:

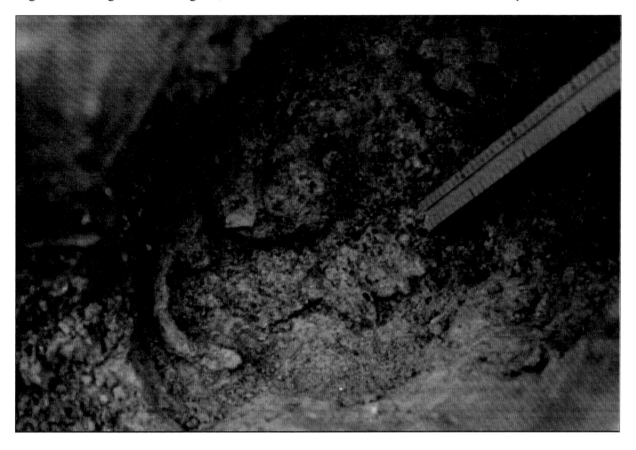

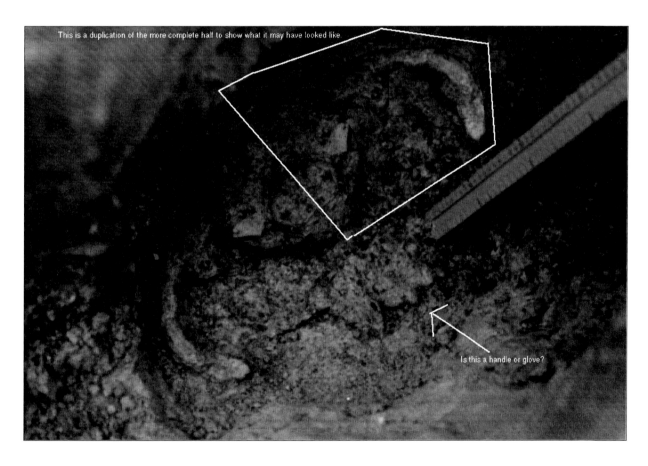

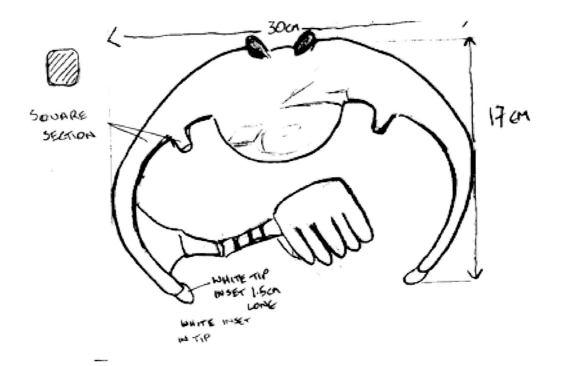

SQUARE SECTION

30cm

17 cm

WHITE TIP INSET 1.5cm LONG

WHITE INSET IN TIP

The problem with these images is they were taken with a film camera, when this work was done in the 1990s - a long time ago. Long before the Norman Invasion site was located at Wilting Farm. This is not the place to get involved in discussions as to how this object was found, or why I did not continue my research into the Battle of Hastings on this site. All I will say is that I had reasons, which will become apparent in the course of time. Some would say it was an act of faith and that would be correct in that I understood that what I saw confirmed my belief that there was information hidden in these fields.

I assumed that the discovery of this object as *'Norman armour'* confirmed my belief that the information that had led me to this site was correct. Any man who finds himself in the middle of a field, in what to all intents and purpose was the middle of no-where in a historical research sense, would not be able to disregard the evidence of his own eyes. Firstly the object, what ever it was, existed and to my untrained eye appeared to have a metal appearance. But it wasn't metal, because there was absolutely no metal signature from the metal detector. It is easy to go and look for something, but quite another matter when you find something like this. Having had some experience at digging these sorts of exploratory holes I can tell you with certain knowledge that you can dig down 80 centimetres in any field in England and be almost certain to find nothing. Certainly nothing that looked like this. The mystery at that time was trying to understand what it was, if it was not metal, and required me to investigate and understand the nature of truly old metal excavation.

The discovery at the time was not for public consumption, but provided me with the inner knowledge that I needed to continue my research. The focus of that research moved away from looking for the battle site, because I believed at that time I now knew where it was. It was with this knowledge it was possible to work backwards, using the Bayeux Tapestry as a map, to locate the correct site of the Norman camp. The Bayeux Tapestry confirms both events as one continuous history. One cannot exist without the other, and so the two are linked in a way that effectively reveals the two. It is for this reason I shall deal with the Bayeux Tapestry in the last chapter of this research.

It was my conviction then that once the Norman Invasion site was established, then and only then would the battle site be able to be confirmed. As a result I put the photos into the drawer to be taken out now. I stand by that conviction, because now I have seen enough to know myself that the work that has been reported here is correct.

Before I came to that conclusion I posted copies of the above photos to the Royal Armouries to ask if they knew what the object was. I also posted the photos to some history news groups in the early days of the internet, but unfortunately no-one knew what it was. I put forward the hypothesis that it was a crossbow, because that is what it looked like to me. I had drawn an image of what it looked like and I have put it here in the hope that someone else will have seen something similar.

In many respects it was a mystery, because when looking for crossbows in research journals and on the Internet I could find nothing that looked exactly like this. The image that could be seen in the soil, at the bottom of the hole in the field in Crowhurst, appeared to have some sort of glove attached to it. That glove might have simply been beneath the object. The definition was not clear enough to be specific.

Upon re-examining the drawing against the photo it can be seen that the drawing was done before I finished the excavation. It shows a wide armature in the central section, whereas the photos confirm that this is not the case. In the first picture of the excavation, it can be seen that the curve of the arms drops back down on the left hand side. I also assumed that the glove was attached to the crossbow section, but it may not have been. I now can see that it probably was not and probably lay underneath the object.

There were also other objects close to the main image. An object that looked like a mace head, in the top right of the photo, but again not well defined. In order to reveal them properly it would be necessary for a specialist recovery archaeological team to firstly uncover the item to the right depth and then impregnate the soil with resin. At that stage the whole excavation could be removed and taken back to the lab for specialist recovery.

I tried to get people interested, but no one would take the concept of the Battle of Hastings being in the wrong place as even a possibility. No-one knew what the photo was and as far as I could make out it could just as easily have been the back axel of a Morris Minor, as far as getting any expert identification was concerned. Someone would have recognised it if it were!!

I did show it to friends and covered up the excavation in the belief that when I went back one day it would still be there. Given the fact that I had opened it to the air I now realise that this is unlikely. I then left a plastic bag over the item so that when the time comes finding the depth will be easy located. It will assist any excavation, which can be widened to look for what else is there. If there is one thing there will be more.

In that respect the crossbow story finished and for the next fifteen years I was involved in research for the Norman Invasion site. Then one day Philip Brown, the eminent local historian who wrote the trilogy on places connected to the Norman Invasion, rang me out of the blue. He told me that he had kept the photos of the crossbow. I had sent them to him and he had shown them to his friend, who owned the Filching Armoury Museum in Wannock, Eastbourne. His friend was Paul Foulkes-Halbard and he wanted to see me.

At a meeting Paul showed me drawings of crossbows from Turkey used in the Crusades. He was completely convinced that I had a picture of one of those. I could not see the similarity at all because the bow looked as if it were the wrong way round to me. He said that these were composition bows and because they would be unstrung they would revert to the shape shown in my image. He was completely convinced and was prepared to pay to recover the bow. Unfortunately Mr Foulkes-Halbard passed away in 2003 and as a result he can no longer be consulted. All I can say is that he appeared to have an extremely large collection of armoury in his museum, was very well researched, and despite my own reticence he was completely convinced that the object was correctly identified as a composition crossbow. He considered it of Turkish origin and offered me a remarkable sum of money to recover it, but I had to decline because of the circumstances.

It seemed an unlikely confirmation, but research confirmed that the Normans probably employed Turkish mercenaries to fight with them at the Battle of Hastings. It is therefore possible that Mr Foulkes-Halbard was completely correct. He was after all an expert in these matters and I am not.

The crossbow will now be a matter that can only be resolved by reinvestigation, should the man who owns the field decide to allow me to go back. His name was Dee Oliver and he now lives somewhere in Bexhill and I have lost touch with him. It was most unfortunate that the disturbance of the ground caused the emergence of thistles. One good thing came out it though. As a result of finding the bow I went back a few years later and found his mother at work in her garden. We had a chat and over the next few years became really good friends. I enjoyed her company a great deal. She too is now unfortunately departed, but her wisdom and knowledge of the village was invaluable in providing local history knowledge and helping me through some very difficult years.

Now the story has come out, as a result of bringing all the pieces of the puzzle concerning the Battle of Hastings into one place. Other experts have now been kind enough to contact me, including Arthur Credland, who is editor of the Society of Archer-Antiquarians. He kindly sent me a lot of information, together with documents and photocopies of early crossbows. He too could not identify this as a crossbow. At the same time I sent the image to Adam Karpowicz, whom I believe is probably one of the worlds leading experts on Turkish bows. He too produced a negative response.

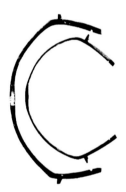

Looking through the articles which I was sent there is nothing that is identical to the image I found in the ground, which Paul Foulkes-Halbard identified as a Turkish crossbow. This is one element that caused me to think that perhaps Paul was instinctively right.

In the Journal of the Society of Archers - Antiquaries 2008 on page 9 is an article about a heavy Manchu composite bow. Composite bows were made to produce high poundage of pull, so that the resulting arrow, or in the case of a crossbow, a bolt would achieve maximum distance and power. Certainly crossbow bolts could destroy shields, as we have discussed earlier.

The article discusses in some detail the historical background to the bows and makes the point that they are hardly ever found in a strung condition. The reason for this being that the pull was so great (in this case estimated at 240 pounds), they became too difficult to string and unstring, except by an expert.

The image above shows two unstrung versions. In consequence in order to understand how they worked you have to recognise that these are composition bows that have reverted to their original unstrung shape. When strung it is necessary to invert them so that the wings, that currently point to the right, are bent backwards until they point to the left and are creating the maximum pull outwards. Strings are attached so that the grooves that can be seen on the inside unstrung are on the outside of the bow when strung, with the projections that are currently on the outside pointing inwards when strung.

These projections are called ears I believe. It was these ears that I can see on the object found in the Crowhurst field, which first caused me to question what these projections were for. It seems a strange design. You would think that there must be a reason to include them. Did it make the object stronger?

194

Was it in order to reload or fire the object? This is a small hand held bow, if it is a bow. It can be seen that both this object and the Manchu bows have the same projections. Both would have a similar shape when strung, if Paul was correct and it was actually a composition bow. If that were the case then what we are looking at down the hole is the round end section of the bow. The wooden shaft would have been attached to the north-east of the object running into the side of the pit. I had assumed the curve of the bow would mean the wooden shaft that is no longer there would run towards the glove, because that is what a normal person recognises as the normal crossbow shape. Perhaps Paul was right, because the composite construction would unbend when broken, forming an upturned Y shape. The shaft attachment would be made from wood and looking carefully it looks like a plate is attached to hold the composite structure beneath it? That is why the ears are there. Bows from this period often had round metal ends or rings, to attach them to your belt and in order to fire them. The round end could easily be a corroded ring.

25. Matthew Paris Chronica Minora c.12?? (Corpus Christi College, Cambridge, Ms.16, f.138v

28. Luttrell Psalter, c.1325-1346 (Bl., Add. Ms. 42130 f.56)

Here we see the ring held high and the other man has his foot in the ring - the reload mechanism. If you look carefully you will see that he has a belt and hook attached to the string, so that he uses his whole body and legs to reload. I had assumed the round element of our picture was solid. Here again I can see I am probably wrong, because it can be seen from the pigmentation of the soil that the centre of that circular section is not the same colour. It may well have a ring attached to the front. The soil is lighter in the middle. The conclusion I must draw from this is that Paul Foulkes-Halbard knew what he was looking at and this is likely to be an early crossbow.

The construction appears to consist of some form of plate which holds the composite arms in position. It has corroded to the point where all the ions have migrated, but the presence of two dark patches of brown, where the bolts or weld fitted into place, can still be seen on the left above and by the flange. That plate would allow bows to be made in number, without the need for a skilled bowman to individually make each bow. I have drawn the outline of my understanding now of how this bow is probably constructed and it confirms to me why Paul immediately recognised it as probably a crossbow.

The drawing above shows the position of the original crossbow in relative to the photo of the crossbow excavation. The red sections are the crossbow arms as we see them now in the photograph and the shaft has of course gone. If this were a composite bow it would be expected that the composite section would also have long gone. If it was soaked in resin then what we see may be the result of that process creating the image.

After starting out having great difficulty in believing the object in the field, found where I believe the last Saxon defence took place, was a crossbow, I have much to my surprise come to conclude that it is. The conclusion comes from re-examining the photograph in close detail.

It might be thought that this was an obvious thing to do, but when you have lived with it in the drawer for many years there is a tendency simply to accept what you are told by an expert, even if you might not completely understand what is being proposed. I had made an assumption on what I was looking at based upon an excavation, and my memory of it.

Now I understand which way round I should be looking at this. I also understand that there is a ring at the front. This means this is probably what archers call an early footbow. A footbow being used by Turkish troops of the time - and hence the assumption that Paul had made.

16. One of the horseman of the Apocalypse from Beatus' commentary on Revelation. late 11ᵗʰ century (Cathedral library of Burgo de Osma)

Above we see an image taken from a Catalan manuscript c1086, in a commentary on the Apocalypse (though originally from Astorga), Cathedral Library of Burgo de Osama, Spain. This is a very small weapon, probably one of the smallest of the age, but to my mind important, because it is exactly the era of the Battle of Hastings.

This crossbow is I believe the same construction as the one in Crowhurst. The only difference is that ours is designed as a footbow and the one above is for use on horse.

Whilst this is a stylised drawing the similarities are remarkable. It has some form of attachment at each end for the string. I noticed during the excavation that the end of the composite section had some sort of white attachment - this is not present on other bows of this age. I know of none that have ever been found.

Lastly the stock is attached to the composite wings via some form of plate and not attached by leather or rope, as was normal. I believe the artist is attempting to show the plate holding the wings and at the same time sitting under the level of the stock, but hasn't understood how to do that. Very early bows suffered from loss of power through the string rubbing along the stock as they fired. If built with a plate it would be possible to fire the bolt by passing the bolt through a groove in the plate, without the loss of power through friction on the stock.

The use of the imagery of a warring avenging angel, with such a crossbow in his hands, is exactly the sort of image that would have been suitable for the time. The Pope's forces were seen as victorious at Hastings and their weapon included the crossbow.

The author of this work clearly knew the construction of this item. The fact that one has never been found, does not mean it does not exist. I would suggest that given the circumstances of that time it is highly likely that this representation of that very early crossbow was based upon knowledge of how the item worked. This image supports the view that such an object may well be located on the site of the Battle of Hastings.

All I can say at this point in time is we shall have to wait for a proper dig to discover more. The discovery in the Great Field at Crowhurst supports the claim that this is probably the site of the Battle of Hastings in a way that could never be expected. The story of the discovery happened exactly as I have told it, warts and all. I would like to tell you that experts agree with me, but that is not the case at this point in time. It adds an intriguing dimension to the historical research, because it shows artefacts of unknown origin, in a field of no significance, exactly where the Chronicle of Battle Abbey states the Abbey was meant to be built. That same abbey was ordered to be built upon the site of the Battle of Hastings. It is not an illogical leap of faith to conclude that the object is in some way connected to that battle, given the cross-referencing of the known information.

Chapter 71: THE BAYEUX TAPESTRY CONFIRMATION

This penultimate chapter before the summary does not alter any of the evidence to date, but simply provides further confirmation of the correct site of the Battle of Hastings. Rather than work from prints, I needed to confirm what I believe, by seeing the Bayeux Tapestry in person again. It has been fifteen years since I was last in Bayeux and a lot of information has come my way since then. Those documents that exist upon the internet are relatively low resolution and do not have the same continuity that is present in the observation of the person viewing the actual cloth. Anyone who is seriously interested in Norman history must visit Bayeux and see the Tapestry for themselves. It is almost a miracle that it exists at all, simply because it was found covering a cart during the French revolution. It was very nearly burnt, as a symbol of French decadence, but as we know common sense ruled and consequently it exists today in pristine condition, as a testament to the endeavours of men.

We have studied elements of the Tapestry before in the earlier chapters relating to the Invasion. Now I travelled to Bayeux again to see if the evidence of the Tapestry would support those new parts that had recently been introduced into my thinking - namely the site of the battle being in Crowhurst. The second element that interested me was whether the Tapestry supported the use of crossbows, since it is the discovery of remains believed to be a crossbow in Crowhurst that points directly to the site of the Great Field in Crowhurst, as the site of the Battle of Hastings. If there is absolutely no evidence in the Tapestry, then it might be concluded that the Carmen of Hastings must be wrong to have named 'ballistas' (crossbowmen) as being used in that battle by the Normans.

It is known that the Pope banned ballistas not long after the Battle of Hastings. It must be remembered that William had played the Pope card, in his power game with Harold. He had sent emissaries to Rome, to enable him to carry the Pope's banner into battle.

This was a powerful rallying cry to men of good character throughout William's own realm, but also those across the whole Christian empire. William was able to do this, because he had argued that Harold had lost his right to rule, because Harold had sworn allegiance to William upon the most sacred objects in Christendom - the bones of the saints in Bayeux Cathedral.

Wace tells us that Harold did not know about those bones because he:

'Neither saw them, nor knew of them being there; for nought was shewn or told to him about it; and over all was a phylactery, the best he could select; OIL DE BOEF, I have heard it called. When Harold placed his hand upon it, the hand trembled, and the flesh quivered; but he swore, and promised upon his oath, to take Ele (one of William's daughters) to wife, and to deliver up England to the duke: and thereunto to do all in his power according to his might and wit, after the death of Edward, if he should so live, so help him God and the holy relics there.'

This is shown in the Bayeux Tapestry here:

Then Harold is let free to return to England in the same sequence, clearly identifying that Harold was released as a result of his oath, as there is no commentary between the images. There was no reason for Harold to remain any longer and immediately he is released.

In many ways this identifies the reason why the Battle of Hastings took place. Harold gave his oath under the duress of being held hostage. He would never be freed by William until he made that oath. Having made the oath Harold, in common with English law, did not see it as binding - since an oath made under duress was not and never has been binding.

William recognised this as a weakness in his position and consequently sent emissaries to ensure the support of the Pope. He in turn provided that support along with the Papal banner.

This must all be understood as background to the events of the battle sequences that followed later.

William understood his position to be absolute, because irrespective of the issue of duress, this was a matter of honour. Harold on the other hand did not know that the oath was given upon holy relics. Irrespective of the duress of being held a captive Harold did not consider the oath binding. This led to the inability for either man to retract their position later.

What this meant to the Pope was of little consequence, but must have had a direct concern later, when it was found that William employed ballistas (crossbows), for the first time in England, to destroy the Saxon nobility and the Saxon blood line. Today crossbows may seem innocuous, given the array of armour and weapons developed over the past thousand years. At this time in history the first ethics of war were developing amongst the nobility of Europe. A man wore his shield in battle as an extension of his arm, often painted with his personal coat of arms - hence the term arms and armaments. Chivalry was established as a code of ethics of how a man of nobility would live and die, often on the battlefield.

The crossbow was a new weapon and it was, when used for the first time in England at Hastings, the supreme secret weapon, because unlike an arrow, a crossbow bolt could split a man's shield in two, leaving him completely defenceless to further attack. It was in effect the first unethical weapon. Consequently when this was explained to the Pope, after the battle, he banned crossbows.

This is exactly at the time the Bayeux Tapestry was being made, as a grand piece of political propaganda. It has been speculated that it may have been made in France or possibly Canterbury. Its great value to historians is the fact that elements in the Tapestry appear to be correct in all respects, as understood at the time. Elements such as buildings, clothing, armour and the story appear to hold an element of truth not present in many texts which came later. Those other manuscripts were often influenced by the political positions of those who wrote to receive favours.

The Tapestry holds an element of truth that is difficult to deny. It therefore holds an important position as a pre-eminent source for any analysis of the events of the Norman Conquest. Much may be open to debate, but if the Tapestry does not support any such thesis relating to crossbows, then any such thesis cannot be considered worth much weight.

With that in mind I wanted to first look at the issue of the arrow in Harold's eye. I want to do this in order to understand that everything you see in the Bayeux Tapestry is not as it was made. Even the Bayeux Tapestry is a document that over the last thousand years has been subject to change. The issue of Harold being killed by an arrow in the eye is probably the best known event in English history. It is information that for some reason has passed into legend that most people know.

If we look at the Tapestry we see this famous scene:

A man - presumably Harold, under that name, shot in the eye with an arrow on the left and a man killing a man on the right with a sword from a horse. The man on the right has lost his shield and is being cut down on the thigh. So the question arises - is the man on the right being killed Harold?

Wace answers that for us. He tells us in his 16,000 line account of the battle that Harold's eye is put out by the arrow above the eye.

The Battle continues and Wace reports much later after detailing the gore of battle, telling how many named knights died:

'And now the Normans had pressed on so far, that at last they reached the standard. There Harold had remained, defending himself to the utmost; but he was sorely wounded in his eye by the arrow, and suffered grievous pain from the blow. An armed man came in the throng of the battle, and struck him on the ventaille of his helmet, and beat him to the ground; and as he sought to recover himself, a knight beat him down again, striking him on the thick of the thigh, down to the bone.'

At this point Harold dies.

If you look closely at the fallen knight, you can see that Harold has had the arrow removed from his eye, leaving a neat row of stitch holes:

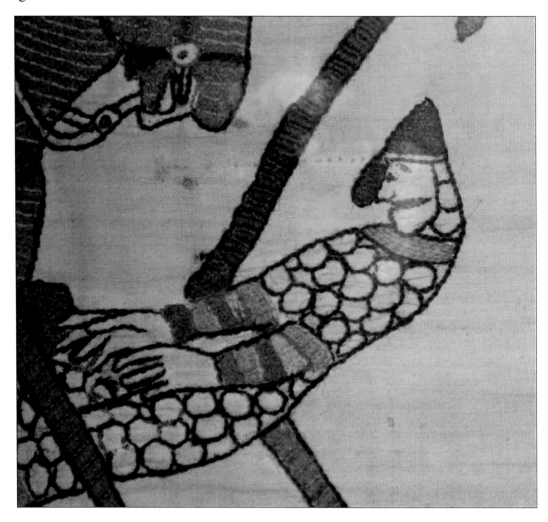

The original stitch marks can still clearly be seen approaching a thousand years after the original work was done. But contrary to what might be the initial assumption, this alteration could have been done at any time since the Tapestry was made. We know this because drawings of the Tapestry by Bernard de Montfaucon in 1729 show the arrow is not present then. It could therefore have been added later and removed or removed at any time since it was made - there is no way of telling.

The important point, which I wish to draw to the attention of the reader, is that because the Tapestry exists it does not mean that it is immune from alteration. It may be easier to alter a tapestry, simply because any competent woman could do this upon the orders of the owner.

Unlike dealing with documents, alterations on cloth are in fact harder to conceal - resulting in ultimate exposure, because what we see on one side of the cloth will be different on the reverse, when it can be examined. Certainly where stitches are removed they leave tell tale holes. Note in the above image stitches are also missing around Harold's eye, also on his hand and along the rear edge of Harold's back, below the sword. (*Note: The missing arrow also penetrates above the eye*.)

To look at the stitching was one of the reasons I needed to come to see the Tapestry again. If the Pope had banned crossbows at the time the Tapestry was commissioned, the question arose in my mind as to whether it was possible that the Tapestry had been altered to accommodate the politics of the day? With this in mind I wanted to examine closely the archers that are shown in the battle scenes. If the Pope banned crossbows, and they had been used at that battle, there might be some telltale sign of alterations to those archers.

Chapter 72: THE ARCHERS

The first observation that must be made is that the Tapestry has clearly been repaired. The repair work is of an excellent quality, where torn parts have been sewn back into place expertly. Indeed so expertly that the casual observer may not even notice.

At the same time it is noticeable that the quality of the stitching throughout the Tapestry is also of the highest quality. It might be expected that there would be many sections with stitches missing or replaced with new thread, but this is not the case. Looking closely at the stitch work it remains of the highest quality and impeccably accurate. It is almost impossible to find any elements that could be considered possible to alter on the vast majority of the cloth. There were none that I could see, except for the section dealing with the death of Harold and the archers.

ARCHERS 1-4

There are 30 archers shown on the Bayeux Tapestry. The first four are numbers 1-4, marked in red on the following image from the start of the battle scene:

My comments are based upon my own observations from the Journal of the Society of Archer - Antiquaries, as well as having received considerable correspondence on the construction of bows, crossbows and their use, from those who have read about my claim that crossbows were probably used at the Battle of Hastings. Bowmen, who love their bows, have a different understanding of these weapons from us mere mortal men. I recognise that I am not an expert, but I have no reason to disbelieve what I have been told and include this in my thinking. I am sure that some will disagree, but that will always be the case I am sure.

The first thing to note about the four bowmen, shown together, before the battle begins, is that these four men have two distinctly different types of bows. Bowman number one is a normal longbow type construction - but it is far too short to be a longbow and must therefore be considered to be a standard straight-limb short bow. It is probably made from wood and shows two colours of thread on the main limbs. When the bow is pulled it arches from the top to bottom and was probably made from Yew or some similar wood, which is flexible, or two woods glued together.

Archers 2, 3 and 4 are using a different type of bow, as can be seen from the shape of the bow when pulled. These are in the recurve bow shape. A recurve bow stores more energy when the bow is strung. It was usually made from composite material and has higher draw weights - meaning it could shoot further. Composite bows were often constructed from a variety of strips of wood glued together to provide as much tension as possible when strung. Many of the original composite bows were designed in the Middle East and subsequently were taken into the local population as warring armies migrated across continents.

William's army, like the Romans before him, used composite bows, as well as the traditional short bow. These bowmen do not stand their ground correctly in the field. Bowmen 1, 2 and 4 are in the traditional firing position for a bowman, but number 3 is completely wrong. You cannot fire this weapon properly holding arrows in the left hand, because it would not be possible to create the necessary pull poundage and still keep your feet together and grip the bow without falling over.

Bowman 3 has his quiver, which holds his arrows, tied around his waist. Short bowmen and longbow men should never do that. Those bowmen wear their quivers in the position of bowman 1 - yet bowman 2 and 4 also have their quivers set at their waist.

It could of course be argued that the women who made this Tapestry didn't know the detail and just drew what they thought should be shown. That is wholly inconsistent with almost all other aspects of this work. It suggests to me that the designer of the Tapestry knew only too well that there were differences between the various elements.

What I see is evidence that supports archer number 3 as a French crossbowman. My reason for believing this is primarily the way he is dressed, the way he stands, and the fact he is holding his crossbow bolts (shorter than arrows) in his left hand as he readies to fire. More important to me is the fact that the bowstring does not cross the archer's chest.

Close examination of that archer shows the bow string goes under his arm, meaning his left hand was above the bow and so what we are seeing is a crossbow without the wooden shaft showing. Either the design left it out deliberately, or by design it was made to show the bow side on, although it was meant to be held parallel to the ground.

The experts at the Bayeux Tapestry Centre have noted that all the bows were of a small uniform size and have made the supposition that this was in order to make the design fit. I truly doubt that, because the men are drawn in all different sizes and scales. Even with these four archers you can see that number 2 is much larger than number 1, but the scale is the same. It would have been easy to adjust this and I must conclude that the bows were drawn small, because they were small, and the quivers were at the waist because 2, 3 and 4 were probably William's secret weapon - his crossbowmen.

There is no adaptation work that can be seen here. All the thread is of the correct colours. Great attention is paid to colour and style of each of the four men. There are no missing stitches or holes in the canvas. Bowmen 2 and 4 I believe are also passing the bowstring under their lead arm. This is not clear from the image, but as plain as day in person, as the bow string is a specific colour and the clothing is not the same. The assumption to a casual observer is that the strings go over the arm - they do not and this is a major revelation. It probably means that three quarters of Williams' archers may have had crossbows with them. At this point I would say the Tapestry confirms positively the supposition that crossbowmen were present. When it is understood that the bowstring goes under the arm it is strange that the perspective can easily be understood to show crossbows.

Whilst you and I know what a crossbowman might look like we must remember that there is no record of crossbows ever being used in England before this battle. William is known to have had a contingent of Turkish mercenaries in his pay. It seems to me wholly consistent that these should have been equipped with a weapon that was at that time already common in Turkey and able to win battles. It would also fit the opinion of Mr Foulkes-Halbard, the military expert who concluded that the crossbow found in Crowhurst was of Turkish design. It doesn't take a lot to put two and two together.

We should now look at the section of the Tapestry where the battle is won. No more Norman archers are shown until William raises his visor to show his face. This is during a critical part of the battle. The Normans probably believed the battle was lost, since it is now 3pm in the afternoon according to some later sources and at this point William rallies his men on the battlefield, showing his face and giving his famous rallying speech.

The lower border now shows archers numbered 6 through to 28 (23 in total in this sequence) flowing through the scene, where William wins the battle, just up to the point before Harold is killed. A clear statement of the important part the archers played in winning that battle.

Up until this point the border is to detail dead bodies. We shall never know, but it is probable in my view that those who knew this event intimately would have known who these bodies were by their colours and position relative to those above. What is clear to me is the archers are introduced as the living force on the battlefield, exactly at the point where William turns the battle in favour of the Normans.

When you look closely at these archers there is clearly something different about them compared to any other characters portrayed either in the battle sequence or before this point. The most obvious omission is the fact that only one (archer number11) has been coloured in. All the other bowmen are just outlines. Several have had their quivers coloured, but apart from that all of these archers are in rudimentary format, apart from one.

Close examination also shows very untidy stitching that is loose and there are a lot of missing stitches, as shown where Harold has his arrow removed from his eye. It is in my mind impossible not to come to two conclusions.

The first conclusion is that these archers have been altered at some time in the past. If they had not been altered the quality of the stitching would be consistent and there would be no missing stitches. This is shown by a considerable number of missing stitches marked by holes in the background around the bowmen.

It does not look like this section has ever been completed, because there are not enough missing stitch holes to make that likely. So the second conclusion must be that this section was deliberately left in this condition.

Once the archer sequence is finished the Tapestry reverts to full, high quality stitching, through to the end. So it would not be unreasonable to conclude that there was a reason for this, and it is up to us to seek to find a logical and obvious conclusion.

If we now look at the Bowmen in turn we will see that these men may appear on the face of it to be just like the rest of the Tapestry, but they are not.

ARCHER 6.

Starting at number 6 the reader should look closely at these men, with a magnifying glass if necessary. In the first case (number 6) follow the bow string from the top to the bottom of the bow. There is a suggestion that the bow string passes behind the face of this archer, but may have been sewn in front on the bottom half of the face to accommodate an alteration. The string runs from the hand directly up to the mouth at right angles to the ground in one colour and then changes colour. In the bottom section the string either shows an attachment to the bow, like an attachment to the belt, or the string runs to the archer's waist and is being held too high up and should be attached where the belt is located.

The string colours also change between the chin and the bow, suggesting that the bow string has not all been completed at the same time. We again see a bowman in the stooped firing position. It is quite clear in this case that the bowstring also passes behind the shoulder.

The designer of the Tapestry might have known this was a crossbowman with a belt attachment, since this was the normal way that crossbows were reloaded. In order to facilitate quick loading a man would stand on the bow, in a type of stirrup at the centre of the bow where the hand would hold the stock. He would attach the hook, which was attached to the belt on his waist. The action of standing up and leaning back would pull the bow string into the load position. This man does not have quivers either on his belt or shoulder. He shows his clothing, or a possible belt connecting to his waist.

ARCHER 7.

Archer 7 shows he has part of his leg missing behind the bow. He has his quiver on his right leg below his waist and is also in the traditional crossbowman stoop for firing. There is no doubt in this case that the bow sting runs behind his shoulder - a position impossible for a normal archer to fire unless holding the bow parallel to the ground. This man also wears a beard - and so was almost certainly not Norman, because the Normans were known to fight clean shaven - unlike the English. Most of the archers either have beards or facial hair as moustaches. The inclusion of the beard is to me a clear indication that the authors of the Tapestry were making a clear statement that allegiances were won at the Battle of Hastings, by those foreign mercenaries, who attended as archers on William's side. This bowman definitely supports the thesis that he was a Turkish mercenary, as do many of these men.

My reason for thinking this is because stylistically these men are not portrayed as Frenchmen. The other Frenchmen in the Tapestry wore armour, or chain mail, and were all wearing early western style battle dress. They were also depicted in pristine stitching befitting knights who would win such a battle. These archers are on the contrary all wearing skirts in the Turkish style (with the sole exception of Archer 11). The faces of these men are shown with large noses and typical recursive bows. The conclusion I have to draw is that these men are not normal French infantry, because I believe they would have been shown in the same style as those featuring in the main tapestry sequence, as shown by archers number 1 - 4. These in the border were not worthy of inclusion in the main sequence - they were foreigners, and portrayed in the margin along with other unimportant elements of the battle, with associated information known to those who attended. None the less this registers the part they played and the battle could not be portrayed without their inclusion at the appropriate point. It is for this reason I believe they were included to mark their importance. It is difficult to draw any other conclusion.

ARCHER 8.

This archer, like Archer 7, has his quivers at his waist in traditional crossbow position. This man also shows the bow string going behind the shoulder, but far more relevant is the additional arm, or crossbow stock, drawn behind the front one in dark outline. A close-up of that element can be seen here:

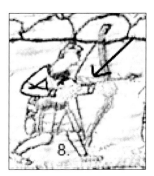

That arm identified by the arrow is not a mistake, but confirms that adaptation work has taken place, because it has not been removed. Either it is the original arm, before the adaptation work has added the firing arm in the front, or it is confirmation that wooden stock of the original crossbows were originally drawn in and either not completed or removed at a later point in time. The evidence presented by Archer 8, together with a number of missing stitch holes around the archer indicates alterations have taken place. The fact that the original stitching is still in place indicates that the quality of the adaptation work was very low - as is indicated by the poor quality stitching and lack of attention to detail.

Looking carefully at the actual arrow it should also be noted that stitch holes can be seen below the arrowhead. At the same time the angle of the arrow looks like it has been changed from its original elevation parallel to the ground. Its original elevation would have meant that it would have been drawn along the wooden shaft. Leaving the shaft in position appears to confirm this man was firing a crossbow, but who ever adapted the work later had little idea what he was doing, probably never having seen a crossbow, but relying upon reports.

Stitch holes on this bowman indicate that this bowman too, at one time held his arrow parallel to the ground.

ARCHER 9.

Archer 9 stands in the classic crossbowman firing position with quiver at the waist attached to a belt. The bowman's leading leg is also missing behind the bow and the firing arm has been reduced in size to less than an a few centimetres below the firing finger. The bow string has not been completed across the arm at this point and is also missing between the chin, where a beard is located and the top of the bow.

The hand and finger position for archers 7 and 9 clearly connect the finger with the bow string. Archer 8 shows a slightly different position, whereas later archers such as 10, 11 and 15 show the connection to the arrow, indicating a number of inconsistencies not seen anywhere else in any other aspect of the Tapestry. It is as if the attention to detail elsewhere has been ignored. A more likely conclusion being that what we are seeing is alteration work that was not present at the time it was first seen.

ARCHER 10.

This archer shows clear signs of adaptation work to the critical eye. He stands in the crossbow position with bended knee and has his quivers in the crossbow position on his waist. He also appears to be wearing a special strap that crosses his shoulder and like the bow loading hook finishes at the bow sting. No hook is actually drawn, but the shape of the strap is significant.

Archer 10, 11 and 15 hold the arrow not the string

This man (Archer 10) is not wearing clothes suitable for an October day in England in 1066. There is very little detail supplied. The thing that jumps out at me is his left bow hand. It holds the bow below a circular hook - exactly like that we have seen attached to the front of a composition Turkish bow of early construction. The horseshoe/loop type fixture is not part of the hand, which holds the bow below this point. It looks like confirmation of a bow with the foot stirrup expected to be part of the sort of crossbow we believe to have been found in the Crowhurst valley. Below are two early images of bows near this era. Note it was quite normal to show the bow side on - despite its normal firing position being parallel to the ground. At this time in history the art of drawing perspective had not been learnt. In consequence it can be assumed that any or all of the archers shown in the Bayeux Tapestry may be using crossbows if other elements known to fit crossbowmen are shown. These two images show different styles of early bows. Note that the construction of the one on the right (dated 11th century) is similar in its scale to the ones shown in the Tapestry:

6. Saracen crossbowman from
Las Cantigas, late 13ᵗʰ
century; detail after Nicolle

17. From Haimo's Book of
Ezekiel, late 11ᵗʰ century of
Ms Lat.12.302) (BN

An enduring mystery continues to this day and is in part the reason why historians have denied crossbows were used at the Battle of Hastings. Great debate has taken place about how the firing mechanism worked on these early bows. Some say it was a ledge which held the string, others a pin which may have been pulled (see right hand image above), whilst others see levered triggers. The Victorians concluded that because there was no record of any crossbow ever being found in this country until much later, that these images in the Bayeux Tapestry could not therefore be crossbows. At that time the Carmen, which confirms ballistas (crossbows), was not accepted as authentic, and so it was easy to dismiss the allegation. Now it is starting to become clear that this assumption, like the one that the Normans landed at the town of Pevensey, can be seen to be flawed by a lack of understanding of the references being made.

Lastly in relation to Archer 10 we see the bowstring has almost certainly been altered at some point. This can be seen because it changes thread weight and direction, between what is assumed to be a beard and the flight end of the arrow. It is notable that the bow string does not follow the curve you would expect. The arrow is above the firing hand, suggesting that this arm might also once have been a wooden stock, with firing finger below the stock. It may have been altered, but the design fault remains, even when the alteration has probably been made.

ARCHER 11.

This archer is the one and only archer in this section who is coloured and detailed, like the first four archers (1-4). He is in the stooped crossbowman firing position and holds his quiver of arrows at his waist. I would conclude from his style of dress and also facial features that this man is a Frenchman and that is why attention has been paid to the detail of his clothing.

It would be easy to conclude that no alterations have been made to Archer 11. but there are anomalies on this archer too.

It is as if when making the alteration the yarn used to embroider the original image was used, but because there was not enough when the alteration was made different coloured yarns were introduced in key places. Perhaps the original bow string went behind the arm, in the same way as the previous archers and the alteration has over embroidered the connecting yarn across the arm. This has resulted in the green yarn for the bowstring now stopping just by the knee, instead of continuing down to the bow arm at the bottom.

The arrow is also misaligned, rising at the hand on the bow. A large image of this section is detailed below in order to discuss the next two archers:

ARCHERS 12 and 13.

These close-up images are unfortunately not very good due to low light. The centre archer wears a full beard and is almost certainly not French. He, like Archer 11 also wears his quiver at the waist and both are in the crossbow firing position - suggesting strongly that all the archers from 6 through to 14 are crossbowmen.

If the stitching here is compared to the normal Tapestry stitching, such as shown in Harold's death scene, there is a noticeable drop in quality.

The most obvious observation to the untrained eye is again the irregular use of thread colours. Archer 12 clearly shows what could be interpreted as a crossbow stock, which has been adapted to look like an arm. If you look closely at the top edge of the armband, along the light fawn coloured yarn under the arrow, by the bowstring, there are stitch holes confirming the alteration. The use of the fawn coloured thread at both ends of the arrow, and the use of the parallel lines, exactly where the crossbow stock should be located, cannot be a coincidence.

As if to confirm this Archer 12 has no proper arm embroidered, but still retains a crude attempt to show a crossbow stock. Who ever did this work could not in my view possibly have been in the same team who made the Tapestry.

The bow strings on both archers show they have been adapted, because Archer 12 is missing the stitches across the front of the arm, at the top of his arm under the beard where there is a strategic gap, Archer 13 also shows a string colour not used anywhere else. This archer also shows the tell tale stitch holes between the bow and the head of the archer. The suggestion from this observation is that the original stitching showed the bowstring running from the top of the bow (like the other archers), behind the front of the face and behind the arm. It suggests that the change in string colour is simply due to lack of appropriate coloured thread.

Much of this might be considered speculation, which it is without confirmation by the Tapestry authorities. None the less the observation is valid and cannot be explained by simply stating that it is how it looks now. In the same way that a conclusion regarding Harold's arrow in the eye being removed shows that adaptation work has taken place, I believe it is impossible not to conclude that who ever did the adaptation work in that sequence most probably had a hand in adapting these archers.

ARCHERS 14 to 28.

It is important to realise that what we are looking at is a story. It is not a snapshot of one particular moment when we are looking at all the archers. The story is telling us that the crossbowmen were used when William was showing his face to his men until the statement *'Here the French do Battle'*.

At the point when we reach Archer 14 in the Bayeux Tapestry the battle plan changes. At that point the archers are shown without quivers and from Archer 14 to Archer 16 we see the archers change from crouching to standing positions. This is to my mind telling us that the battle was moving forward. It was normal in battle in those days to reuse arrows that were fired at you. The fact that the English had few archers (as registered by the solitary archer in the middle of the battle scene) may go some way to explaining why the battle lasted all day.

There is a clear gap between archer 16, 17 and 18. showing distance, meaning that the battle moved forward and at the same time, as we learn from the various manuscripts the archers raise their elevation. These later archers are not crossbowmen because of their firing positions and because the quivers are being stored on the ground. The process of reinforcement had at that time brought new supplies of arrows and consequently the tactic of shooting high was employed - resulting in Harold and others being hit above the eye.

It is clear to me that the reintroduction of dead bodies in the border between the archers shows that the Normans were not only able to win ground, but moved over the dead bodies of the English as they progressed. In short the Bayeux Tapestry faithfully records what the different chronicles have recorded in their different ways.

My view may not be the old view that the Victorians took, that crossbows were not used at the Battle of Hastings. My view I believe is sound, because I have information that the Victorians did not have.

They had come to that conclusion, because they had discredited Wace, as a result of the battle site being identified in the wrong place. In a similar vein they had also discredited the Carmen, because it did not agree with other elements that they wished to impose as the authorised version of events.

Now with the benefit of hindsight, a lot of new information, and now a scrupulous examination of the most eminent source for the period - The Bayeux Tapestry - we can see clear indications of adaptation work and even elements of crossbows still in the Tapestry.

The question that arises is *'why would someone do that adaptation work and who?'* This is I believe one of the easier questions to answer. We do not know who made the Tapestry for certain. Most authorities believe that it was probably made in Canterbury in England close after 1066. Voices are not unanimous on this point, since I have seen that the French seek to claim that it might have been made in France (source the Bayeux Tapestry Centre, Bayeux).

I suspect this is more to do with Gallic pride than the quality of evidence of what else was embroidered of this high standard at that time in France. I, like most authorities, am happy to accept that the Bayeux Tapestry was probably made in Kent and moved to Bayeux in 1077 for the consecration of the

Cathedral. Bishop Odo was based in Kent and it seems highly likely that his hand was the motivating force, because of the inclusion of three of his bishops in the script.

Given that the Tapestry appears to almost perfectly fit the nave of Bayeux Cathedral it looks like it was effectively made to measure for that building. It was a wonderful piece of political propaganda, aimed at those who would attend the consecration of that cathedral, empowering William's position as head of state.

In April the Second Council of the Lateran was held by Pope Innocent 2nd. It implied a ban on crossbows and bows ruling: '*against readily available and all too effective projectile weapons.*' These weapons rendered the chivalry of Europe (those men who sought to fight with honour) liable to fatal attack from afar and undermined the ethics of that age.

The ban was proclaimed again at the 4th Lateran Council and whilst it had political implications it was generally ignored. The crossbow spread throughout Europe in these years and like the longbow became a must have weapon of war by the 14th century.

This explains exactly why the crossbow men in the Bayeux Tapestry needed to be changed. The Tapestry was hanging in public display in the cathedral, which effectively was William the Conquerors personal mausoleum. To leave the crossbowmen in plain view was to deface his name in the eyes of God and the Church in the face of a Papal edict.

It is my contention that the reason these alterations are not very good, and also the Tapestry is incomplete in elements of the stitch work, in the section detailing the bowmen, is explained by the history. Taking the Tapestry back to Kent from Bayeux would have been impossible, so it had to be done on site and in secret. This meant that the people who had learnt the art of creating the Tapestry could not be involved. We see the results today in different stitching and missing stitches, as well as different coloured yarn with incomplete colouring.

If these archers were unaltered I could not conclude that crossbows were used at the Battle of Hastings with any certainty. The fact that they have been altered, and because the alterations have not been carried out with an eye for the artistic endeavour, we can still see elements that confirm crossbow use, such as the stock still in outline.

I must therefore conclude that the statement by Guy Bishop of Amiens was correct, when he wrote that William did employ crossbowmen in the Carmen. The fact that we now understand the Carmen to be authentic means we should actually expect crossbows to be used at the Battle of Hastings. It would be quite strange if they were not. What we have now is a completely logical explanation of why the Tapestry shows what it does. It confirms the Carmen by virtue of recognising that alterations on the Tapestry exist.

Historians may have in the past denied crossbow use at the Battle of Hastings, because they could see no evidence at the authorised battle site and there are no other archaeological records of crossbow use in England before the 13th century. However there is a well recorded case of William the Conqueror having his horse shot from under him by a crossbow. This is recorded in the Anglo-Saxon Chronicle of 1079. It is therefore quite clear that by 1079, thirteen years after the Battle of Hastings, crossbows were in common use in England and probably were introduced by the Normans. The fact that archaeology has not been found does not mean the record is wrong. Given that the conclusion of this document is that the site of the Battle of Hastings is now in dispute, finding a relic that is claimed to be a crossbow adds fuel to that debate, which will only be resolved when the new site is examined by experts.

When I created the original thesis in 1997 stating that the Normans camped at Wilting the elements that supported this conclusion were drawn from the Bayeux Tapestry. A key element of that evidence being the Tapestry showing the correct landing site, by virtue of the ground and buildings depicted. It would therefore be inconsistent to ignore the ground of the battle sequence, even if there are no buildings that can be compared.

If the battle site were correctly displayed in the Tapestry, according to the logic previously employed to support the landing site at Wilting Manor, then the battle sequence must also show the correct terrain. It is not logical to rely upon one principle simple to ignore it in relation to the connected battle site.

I have therefore taken the Bayeux Tapestry, again from the point where the Normans leave their camp at Wilting, through to the conclusion of the battle. This time I have coloured the ground according to the type of ground shown, with a commentary. This commentary explains why this image is depicted in the way it is.

In simple terms the ground is coloured black when it is uneven, white when it is level pasture, and blue when water.

The Normans leave their camp at Hastings (Wilting Manor) which is located on uneven ground next to a plain (as reported by Wace). At the rear is Monkham Wood (the tall trees) and Redgeland Wood the small one at the front. Monkham Wood is behind the Normans as they leave their camp behind them as the ground rises.

At this point William asks Vital whether he has seen King Harold. There is a large hill (Wilting Manor hill with a wood on the far side (Chapel Wood) and a valley from where Harold's scout can see the Normans. The Saxon scout looking for the Normans stands on the lower hill, turns and reports to Harold, who is on horse with a tree (shown in the next section) at his rear.

Wace calls that slope *'rising ground'* over which the Normans first appear on the battlefield. It is drawn twice because it is recording two events in the same place and is marked between two sets of trees acting as scene markers. The tree behind Harold is the Crowhurst Yew shown in this plate after William has passed that point on horseback.

Now the Norman Knights engage in battle. The ground is uneven, but there is a ditch or flat section where the archers first engage. There is a rise in the ground and then another plain or level ground (white) exactly in front of where the Saxon defence line is located. This same level section is shown later in the Tapestry when identifying the same location.

The battle rages with Normans on horseback. It should be noted that it is not exclusively in one location, confirmed in the Carmen as being over an extended area. At this stage the Saxons take the initiative by bringing the fighting to the Normans and undermining William's plan for knights to follow up archers (Carmen).

There is a swamp or stream in the battle site in front of the very large hill that is higher than the hill where the Normans left Hastings camp at the port. The ground is agricultural and tilled (brown wavy line) and although uneven it was managed as opposed to uneven pasture. This section shows horses falling in the stream/swamp and a large tree at the rear of the hill.

This section shows where the Norman cavalry is in action where William raises his helmet to identify himself to his men. At this point the Norman archers and crossbowmen appear in the borders showing their deployment.

Here we see the arrows shot from the archers who are shown firing high in the border. The ground over most of this and the previous scene rises to the point where the level ground and *'the plain'* section is shown again in front of where King Harold and his men are shown.

This is the final scene; Harold is killed where the ground rises to a flat section at the top of the hill, with a tree drawn next to it. This tree is the end marker for the battle and shows the Saxons exiting from the battle being pursued by Normans on horseback at two different levels.

The conclusion that I am drawn to after conducting this exercise is quite clear and logical. Knowing where the Norman camp is located plays a key part in understanding that everything drawn in the Bayeux Tapestry is there for a reason - including even the way the ground is displayed.

The traditional view until now has been that the ground and buildings shown in the Tapestry are simplistic approximations of a cartoon type story - where the only elements that can be relied upon are the characters being deployed in the story. The work that we have done here shows us that this view can only be adopted as a means of seeking to credit the site at Battle Abbey as the battle site. The reason for this is that none of these elements fit in any sort of chronological order when applied to the Battle Abbey site.

The problem with the Battle Abbey site is that whilst it has a very small ditch half way across the battle site there are many missing and key ingredients that the Tapestry show us. In order to accept the Battle Abbey site as authentic you have to discredit the authors of the Tapestry, by seeking to claim that there was no purpose in showing one hill larger than the other. You would need to believe there is no purpose in showing the valley with the trees where Wace says the Normans first saw the English. You must also ignore the evidence where Wace tells us the Normans crossed a valley and plain before reaching where the first engagement took place.

It doesn't stop there though, because there is no Malfosse at the Battle Abbey site. Yet we see horses falling into a wide area of water just next to a flat and unexplained area at the bottom of the main hill, which the Normans are fighting. There are different sections of ground shown in different ways. You are asked to believe that all representation of the ground in the Tapestry is simply artistic temperament. The Battle Abbey hill is dwarfed by the one that forms the Ridge to its south at Hastings, but we are asked to believe that this is ignored by the authors of the Tapestry. We are asked to believe the two hills taken from the landing site are in reverse proportions to those of the two main hills shown in the Tapestry. In fact the proportions are exactly the wrong way round - which might just suggest that someone - including William - might query this when he saw it, if it really was that wrong. Of course it was not wrong and that is why no-one queried it. It can only be wrong when you apply these images to the Battle Abbey site – which the Normans did not because they knew the ground and where these images referred to.

If you continue to believe that the Battle site was at Battle Abbey you also have to completely ignore the smaller lesser hills between the battle site and the Norman camp. The only solution for such a conjecture is to discredit the Tapestry, in terms of the ground, and I believe to do that shows a lack of understanding of how we got to this position in the first place. Most people would like to think that history and truth always walk hand in hand. This is not always the case. Here at Hastings we have probably the most important battle in British history and one that formed the backbone of the future development of Europe as we know it today. Much of what happened in 1066 sits at the root of what happened since, not only in England, but France as well.

When this matter came under scrutiny, in the Victorian era, history played an important part in the English psyche. It required investigation of every element of every statement, from every source that could be found regarding this battle. The Victorians wanted to know all they could and as a result examination of the documents simply did not align with what they considered the *'known facts'* - the most notable known fact being the location of the actual battle site at Battle Abbey.

Faced with the apparent fact that the Battle Abbey site was the actual battle site, because they believed it was recorded correctly in the Charter from that time, there was no choice but to throw away the key documents that contained the references that discredited the Abbey site. These were Wace and the Carmen, but also there was the reference to the ground structure in the Bayeux Tapestry. Whilst this would be an easy conclusion to draw, it was also one full of errors. Those errors are now shown in their full glory, once it is known that the Chronicle of Battle Abbey confirms that the current Abbey site was not where the battlefield was located. Mr Wace is as a result of this historical research therefore reinstated as the foremost expert witness of the events of the Invasion and battle. His version of events is shown to be the most accurate document of the time, with the most detail. The embittered critic of Mr Freeman, Mr Round, who was so sure he knew exactly why Mr Freeman was wrong, will turn in his grave. His expert opinion is now shown to be no greater than his ego and a name that will live in the annals of history as a testament to the mistake of failing to check his source documents – a mistake as common then as it still is today.

It is now July 2010, twenty-four years after first starting this work, as I conclude this last chapter before the summary of conclusions. Even now a last minute revelation occurred to me, as I visited the Bayeux Tapestry one last time. As I looked at the images of the trees that have been used as scene markers in the battle sequences, I wondered why they had each been created differently from each other.

It seemed strange to me that who ever had created this work had meticulously ensured accuracy down to the elements of the ground at each stage of the battle. Yet the trees were not a uniform style. If you look at the first three that separate the scene where we are told the soldiers have gone out from Hastings, we see that the centre tree is in a strange shape, with what looks like a graphical impression of water inside its head.

The second set of trees is where they leave the Norman camp just before crossing the valley, which is wooded and Harold's man informs Harold that the Normans are coming. This tree in the centre has a brown wiggly line under the branches.

The third tree is at the back of Harold when that man makes his report. This tree is similar to the first tree, but instead of an image in its head of water there is what could be interpreted as roughly shaped rectangular blocks, or possibly tiles similar to those shown in the manor house shown earlier, which we thought might be adjacent to Wilting.

Next there is the tree at the rear of the Saxons fighting off the Normans at the top of the battle hill. The hill is drawn specifically with the brown wiggly line, exactly as included in the second tree discussed above. The tree on this hill is normal and does not have anything added to it. It is shown on the slope of the hill.

Lastly at the end of the battle scene there is a final tree set where the English leave the battlefield on an upper and lower level. This tree clearly has a circle at the top with nothing in it. The branches are regular and stunted. More important than that is the fact that it is drawn in two halves and the bottom right hand branch of the tree shows a red apple falling, since there is a clear gap between it and the tree or ground next to it.

I had to smile when I saw these, because it seemed so strange that having looked at these scenes many times, as I am sure many of my readers who study Norman history will also have done, and never have given these elements a second thought. What the author of the Tapestry was telling us was these were no ordinary trees. They were trees specific to the time and place. They were scene markers and who knows; one day maybe someone would dispute the authenticity of the Tapestry. Then perhaps, and only then, would the significance of these trees be known. That is what made me smile, because these trees could only fit the description of the events that took place between Wilting Farm in Hastings and the Crowhurst valley.

I know that now, because the first tree is embroidered with water in its branches. This is because it was located at the port of Hastings, next to the Norman camp at Redgeland Wood. The second set of trees was embroidered with the wiggly line, because it was next to the tilled land at the top of the hill at Wilting Manor. This is the reason that the hill in the main battle site is shown in the same wiggly brown format - it is because it too was tilled land, which was rough tilled soil. The tree which Harold has his back to, has roughly caste stones or tiles in its branches, because it is where the low stone wall is located, where the Crowhurst church now stands next to the manor house. The stones or tiles represent the location next to the manor house. It must therefore have been the Crowhurst yew. The tree shown half way up the battlefield hill has no identifying marks, because it was identifying trees adjacent to the hill as a wood, with no particular merit. Finally the last tree drawn in the sequence, which has a circle at the top, with nothing in it, shown in two halves with clear space in the centre and a falling apple, is clearly identifying the '*hoary apple tree*', after which the battle was named by the Saxon Chronicles. How do I know this? It is because the circle has nothing in it. We are being told that this tree was hollow, exactly as we would expect such an old tree to be. The apple is the final confirmation.

Now with the benefit of hindsight, and a lot of historical research from investigative historians in Cambridge and elsewhere, we know that the Carmen was correct and so was Wace. Armed with this information any straight thinking man who looks at these matters afresh must come to the same conclusion. I therefore conclude that the Bayeux Tapestry was also correct in all the details given. To deny this simply begs the question why include the different terrain and dialogue if it is not correct, when a site can be identified that fits every feature of the story as shown, and in the chronology shown, exactly where it is supposed to be?

It may not appear obvious to the casual viewer, but I knew when I revisited Bayeux that what I was looking at was the detailed and specific land between the Norman camp at Wilting Manor and the hill known as Telham Hill in Crowhurst. That is for me direct confirmation of everything else that is written in this document. Consequently I can confirm that the Bayeux Tapestry is a work of undisputable authenticity. It directly endorses the site in the Crowhurst Valley as the site of the Battle of Hastings, as well as the site of the Norman camp and invasion at Wilting Manor on the outskirts of Hastings.

The annual anniversary of the Battle of Hastings approaches on 14th October each year. It is the time when those who care about English history and heritage gather on what they believe to be the sacred soil of the ancient battlefield at Battle Abbey. Thousands gather for the annual re-enactment unaware of the lie perpetrated not only on the gate, but in almost all history books and all the online literature that you can put your hands on.

This story is therefore about revealing a long lost historical truth, which at the time I started my quest, was unknown to any man. Even those who saw the raw information in the books and documents I have examined had not recognised the underlying truth, or questioned the reasons why inconsistencies existed. They, like those before them had sought to justify previous misunderstandings, rather than face criticism from their colleagues, or seek to find an explanation that removes those inconsistencies. For what ever reason, it appears to have fallen upon me to expose what was a fraud, in order to bring the matter into focus and the correct site of the Battle of Hastings be identified. There are many who understand that there are just too many inconsistencies in the historical record to justify the Battle Abbey site as the site of the Battle of Hastings. Having travelled with me over these 24 years you now know what those reasons are.

I do not intend to repeat the conclusions drawn earlier on the Invasion site at Wilting Manor, detailed in the manuscript presented to the Highways Agency inspector. The landing site and camp play an integral part in the events of the Norman Invasion that cannot be disconnected from the battle. They were connected by the manuscripts that recorded the events of those days in writing, by a number of eminent authentic sources. These are primarily the Chronicle of Battle Abbey, upon whom the authority of the Abbey was based, the Domesday Book, which recorded faithfully the values of the 1066 manors for William the Conqueror and cannot be called into doubt. In addition to these there is the Carmen by Guy Bishop of Amiens, an 835 line long song of the Battle of Hastings and Wace's Roman de Rou containing in excess of 16,000 lines of detail. Both of these last two were documents discredited in Victorian times, because they could not be reconciled with Poitiers version of events, in conjunction with the then current interpretation of the Bayeux Tapestry. This last element being considered the weightiest in concluding that the Normans could not have landed at Hastings, because the Tapestry records the Normans as travelling to Pevensey half way through that work.

As a result it was not possible for any single version of the Battle of Hastings, or the Invasion, to have been recorded without inconsistencies between each document. Historians have therefore throughout the whole of history sought an explanation that gives precedence to one document over another, depending upon your particular preferences. In consequence when one author notes that there is a site where many Normans are killed at the end of the battle in a large ditch, which the Normans called the Malfosse (bad ditch in French), the absence of any such ditch adjacent to or on the battlefield at Battle Abbey, is ignored by those who support that site. Later when the issue is called into doubt, a so called cleft in the land is found that suits those who propose that particular document, even though the cleft in question is a good mile from where the fighting is supposed to have taken place. In the same way in other documents there are places named, such as the specific naming of the Norman camp site, at the port of Hastings, at a place called Redgeland. In this instance those who seek to avoid the implications of what they are reading seek to claim that there is no evidence of the port, because '*it has been eroded from the coast*' In order to deal with critics, I have, I believe, dealt in this document with many myths and legends regarding the Battle of Hastings and Norman Invasion that persist to this day. The principal issues, whilst not exhaustive of the document as a whole, cover the main points as follows:

COASTAL EROSION

We studied the myth of the old Hastings port being situated below the current castle As we have seen by our detailed analysis of all of these claims and counterclaims there is no evidence to support the port of Hastings being removed by coastal erosion. Coastal erosion cannot have removed the port because as Simon Jennings, the expert sedimentologist from the University of London told me, and it is an easy observation for people to understand, chalk cliffs cannot erode to reveal petrified forests made later than the chalk that erodes away. The whole story was made up in Victorian times to seek to justify something they had no evidence to support. Those who claim coastal erosion, to support the lack of evidence at Hastings, have not performed their due diligence in the study of the sediments of the land and sea area under discussion.

HASTINGS PORT

We have established through the location, together with the expert evidence of sedimentologists, who have conducted substantial numbers of bore hole studies in the Combe Haven valley, that the underlying proposal that the Hastings port (the largest and most important of the Cinque ports) developed through continuous occupation from the Bronze Age, through the Iron Age and Roman period, and was situated next to Wilting manor in the parish of Crowhurst pre 1066. The evidence for this is established through sedimentary studies of the Combe Haven and the Hastings Castle valley, as well as through expert sedimentary studies. Evidence was found of stone tools and aerial photographs revealing pits as well as settlements throughout the 200 acre Wilting Manor site. The Wessex archaeological survey conducted in 1996 produced substantial archaeological evidence (external link http://www.secretsofthenormaninvasion.com/corresp/trenchal.jpg) to support the conclusions produced in this document.

Expert evidence to support this claim, by Wessex and others, is contained in the external correspondence pages of the web site (www.secretsofthenormaninvasion.com/corresp/index.htm)

Discovery of a Bronze Age log, with man made cut in the section known as the earthen bank, dated by carbon dating at between 1890BC and 1520BC, provides positive proof of the importance of the Wilting site, as a site of man's first development on the south coast of England. The accumulation of finds covering all human periods since that time confirms the thesis of continuous development. It should notify the authorities of the need to protect this important site for the study of human development, where evidence of all of man's developmental ages can be found on one site on the south coast of England. The marsh is already a Site of Special Scientific Interest and a protected environment. Evidence collected over the last 24 years now shows the unique nature of the Wilting Manor extends beyond the 200 acres of land, but into the marsh as well. Expert appraisal and investigation is required to establish whether this site is earlier and/or more extensive than the nationally renowned site at Shinewater some thirty miles along the coast at Eastbourne. With such a wealth of historical and archaeological, as well as environmental evidence available in one place it should be a site worthy of attracting a large number of tourists interested in the country's cultural and environmental heritage. It would seem highly likely that Wilting developed first, by the nature of the protected harbour, and from the archaeology of the site that has come out of the ground over the period I have been studying this subject.

The stratigraphic record, completed by Simon Jennings and Christine Smyth of the University of London confirms a deep water inlet at both Redgeland and Monkham Inlet suitable for seafaring vessels, where I believe there is evidence that the Norman fleet landed. The subsequent development of the London to Hastings railway in 1843 caused the site to be effectively cut off from building inside the borough boundary. Hence even today the site at Wilting remains almost the same as it was when the Normans landed. The marsh is now drying out, with climate change, and is in need of protection as the environment takes its toll.

We discovered the Romans were active at Wilting through the discovery of an extensive network of tracks used to take iron ore from the bloomeries at Crowhurst Park, Bynes Farm, Foreword and Beauport Park, to the deep-water port at Hastings within the Wilting Manor site. Excavations by Wessex Archaeology confirmed finds in over 108 locations in their report held on the web site (http://www.secretsofthenormaninvasion.com/corresp/wessex6.htm) along with evidence of industrialisation on the edge of the marsh in the port area. Aerial photographs revealed ancient tracks and sites of habitation consistent with the thesis that Wilting Manor was the site of the port of Hastings pre-1066. That thesis showing the port developing through continuous use from man's earliest settlement of that protected waterway.

Place name evidence was confirmed by Margaret Gelling, the place name expert, who identified the name Bulverhythe at the entrance to the Combe Haven valley, as meaning an inland port, with the name coming from the olde English *burhwara* meaning *'the landing place of the people.'* Other as yet unidentified features of the port area include a defensive structure in Redgeland wood, probably the Norman castle mound pre 1090, as well as and earthen jetties, most probably used in the Roman period.

THE LOWER FORTS

Resistivity surveys were carried out both on the lower and upper forts at Wilting Manor. The evidence of those surveys shows the existence of an enclosure, which we claim is the site of the first Norman camp of William the Conqueror, confirmed by post hole evidence, and evidence of a hidden ditch (shown being dug in the Bayeux Tapestry) when William landed his ships at Monkham Inlet. Those surveys show the Norman enclosure on the site of a previous Iron Age fort, on the headland below Monkham Wood.

It is my contention that this inlet has been earthed up at some stage in the past. The earthen dam found on the site was examined in detail and is consistent with the thesis that the dam was created by William the Conqueror, when he ordered his men to earth up his boats (as described in the Carmen), whilst in contradiction he orders them to dismantle his boats in the Wace manuscript, and in another burnt his boats as detailed in the Chronicle of Battle Abbey. The discovery of charcoal, boat parts and an earthen dam all in the same inlet appears to provide convincing evidence that all three manuscripts were describing the same event of the Invasion, without any contradiction. Rather than reporting separate events each author recorded only the element that they knew about – throwing light upon the events of the landing and further supporting the legitimacy of all the manuscripts involved. Auguring work (digging core samples) confirmed that the inlet was navigable at the time of the 1066 Invasion and that the whole of the Combe Haven was a tidal estuary capable of holding at least 1000 invasion boats. That inland water way was open to the sea until the 13th century, but was closed by storms caused by the longshore drift of shingle moving along the coast and closing the entrance to the port.

UPPER FORT

The top field at Wilting Manor is claimed to be the site of the second camp of William the Conqueror, as shown in the Bayeux Tapestry. This claim of two forts on the site of the Norman Invasion is unique to this document. No other historian has made this claim. It is as a result of an observation of two forts - one at the bottom of the hill, built when the Normans landed, and one at the top, built over the following week. Documentary evidence supports this in reference to forts (in the plural) in the Carmen manuscript. The discovery of forts that existed at this site confirms authenticity of the Carmen, when previously this information was not trusted.

Further evidence to support the location of the second camp on the top of Wilting Manor hill is provided by confirmation of line of sight between the camps of the Normans and Saxons on the night of the Battle of Hastings. This is not the only evidence collected over the 24 years. Wessex Archaeology confirmed the presence of two parallel ditches exactly where the Normans are claimed to have erected their barricade at the top of Wilting hill, within the defensive bank, as shown on the Bayeux Tapestry. Post holes and enclosures were found showing a large building located where it is claimed the Castle of St Mary in the Castle was located and 11th century Norman period pottery found in the post holes.

The Norman period pottery is important, because no other 11th century Norman period pottery has been found at any other site associated with either the Norman Invasion or Battle of Hastings. None that I know of has ever been found at Battle Abbey, Hastings Castle or Pevensey. The pottery was found in enclosures, which were located in the same orientation on both sides of the top field at Wilting Farm, suggesting the whole of that field was probably the original site of the town of Hastings pre1066. Speculation that the house being burnt in the Bayeux Tapestry was the town of Hastings, may be correct if that town was located at Wilting Manor. This is because all traces of Hastings were removed, and no entry found in the Domesday Book. The archaeological record at Wilting shows a remarkable site, packed with unexplored archaeology, which awaits investigation. The site is planning a heritage centre and archaeologists are I am told welcome to visit and work with the trust, who are set up to develop the site for educational purposes.

We examined the so called lynchet on the top field at Wilting and confirmed that it could not be a lynchet, because the slope was too small for one to for. A lynchet is a natural bank formed on a slope which requires a minimum 5% slope. My conclusions in that respect are that this top field has had a major earthwork at some stage in the past, as earth from one side of the field is stacked on the other giving the appearance of a lynchet. Even a cursory inspection will show that this is not possible to form at the top of all four sides of the same hill. The conclusion therefore is that this flat hilltop is man made. It cannot be confirmed as man made in Norman times, but it cannot be ruled out, since it is reported in the Carmen that they 'restored the dismantled forts'. Given the evidence of Iron Age activity on this site it would seem probable that this is what the Carmen is referring to. No such forts (in the plural) exist anywhere else along this coast, providing yet another explanation, having never before been revealed in any analysis of the events of the Norman Invasion. The discovery of these unreported and archaeological records further confirms the authenticity of the source documents examined and by inference the authenticity of the site as the Norman Invasion site.

The evidence we looked at up till now contributes to our understanding of exactly where the Norman Invasion took place. The next element provides absolute documentary and scientific evidence that cannot in my view be discredited. That evidence comes in the form of the Domesday Book evidence.

The Crowhurst battlefield 'plain'

222

Our journey has caused us to re-examine the documents written within 150 years of the battle in the light of a new understanding of where the Battle of Hastings must have taken place. Having concluded that the camp was at the port of Hastings pre1066 we can see that the Carmen confirms that Harold's standards were visible on the night before the battle. In order for this to be true the Saxon camp had to be much nearer the sea than Battle Abbey, nearly five miles by road over the ridge of the South Downs that surrounds that area. The Carmen also confirms Harold's standards were set on the top of the hill. The highest hill in the area is the Ridge that surrounds Hastings, which cuts the view of the sea off from anyone behind that ridge.

At the time I did the investigation into the Norman Invasion site I did not know for certain where the battle took place. None the less the evidence of the Domesday survey shows conclusively that the most damaged of all manors was in fact the manor of Crowhurst and not Wilting. This is with the benefit of hindsight a conclusion that is hard evidence that Crowhurst is confirmed as the site of the Battle of Hastings, because the battle would destroy everything and leave nothing of value. At least some infrastructure would be left at the Norman camp, since it is reported that the first sheriffs of Hastings took over there when appointed by the Normans after the battle.

The image below shows the amalgamated Domesday data, by geographic area, rather than the isolated manors. The progressive loss of value we saw in our desktop analysis shows the values of manors dropping west of the real battle site at Crowhurst. Battle Abbey is hardly effected compared to those manors that follow the main road to Pevensey, avoiding the pale yellow area of Battle Abbey's lands altogether.

DOMESDAY DATA

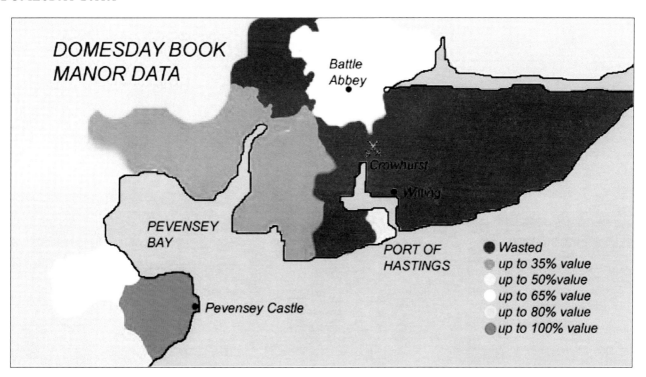

This Domesday data confirms that the manor value and its later value after the Invasion, was directly related to the ability to connect by road to Wilting Manor. Those manors directly connected by road to Wilting Manor, and closest to the Invasion site, suffered the greatest loss. Those located further away from the correct battle site decreased in a logical and progressive scientific reduction, based upon distance (graph2) and the layout of the road network. Hence Catsfield to the west of Crowhurst avoids the greater devastation of those directly west of Battle Abbey. This is an explanation of how the wasted manors of Sussex reveal the correct site of the camp of William the Conqueror, as well as the Battle of Hastings. This is new information not available in any other study of this subject.

The Domesday manor values, by virtue of this scientific data analysis, confirms in a scientific analysis that the town of Battle could not have been the site of the Battle of Hastings, because it suffered the same relatively low degradation as other manors on the London Road, which were quite a distance from Wilting. Percentages alone do not tell the whole story. The record shows Battle still having a value of £30 at the time of the battle (a not inconsiderable sum) and a value of £40.5s when the Domesday survey was compiled twenty years later. There is no logical explanation for these values, if the battle had really taken place at the town or parish of Battle. This is because the value at the time of the battle had to be zero (wasted) if the battle had taken place there. The parish of Battle retained 62% of its pre-invasion value and is well down the list of manors that were affected, because it was off the main route used to forage for supplies. The Domesday Book therefore reveals both the site of the Norman Invasion and where the battle really took place, by the correct interpretation of the manor values recorded in that book.

These manor values provide a compelling logic, since they also confirm that the road from Wilting to Pevensey did not in fact pass through the site at Battle town as the major thoroughfare. The belief that it did is due to inadequate research of the pre-medieval road structure in the Hastings peninsular, by earlier researchers, who appear to have reached conclusions without any data or study of the ground to support such claims. The research reported in this book confirms Telham Hill as being the crossroads at which the Norman army could exit the peninsular via the Forewood along the Powdermills track to Pevensey, not Telham Hamlet on the Ridge, as reported in many books. Harold had trapped the Norman Army in the Crowhurst valley, in the manor he was probably familiar with, because he owned it, as his father did and confirmed in the Domesday Book entry for Crowhurst. This is exactly where the major devastation occurred. Those manors west and north of the town of Battle suffered considerably more the Battle because the foraging route diverted around Battle, avoiding the steep valleys on the direct road to London. Crossing these two valleys made transportation of supplies along the Battle road extremely difficult, as it was a road that was treacherously steep. The development of the Ridge road at a later point in time confirmed the original route's unsuitability and by the 1700's the access to Crowhurst was by coach via Telham Heights, avoiding the original old London road. This was undoubtedly one of the primary reasons that the monk named Smith, who oversaw the building of the Abbey, moved the location of where the Abbey was eventually built. The real battlefield site was not only unsuitable for water, but made access directly along the road north almost impossible, due to the existence of those two steep valleys on the old main road between Crowhurst and Battle.

In many respects it was madness to start building the Abbey where the battle really took place, because there was no infrastructure to support it. The excuse given in the Chronicle of Battle Abbey was that there was no water where Harold is reported to have fallen. Yet supporters of Battle Abbey would prefer to believe that the Abbey site is authentic, as it had all the water it could possibly need. Whilst we can argue such niceties till the cows come home, you cannot argue with the Domesday data; it proves conclusively that the Abbey site was not built where the Battle of Hastings took place, or where Battle Abbey now stands.

The manor values in Domesday similarly prove that the Normans did not land or camp at Pevensey. This is an absurd proposition, built upon the false assumptions made in Victorian times that the references to Pevensey in those manuscripts we have looked at refer to the town of Pevensey. In order for all the documents we have examined to make sense, without any inconsistencies, it is necessary to understand that Pevensey was the area that the castle at the town of Pevensey controlled. Hastings was within that area and consequently all the documents that refer to Pevensey are referring to the area within the control of the castle, this includes the Bayeux Tapestry, which correctly reports the landing at Hastings.

As we established from our investigation of the Bayeux Tapestry Bishop Odo was eating fish at Hastings on the Friday 29th September 1066, the day of the Invasion. It would have been impossible to land at Pevensey and then to ride or sail to Hastings in one day in time to camp and eat supper at Hastings that night, as shown in the Bayeux Tapestry. Confirmation that this meal took place on the day of the landing is found in Wace's Roman de Rou, providing independent confirmation of the event recorded in the Worcester Chronicle.

We know that marching down the coast from Pevensey to Hastings was not possible, because of the impassability of the Combe Haven port area. This was a tidal waterway extending several miles inland. The logistics of moving 5,000 men in 1066 the distance from the old town of Hastings to Battle Abbey, in the time required, proves that this version of events is fatally flawed. William would not choose to sail past the entrance to the safe harbour of Hastings, in the days when boats were exceedingly dangerous, having taken the wind from St Valery the night before the landing. The fleet would have sailed right past the open undefended port. It would be military madness to suggest William would land his troops in front of the largest defensive castle on that part of the English south coast. William would then have to order his men to go come back down the coast to Hastings, by land, on a detour around Pevensey Bay the same day – something there was neither time nor tide to achieve. Even if it were technically possible, which it is not, it is not a viable concept for a man of William's military ability. Even a child could see that when you have an army to land you would not choose the best defended place along the south coast to bring your men ashore.

Wace's record of events tells us a raiding party left Hastings to check out Pevensey the day after the Invasion had taken place at Hastings. He reports that Pevensey was deserted – that is what the Domesday data confirms through the record of values of manors, at and after the Invasion – there is no other possible explanation of this data. The story that the landing site was at Pevensey town was built upon Victorian misunderstandings that sought to justify the understanding of Pevensey as being the town of that name. The effect of imposing that idea was to create many inconsistencies across the eight documents that recorded the events, since six manuscripts tell us that the landing was at Hastings. Simply by understanding that Pevensey was the area, rather than the town, all inconsistencies are removed, confirming the validity of that understanding.

Recognising that all the documents refer to the area of Pevensey provides the solution to identifying the true location of the landing and battle sites.

CHRONICLE OF BATTLE ABBEY

Our examination of the Chronicle of Battle Abbey confirms that the monks who built Battle Abbey held a written record of the place where the Normans camped. This place was detailed as being at the port of Hastings at a place called Hedgeland. The proposition in this document is that the port of Hastings was located pre1066 at Redgeland, a name that was wrongly transcribed by the monks 180 years after the battle. The fact that Redgeland is located in the deep-water section of the Combe Haven (a haven being where boats shelter from storms and is usually a harbour area) can hardly be a coincidence. The fact that it is exactly where the monks at Battle Abbey recorded William's camp to be located also cannot be a coincidence.

In the past this information has not been ignored by historians, because they did not know that Redgeland existed, probably any more than the monks who wrote the Chronicle. This document confirms the location, which is recorded as a wood name on the Ordnance Survey map at TQ778104.

It is my understanding that the educational trust, which looks after this land, welcomes visitors. I recommend that you contact the owners of the site. They need your support for heritage infrastructure and funding that they deserve. If you visit please make a donation. They are planning Norman walks and other educational initiatives aimed at all age groups. Until heritage facilities are in place you need good shoes and a stout heart; it is not suitable for the infirm. The property is owned by Hastings

Council, who have deliberately failed to support the trust tenants, in a disgraceful act of cultural negligence. I hope their embarrassment to be named will be rectified before the film cameras ask who is responsible for the obvious neglect of such an important Domesday property.

The naming of the camp site by the Chronicle of Battle Abbey cannot be ignored any longer. Those who seek to claim that this is just a coincidence rely upon the fact that the monks created a place called Hedgeland in the place they thought the Normans must have camped on the night of the battle. That place was not at a port and like the other place names the monks created around the year 1180AD (Malfosse, Herste etc) they were created in order to support the documents we now know were forged, which entitled them to claim to be free of taxes and state involvement.

It is now known that the documents that the monks created at that time, to protect themselves from attack by the exchequer, were forged along with the charters. Eleanor Searle in her excellent work entitled the Chronicle of Battle Abbey sums up with the words:

'Forgeries of the twelfth century abound, but usually we can only guess at the forgers' motives. In the Battle Chronicle the veil is for a moment lifted, and we can see the living world in which an abbot came to the pass where forgery was his last, best hope of victory.'

The conclusion we are forced to draw from this document and the re-examination of the Chronicle of Battle Abbey is that the monks could not throw away their source documents, because these were the only evidence they had to support the building of the Abbey by William. They therefore sought to create a tradition that the site where the Abbey was built was the site of the Battle of Hastings, in order to legitimise their claims. This is despite the confirmation, in the source document in the hand of the original author, that the Abbey site was moved from the battlefield at Herste, to the site where the Abbey now stands. Not only does that document name the site where the battle took place, but it confirms the name as 'Herste' and the fact it has a low wall as a landmark. It tells us that this place is low down on the western slope of the ridge, exactly where Crowhurst is found, with a low stone wall that was once an enclosure where men would meet; a place that was probably a well know landmark in the area, due to the rarity of stone constructions at that time.

Local tradition has assumed that the place the monks named Herste around 1180 to support their forged documents, was north west of the existing Abbey and therefore confirmed the location of the Abbey as the battle site. Our examination of the Chronicle of Battle Abbey shows that this is not what the document tell us. The tradition that relies upon this understanding of the Battle Chronicle is not supported by the written Latin. This shows without any possibility of contradiction, by an expert in the field, that the final building site of the Abbey was chosen because it was not the battlefield. It is therefore not possible for the Battle Abbey site to claim it is the battlefield, when this founding document shows it is not, and there is no alternative evidence. The tradition is therefore shown to be false, created by the church in order to justify what could not be justified in writing. The church relied upon the fact that it was recognised to have the authority of God and therefore could not lie. That authority lasted even through to the Victorian Age, resulting in the discrimination against documents that challenged this traditional thinking. Now we know better: The church lied.

The local knowledge gained by living in this area confirms that even until recently the people of the Crowhurst valley knew their village by the name 'Hurst' in Sussex dialect. It has a low stone wall, which our research confirms was part of an enclosure, where men met to do business, with the famous Crowhurst Yew growing within two meters of the wall. Evidence provided by Alan Meredith, the world's greatest Yew expert, confirmed that this tree must be at least 1,800 years old and might be a lot older. The confinement of the roots of that tree would make the Crowhurst Yew one of the slowest growing in the world. Our research confirms that the tree and the wall have been co-habiting since long before the Norman Invasion and would be at least 800 years old in 1066. It is therefore concluded that such a tree in the location of the battlefield would be recorded, because the Normans would have seen it.

The examination of the Chronicle of Battle Abbey text, shows without the possibility of contradiction that the monks created a false tradition, designed to reinforce their claim to legitimately be free of taxes or church interference. The battlefield oath, which gave the Abbey its special free services from the King, is fanciful to say the least. If there really were a battlefield oath it would have been recorded in the Bayeux Tapestry – a truly legitimate document designed to hang in William's own Abbey in Bayeux – there is no such oath in the Bayeux Tapestry or any other legitimate document of the time. This evidence should be enough to persuade even those who may still be sceptical.

What we can rely upon are the names given in the Chronicle, because they were surprisingly not invented. They were place names that were passed on to the monks, and that is why those names were included in the first 22 folios of the Battle Chronicle. The inclusion of those names identifies both the landing and camp site at Wilting Manor and also the Battle of Hastings site at Crowhurst. The monk who wrote that document confirmed the names, in order that they would support their case, at the same time noting that the Abbey had been moved from the legitimate battlefield. The inclusion of the original legitimate names for the camp at the port of Hastings and the location of the original battlefield at '*Herste*' is our second and most damning piece of evidence, as it confirms that the monks moved the Abbey from the battlefield. It is confirmed in that original hand that the Abbey had been moved '*not far off*'. Indeed, by the standards of the day it was not. This proof effectively reinforces the Domesday data, since one confirms the other – something that should be expected of true historical proof of evidence.

The battlefield oath is not supported in any other description of the Battle of Hastings, because it could not have happened. It, like the claim that William wanted to move the Abbey back to the '*original*' site at Battle, was a deliberate invention, designed to justify starting to build the Abbey in the place known as Herste. Any investigation by the King's men at the time would immediately identify the fraud if they visited the area, since the correct site of the original battle would be known, because the foundations at the original Abbey site had reached an advanced stage. The site of the '*hoar apple tree*' would also probably still be known (the original landmark for the Battle of Hastings according to the Saxon Chronicles). The inclusion of the original battlefield name (Herste) in the redrafted Chronicle was a brilliant deception that has lasted to this day. The lack of any archaeology or supporting documents for the Battle Abbey site reinforces the concept of a fraud designed to avoid taxes. Those who have researched the Chronicle know it to be a forgery, along with the Charters and land named after places in the Chronicle, all created around the same time at least 100 years after the battle. The purpose for which those places were re-created is known, but it has not been recognised that the tradition, which was created at the same time was the same fraud, without the documents to support it. The Chronicle of Battle Abbey was not made to be seen by you or I. It was designed to support the legal claims being made against the Abbey by the King. It was noted by Eleanor Searle as '*a last resort*' which failed. We now know that the whole of the document cannot be relied upon in regards to the elements that the monks needed to add – namely the oath and the moving of the Abbey back to the battlefield. As we know, the Chronicle never says that this occurred. It lets the reader assume that it was moved back. As I have stated before I consider it brilliant drafting and misinformation in the interests of God's work, but none the less a lie. That lie required those who believed in God to believe that their church was infallible – a conclusion that we now know was seriously faulted in the 1100s.

I recognise that the Chronicle of Battle Abbey is the document which the monks hoped would get them out of a legal hole with the King. It was a forgery, which was undoubtedly copied from an earlier document. The evidence to come to this conclusion is in the fact that the names from the original document must have come from somewhere. Since these names were of real places, originating prior to the writing of the forged manuscript, the conclusion must be drawn that the names where in an original source document from which they were copied. It may explain why the first 22 folios are in one hand, the hand of the master forger, whereas the bulk of those that follow are in a different hand – thereby removing the person concerned from direct contact with those who were required to finish the manuscript legitimately.

As part of the process of laying out their case the forger took the original information, written in the original hand by what may have been an original witness of the Invasion, putting in the battlefield oath paragraph and the one where William is told that the Abbey has been moved against his wishes. At this point another new paragraph is added laying out the terms of the oath, whereby the monks will receive 'wine... more abundant than any other great Abbey'. It is at this point I found credibility starting to stretch, since the monk states that it is 'a tradition', as if to avoid confirming what he knows to be a lie. After all why would those who built the Abbey need a tradition, as justification for the building of the Abbey, or any of the terms of the oath they stated had been made by William, if what they were telling us were believed to be true and recorded from the time of the events? If it had been written at the time it was claimed it could not have been a tradition, but based upon certain knowledge. The admission that at the time of writing the forged document (one hundred years after the Invasion) the Abbey was built upon tradition reinforces our knowledge that the monks rewrote the document later effectively confirming it was written much later? That lie, relying upon tradition as justification for the existence of the Abbey on the battlefield, has been repeated to this day. They even named the town Battle to create the tradition – brilliant misinformation and an orchestrated deception.

There is one further element that I have realised since writing the chapter on the Chronicle. I realised that the evidence in the Chronicle shows that the monks started to create their Abbey at Herste (Crowhurst) and then moved it to Battle, when the monk Smith came from France on the orders of the King. However the evidence we have recognised in our examination shows that the monks started the original battlefield Abbey at the bottom of the western side of the Ridge. They did not start it at the top of the hill (Ridge) where Harold was reported to have fallen – despite the clause in the Chronicle that states they planned to build the Abbey upon the very place where Harold fell.

At first impression this appears to be an inconsistency – and as I have stated on a number of occasions inconsistencies tell you that any document based upon an inconsistency reveals a flaw in the explanation.

In this case the inconsistency is in the belief that the battlefield oath took place. We have in front of us the evidence that shows it did not. This is exactly because those monks charged with building the Abbey on the original site, before the involvement of the French monks, knew that they were charged with building the Abbey on the site of the battlefield. They could not possibly have been charged with building it on the place where Harold fell. This is of crucial importance because if they had really received instructions to that effect they would have started to build the Abbey at the top of the Crowhurst Great Field. They did not – they started it at the bottom. This confirms that the battlefield oath was a later lie.

This explanation of events tells us quite clearly that the battlefield oath, if made by William, was not specific as to where the Abbey should be built. This in part explains why the monk Smith had the freedom to move the Abbey where he liked. If, as has been supposed, he moved it without the consent of the King, to a place that was not the battlefield, then that would probably have been a capital offence if true. In the absence of the battlefield oath he made the decision to move it because it was in the best interests of the Abbey and his King. The fact that the Abbey was started down at the bottom of the Ridge indirectly confirms that the clause in the Chronicle requiring it to be built where Harold's banner fell was a key lie, otherwise building would have started at the top of the hill. This oath is then backed by the inserted fraudulent paragraphs that tell us the King was angry, which is out of chronological order and is the same dubious paragraph as the text confirming the Abbey remain free of taxes. That last paragraph can therefore be shown to be the lie, by confirmation of the events that actually happened. The monks sought to justify their presence as a tradition, as the last throw of the dice, which ultimately failed.

The conclusion form the Chronicle' of Battle Abbey is that this document not only supports the Domesday data, but actually gives us the name of the battle site as Herste. It also confirms the location of the Battle of Hastings, at Herste (phonetic pronunciation) and confirms that building work was started on the Abbey before it was moved a number of years later – as we have always suspected from other analysis of our evidence. The final piece of evidence provided was that as well as the location being known it had a landmark in the form of a low wall, most probably made of stone, as stone walls were very rare in those days – exactly as found in the place the research has identified as the Crowhurst battlefield.

WACE

Our study of the Wace manuscript (16,000 lines of battle poem) provides insight that no other document can provide. It is now known to be an authentic record of the Norman Invasion, because it identifies line of sight observation between the Norman and Saxon camp on the night of the battle, as well as other information, such as the layout of the battlefield, which we have confirmed as correct. Harold's standards at Telham Hill could be seen from the Norman camp at the correct location of the port of Hastings on the day the Saxons arrived and night before the battle. Wace is the one who tells us that the Saxons build a ditch across the battle site. He also reports that the battlefield is enclosed at three places. It is our contention that the Great Field at Crowhurst is where the Battle of Hastings took place and we have identified such a ditch where evidence of the defence remains as a tree line and lynchet. This is where the Saxon defence was located.

Wace tells us the Normans would '*have to come to Harold*' and this is the reason that stakes were placed across the battlefield – in order that William's horses were rendered useless. This forced the Normans to fight all day. It is clear from Wace's document that the Normans were at several times in danger of losing the battle. We are told that the battlefield starts with rising ground, over which the Normans first appear and then there is a plain where the army assembles. We are told that there is a bad ditch next to the plain and the English fall back on their rising ground of a steep hill.

Wace provides information on the battlefield that is wholly supported by the site we have identified at Crowhurst as the Great Field. The name Crowhurst, being identified as the name for the village of Hurst as pronounced in that village in old Sussex dialect. Not only does Wace identify the place known as the Malfosse immediately adjacent to the battlefield, but we have located the path that leads through the undergrowth, from the battlefield to the bridge that once crossed the ravine where the Normans died. That ancient Roman track is cut into the access way over a meter deep, showing its construction and usage over a long period of history. It is still exactly as described in the Carmen: '*waste ground it was overgrown with brambles and thistles, and could scarcely be seen in time; and it engulfed great numbers. ...*'

Wace's manuscript was discredited in Victorian times, but we have shown that it is wholly reliable. Wace is the only scribe to report Harold being shot over the eye with an arrow and living on to near the end of the battle. Evidence which we have seen in the Bayeux Tapestry confirms this to be correct. Wace also is the only person to confirm that Harold was tricked into making the oath of allegiance in Bayeux Cathedral, whilst being held hostage in France. Whilst we cannot know whether this is true or not we do know that the French accept Wace as a legitimate source and the conclusion must be drawn that Wace is the best available written source for the information concerning the events on the battle site and the events of the Norman Invasion. What we can establish beyond doubt is that the main descriptive dialogue confirms both the landing at Wilting and the battle taking place in the Crowhurst valley. This is by virtue of the detailed description given by Wace, which is not included in any other manuscript.

TITHE MAP

We looked at the 1843 Tithe Map of Crowhurst, because it reveals information that is useful in confirming events even as long ago as 1066. It is a written record made before modern changes when the railway came through the south of England. It shows the roads in existence at that time and also includes details of roads and tracks that have long since disappeared, allowing me to recreate the elements that would have made up the battlefield in 1066. The map shows that the Great Field of

Crowhurst, where we believe the battle was located, adjoins the Crowhurst Parish boundary. Whilst studying the map we found evidence that it was common practice for trees on parish boundaries to be used as marker trees. We identified the field next to crossroads at Telham Hill on the parish boundary as Apple Tree Field. This provided colloquial evidence that the name of the Battle of Hastings, recorded as the battle of *'The Hoary Apple Tree'* in the Saxon Chronicles, ties directly to that site. We also identified the location of the tracks connecting the crossroads at Telham Hill, along the parish boundary towards Pevensey, thus avoiding the need to travel to Battle in order to get off the peninsular upon which the Normans were based. This observation was supported by the Domesday data.

Dawson in his classic work called Hastings Castle identifies 19 examples of where trees are used to mark parish boundaries, introducing the confirmation that the use of the name the *'Battle of the Hoar Apple Tree'* was probably because that tree was located on a parish boundary. The tithe map also confirms the name of the field that stretches from the bottom of the hill to the top was called the Great Field. Whilst it had been subdivided by 1843 enough existed to identify a name that also has a colloquial connection to the site of the Battle of Hastings.

Knowledge of the local track ways, confirmed by looking back in time at the pre1843 map of Crowhurst, provides compelling information to support Crowhurst as the only logical battle site.

CROWHURST MANOR HOUSE

We examined the ruin of the Crowhurst Manor house site, because it fulfils all the requirements of the Chronicle of Battle Abbey. It appears to be the marker for the true site of the Battle of Hastings, where the original Abbey was started, before it was moved upon the orders of the monk from France. It is located at the bottom of the western end of the area known as the Ridge, and has a low stone wall that marks the spot. The wall has been there for at least 1,000 years, because it confines the roots of the famous Crowhurst yew, and one of the slowest growing in the country. That wall marks an ancient enclosure and was known as a meeting place long before the church was built next to the same site in the centre of Crowhurst.

The Manor House was shown to be incorrectly catalogued as a 13th century manor house. Our research confirmed there is no written record of it ever having been built by the De Scotneys in the Crowhurst parish records. Recent archaeological work by Samantha Worrall Bsc on the other hand confirmed the presence of two buttresses and more previously unreported walls, which suggests that the Manor House was where the monks started to build William's Abbey before it was moved.

The original assessment of the building carried out by W. S. Walford in 1854 and was shown to be flawed because he did not have all the relevant information. Whilst the building is large enough to be a seat of government he concluded it must be attached to a wooden hall, with no evidence to support this. The new evidence shows the whole building was built from stone and was probably a two storey ecclesiastical building.

As a result of recent excavations by Ms Worrall we now know that there are hidden walls made of stone where Walford believed this wooden hall was located. We have also seen the part of the original building that still remains has Norman arches similar to the undercroft of Battle Abbey and a style and scale similar to that employed by Battle Abbey. Whilst it is recognised that the building is mainly 13century it is clearly adapted from an earlier building and must have been at least two stories high because of the buttresses. It is my contention that the examination in depth of this building will confirm that it was built as the original Abbey, which William ordered to be built upon the battle site. It is also in an east/west elevation and only proper archaeological excavation can confirm its original use and purpose. The owner has agreed that this work may be done and so there is nothing to stop English Heritage, who are in charge of this ruin, to undertake the appropriate exploration work. I believe it is their duty to undertake such work in the national heritage interest.

CROSSBOW

An excavation was carried out in the Great Field, Crowhurst, in order to satisfy my curiosity as to whether any remains of the Battle of Hastings still remain in the soil. As a result of one exploratory pit being made in the Great Field an object was found, which armoury museum owner and historical expert Mr Foulkes-Halbard of the Filching Armoury Museum confirmed to me as being a very early medieval crossbow. That excavation was photographed and then covered back up, where it may remain if it survived the initial exposure.

The existence of altered bowmen in the Bayeux Tapestry appears to endorse the existence of crossbowmen at the Battle of Hastings. The Carmen quite specifically confirms they were there. In consequence the identification of the unusual object as a crossbow should be of great interest to historians. My research appeared to confirm that it was probably a Turkish footbow of a very early type identical to the design known as the Mathew Paris Chronica Minora c 1240AD. The conclusion I reached being that the bow was of a composite construction, with ears. Further examination of the colour photographs confirmed that the front of the bow almost certainly has a ring attachment and originally of metal construction.

Our investigation of this element of our search for proof of the Battle of Hastings confirms that crossbows were certainly used at that battle, introduced by the Normans. The documentary evidence of the Carmen supports this and our further extensive study of the Bayeux Tapestry also confirmed the alteration of the Tapestry. Those alterations appear to have taken place around the time that the Pope banned crossbows. Consequently we have a motive to explain why the alterations may have taken place quite some considerable time after the Tapestry had been made. By that time it would have been hanging in Bayeux Cathedral and so local seamstresses would have been forced to carry out the adaption work without the relevant coloured threads.

BAYEUX TAPESTRY

I revisited Bayeux in 2010 to check all the details that had come my way over the 24 years doing this research. I wanted to know if the Tapestry, like the documents we had looked at, could support matters in relation to the battle site not being located in the traditional location. I wanted to know if like the Invasion site there were clues that had previously been ignored, due to a misunderstanding of where the battle actually took place.

It might be thought that the Bayeux Tapestry is quite unspecific in terms of where the battle took place. Looking at it with new eyes I was not surprised to find that like everything in those scenes, there is a well-defined element that allows you to confirm the specific location. This was not only the Invasion site, but the battlefield as well.

I have saved this element of the rediscovery of the site of the Norman Invasion and the site of the Battle of Hastings until last, because that was the order of events before writing the book. The thing that is apparent first is not at the beginning of the Tapestry, but at the end. It is the very end section where the Normans can be seen pursuing the English off of the battlefield. We saw that the only way off the correct battlefield site was at two different levels – exactly as shown in the Bayeux Tapestry. Some departing along the top of the ridge and the others along the lower path, where men are being chased on horseback and also caught in briars, as we have been told happened in the Malfosse. That scene makes perfect sense in relation to the Great Field where those elements exist. The idea that escape from the Battle Abbey site in two different levels or locations makes no sense at all and it has never been argued that this is what is meant by the change in scenery.

As a result of the research conducted in relation to the archers, and the battle, the Tapestry gives us a lot of information related to bowmen. The Bayeux Tapestry shows us 30 bowmen using different types of bows. There are two basic types, being short bows and recursive composition bows. Close study of those bowmen confirms that at least 14 and possibly more are crossbow men.

The evidence for this is in the close examination of the Bayeux Tapestry in the way the bows are held and the adaption that has taken place in the stitching. Bowmen are shown to have bowstrings that go behind their shoulders and do not cross their forearm. Something that is impossible unless illustrating the use by a crossbowman. In one case the stock of the crossbow is still present (archer 8). This leads to the understanding that whilst the bows are drawn in the upright position the attention to detail confirms they were intended to be used side-on parallel to the ground. This style follows the graphical tradition of the time in showing crossbowmen in drawings using their bows in an upright manner. Stitches are missing, with threads the wrong colour. Many of these adaptations are in different stitching from the rest of the Tapestry in a lower quality of work. Many of the bowmen are coloured in rudimentary form, with crossbow bolts shown shorter than conventional arrows. Some of the arrows appear to have been extended or altered in elevation. In some the archers are not even holding the string or the arrow.

What all this information tells us is that we are right to conclude that the Bayeux Tapestry is confirming that crossbowmen were used at the Battle of Hastings. These crossbowmen were probably Turkish mercenaries, as Mr Foulkes-Halbard the armoury expert, confirmed his belief to be. The specific information regarding bows does not prove that the Battle of Hastings took place in Crowhurst, but yet again we have the discovery of information that ties the discovery to Crowhurst – namely the discovery of that object in the Great Field at Crowhurst.

We then looked at the ground portrayed in the Bayeux Tapestry and there was an absolute fit between the ground shown on the Tapestry and the route taken by the Normans to the battlefield, from their camp site at Wilting. No-one has ever sought to claim that this could be done, because it can only apply to the correct route. We know exactly where the Normans camped, at the port of Hastings by the wood called Redgeland. We also know that the Battle of Hastings was on the south side of Telham Hill in the Crowhurst valley. Armed with this information we followed the ground as the story unfolded.

We noticed that trees where drawn as scene markers identifying each of the sub sequences of the movement between the Invasion site and the battlefield. We also noted that these trees were each drawn differently.

The conclusion that is impossible to avoid is that both the ground and the trees in conjunction with one and other identify the exact route between Redgeland Wood and the site of the battle on the south side of Telham Hill. Each of the trees identifies a specific identifying character into the branches. Those identifying characters are specific landscape markers that cannot be tied to any other site. The very last tree shown on the Tapestry is identified as 'the hoary apple tree' which stood on the top of the hill on the parish boundary and marks the end of the battle. It is possible to confirm that it is that particular apple tree, because there is an apple embroidered next to the ground where the tree stands.

Many have considered the evidence provided by the Bayeux Tapestry to be circumstantial. It is because they have not had the opportunity to study the Tapestry in relation to the correct battle site. To me it is the additional and a most compelling proof of not only the authenticity of the Tapestry but an absolute confirmation of the correct battle site. We know that there is absolutely no doubt about the provenance of the Tapestry. We know that the people who made it knew that King William was going to see it and it would be hung in Bayeux Cathedral, where everyone else who was important who attended the Invasion would see it. We also know that a great deal of care was taken to ensure every single detail of the Tapestry was correct. It should therefore come as no surprise to learn that the elements that made up the ground and location markers, followed the same rigorous attention to detail.

Knowing the ground between William's camp at Wilting Manor and the battle site in Crowhurst I can confirm that every detail, as I have explained it in the chapter dealing with that matter, is correct. The conclusion I draw is that this is not wishful thinking, because it would simply be impossible for anyone to make what is in the Bayeux Tapestry fit the route between Wilting and Crowhurst by wishing it. The fact is it fits, because the person who commissioned that work wished to make sure that those who attended knew exactly where each of those events took place. In identifying the trees as landmarks and making sure the ground was in the correct proportion it would not be possible at some future time to make a mistake about where the battle happened. Those who claim that the first hill is smaller than the last, because it is not important, have failed to recognise that the size of the hills simply identified where they were. The largest hill was the last hill in the dialogue of events, not the first. The trees grew where they did, because they were fixtures in the landscape, which the Normans had spent two weeks becoming acquainted with.

I do not accept, and never will accept, the hypothesis that there is nothing important about the ground. If that were the case all of the ground would have been embroidered the same. The slope of the ground records exactly where the ground was rising or falling when these events took place. The Crowhurst yew is faithfully recorded exactly where Harold would have been on horseback, when the Normans are first reported as arriving on the battle site. The valleys and plain are in exactly the right place where the Bayeux Tapestry shows them and Wace confirms the same story in manuscript form. The Carmen confirms the place where William's plan to set the cavalry in the front of the attack is foiled by Harold's plan to attack from the wood adjacent to the first Malfosse incident. None of these events can be by coincidence drawn to fit exactly the ground as it is along the main Hastings to London road between Wilting and Crowhurst. It is the same now as it was then, nothing has changed and consequently anyone can walk the same walk and see this for themselves, just by walking it as the Normans did.

Historians would like to believe there is some great mystery about the Battle of Hastings that needs them to interpret the documents written at the time. We have kept our interest within 150 years of the battle to avoid contamination by reported works that are re-evaluations of earlier writings. The tell tale sign that informs you that what you have read is true is the one thing that no other document has claimed. It is that if you accept the proposal that the Normans landed at Hastings, camped at Wilting Manor and then fought the Battle of Hastings in the Great Field at Crowhurst, then none of the documents written at the time or within 150 years of the battle contain any inconsistencies or contradictions. All have perfectly plausible observations of the events with acceptable explanation. The Malfosse is exactly where it was reported to be, next to the battle site. That site was confined and unable to be circumnavigated by the Normans, who were trapped by Harold on the Hastings peninsular. The Domesday manor wastage pattern is explainable, the port of Hastings is revealed to be within line of sight of the Saxon camp on the night of the battle, and the logistics of how the battle could start to be fought within three hours of leaving the Norman camp, is explained.

I am completely sure the Battle of Hastings was just like any other. Men died and left their mark both in the Landscape and by the possessions they left in the soil, when their tunic buttons were torn off, when the horses died and left their shoes to rot on the hillside. Men hid their precious possessions before battle, never to return to collect them. They left broken weapons and belt buckles where they fell – only to be recovered a thousand years later using modern recovery techniques. Those who tell you that there is no archaeological record of the Battle of Hastings are doing so because no one has looked in the right place. Now that place is known the evidence will be found.

ENGLISH HERITAGE

I came into this research project as an amateur who was almost certainly considered by everyone who had any connection to Battle Abbey, Pevensey Castle, or anything to do with writing books about the history of England –a heretic. I had after all committed the greatest heresy of all time. I claimed that the Normans did not land at Pevensey. Now there is the even greater taboo – to claim the site of the Battle of Hastings was not fought where English Heritage says it is – at Battle Abbey.

The reason for writing this book is to make the people who care about the heritage of England aware of the evidence that clearly shows the site of the Norman Invasion was at Wilting Manor and the site of the Battle of Hastings was in Crowhurst Valley. I haven't spent 24 years of my life compiling this work to put my work in the drawer like Wace and the Chronicle of Battle Abbey.

Arguing that the existence of the traditional site justifies the battlefield sign at Battle Abbey ignores historical truth, because as we know there cannot be two sites of the Battle of Hastings. There cannot be one for the benefit of those who make money from Battle Abbey, no matter how important that site may be, and the one in Crowhurst supported by the historical documents. The site of the Battle of Hastings cannot be left to commercial opinion influenced by out of date analysis of the available information.

We could argue these matters until the cows come home, as to who is right, and who is wrong. I take the view that this does not allow English Heritage to charge customers over £15 for a family to walk around a field of no particular significance. Telling those people it is the field where the Battle of Hastings was fought, when there is firm historical evidence that shows this is incorrect, undermines the credibility of the history experts who sit behind them.

My understanding of the law of England is that if you want to put up a sign outside of your building that has information on it that is misleading – and I say that telling people that Battle Abbey is the site of the Battle of Hastings, without any hard evidence of that is misleading. Indeed you are committing an offence. To knowingly take money and continue to do that based upon a proven fraudulent tradition is an offence under the Trade Descriptions Act.

If you cannot prove your case in a court of law, when evidence exists that can show a judge that the authoritative documents of the time identify the battle site is somewhere else, then it is the law that you have to answer to and not me. I am not going to waste my time and yours arguing the niceties of justification of the site of the Battle of Hastings, based upon the likelihood of latrines being used with one bucket of water or two, as has been presented to me by a poorly informed expert who simply seeks to continue the commercial operations at Battle Abbey. I will simply end this document by asking you, the reader, to decide whether English Heritage should be supported in their stand against investigating the true site of the Battle of Hasting or not? They invested quite a lot of public money in the battlefieldstrust.com. Shouldn't that excellent organisation be looking at the evidence at Hastings and employing their brilliant minds to preserve the real battlefield?

I think I might be more than a little upset to have paid my money to walk around Battle Abbey field when it is known that English Heritage know that it is definitely not the right field. Taking money from people in the name of Heritage requires more than English Heritage acting as gatekeepers of the truth, only to be revealed when they like it, or not at all.

My view is that English Heritage are intentionally continuing to operate the fraud at Battle Abbey, which was started by the Church, who clearly knew what they were doing. The wording of the stone they have put in place at Battle Abbey is located here:

It is clear to everyone that there is no Abbey visible above ground dating back to the Battle. It is also clear from the inscribed stone that there is no attempt inside the grounds (once people have paid to get in), to mislead the public by claiming that it is known that this is the battle site. Indeed the very cleverly worded deception is confirmed by its reliance upon the claim of tradition. If it were proven to be the battle site it would say so, as in the case of every other proven battlefield site:

The stone says:

The Traditional site of
The high alter of Battle Abbey
Founded to commemorate
The victory of Duke William
On 14th October 1066
The high alter was placed to mark
The spot where King Harold died

This is a clear and clever deception since it avoids confirming it is the site of the Battle of Hastings. It doesn't even say this is the traditional site of the Battle of Hastings. Indeed the only document that exists dating from this time sits in the British Library and confirms that the abbey was moved from the spot where Harold died on the battlefield. This stone is therefore a lie, as is the sign outside the building and also on every Ordnance Survey map.

The Church admitted they moved the Abbey, because it was the best place to build it, and the evidence to confirm what they wrote themselves is in both the Chronicle of Battle Abbey and also in the Domesday Book. I don't care what the Saxon Chronicles or in fact any of the other documents we have studied tell us. I rely wholly upon the evidence of the Domesday Book. That tells us precisely, in terms that any judge and jury can understand that the Battle of Hastings did not and could not have taken place at Battle Abbey. It confirms the landing and camp site at Wilting Farm in Hastings, as well as the correct location of the battle in the Crowhurst valley immediately adjacent to it. Any expert who says otherwise has not looked at the evidence recently and English Heritage are I believe making a big mistake if they think the public will continue to swallow this fraud, when the details are known and have been known to them for at least ten years. The time has come to take down those signs at Battle Abbey claiming it to be confirmed as the site of the Battle of Hastings, or amend them to confirm that their sole claim to fame of that site is based upon a tradition that is known to be false. In the meantime it would be reasonable for English Heritage or East Sussex County Council to do the right thing and make money available to the Sussex County Archaeologist to allow him to do the job that the people of this country expect. It is his patch and he would be able to appoint independent investigators of the Crowhurst Manor site and battlefield in the interest of us all. Indeed it is a mystery as to why the battlefieldstrust.com have not taken up the challenge to investigate. They received a lot of money from English Heritage to look at Bosworth, but seem to have difficulty recognising the importance of the site of the Battle of Hastings. Perhaps now the matter is documented properly they will be allowed to work with the County Archaeologist to look at the site properly. I cannot think of a better equipped organisation to do a proper investigation.

I understand better than most how the academic fraternity try to deal with difficult persistent people like me, especially when they are caught with their fingers in the till. It is difficult not to reach that conclusion when looking at how this matter has been dealt with by the English Heritage experts Those who resist the correct route that should be followed will, like Harold, believe they have the advantage. However, like Harold, even the best laid plans sometimes come a cropper through unexpected events. Now this matter has been made public, battlefield relics are sure to materialise, because of their value and the identification of the real battlefield. It is a remarkable coincidence that the farm that forms the lower section of the correct battlefield is currently for sale – perhaps a philanthropist will take an interest? Normal relics that would be found on a battlefield would have little value. Those found on the site of the Battle of Hastings would have immense value, once authenticated by their location.

There is, despite having covered almost every single element of the Battle of Hastings another mystery waiting to be uncovered, not by me, but by someone close to this story. I came into this research because of a vision that, like the lady who discovered Sutton Hoo, cannot be explained in conventional historical research terms. It is for that reason I have limited myself to only those things that can be shown to be proven, through the traditional methodologies of historical research.

Any element that cannot be explained is usually ignored in most historical analysis. The one that I leave you with is the one I looked at many years ago relating to Harold's burial. In the Carmen it tells us that Harold was buried quickly under a pile of stones on a headland overlooking the shore and the sea. It was '*in the earth on the high summit of a cliff*' in fact, overlooking the shore and the sea. William commissioned a special marker stone with the epitaph:

'By the Duke's command, O Harold, you rest here king,
That you may still be guardian of the shore and sea'

Wace didn't know who buried Harold, which is a shame given his ability to provide information not found in any other document. He believed the body was taken to Waltham Abbey. However there is no evidence of that. Poitiers tells us that William refused Harold's body to his mother, who offered his weight in gold. William then gave the body to a man named Mallet who buried it by the sea shore.

William of Malmesbury repeats the Waltham story, but this time his mother takes Harold there after receiving the body. Harold's mother came from Thurrock in Essex where she lived.

I believe I know what happened to Harold and if there is any element of this story that explains the mystery of why this story has emerged at this time - it is because Harold was the last Saxon king. William took the crown illegitimately from the last of the royal blood line of the traditional English monarchy - lineage that supposedly went back to Arthurian legend and from there back to the biblical King David. This was a blood line that legend says was appointed by God. William effectively terminated that genetic link with the past. As an act of disrespect he did what the Carmen tells us: he buried Harold under a pile of stones on the headland and gave him a Viking style funeral. I know this, but not from any historical research. You can therefore disagree with me and I will not be offended, since the point of historical research has now finished.

That headland was where Hye House now stands in the Crowhurst valley overlooking the shore and also the battle site. He was buried under a pile of stones where the car park has been built. I used to live at Hye House before this adventure started. The view taken from that position is shown earlier, for those who are still with me. That hye (Olde English) hill was just off the main battlefield and retains that name until this day.

However William remained at his camp at Wilting Manor, at the port of Hastings, for a further two weeks after the battle. During that time he had doubts as to whether he had done the right thing with Harold. William had carried the papal banner into battle and was concerned about the negative effects of failing to bury Harold with the honour that his royal blood was due. It became clear that people were going to the hye hill overlooking the shore and the sea to pay their respects to Harold, in part out of curiosity, but also out of respect. It was easy to see that such a place could become a pilgrimage site and could easily become a rallying point for the revival of the Saxon blood line. That would be a direct threat to the future authority of his Norman authority and descendants.

As a consequence William ordered that the gravestone and Harold be collected from Hye House hill and taken back to the Norman camp. There Harold was buried with honour according to Poitier's version of events. William ordered the new grave to be hidden and I believe the stone hidden in the manor house or grounds of the port, because the sheriffs of Hastings were positioned there to ensure the secret remained hidden, as it has remained to this day.

It was the custom in those days to bury the dead on a headland and so after Harold's body had been taken back to the Norman camp at Wilting the decision was made to rebury Harold in secret. There was no possibility of preserving the body for transport in those days. Harold was therefore reburied on the ridge overlooking the Invasion site, no more than ten minutes from both the manor house and pre1090 castle at the old port. The burial site was in a wood with no buildings near by.

However someone knew, because after the Normans had left to conquer the rest of the country, never to come back, a church was built on the site soon after William died. It was a church which had no supporting population. It was connected to both Wilting and the Invasion port by direct footpaths to the depths of a private wood owned by the Count of Eu and his descendants, who was given Hastings by William. At least three times the church was started and three times the building was destroyed. The story was put out that the destruction of the church was done by the devil in order to keep inquisitive eyes at bay. The people taking the church down were the Normans, who had instructions to keep the burial site secret. The church is to this day called the Church in the Wood and it is my contention that this small Norman church is the final resting place of the last Saxon king of England. However the marker stone, which William commissioned, did not go with Harold's body and remains to be found. When found it will prove the authenticity of the site and also the burial.

According to my vision Harold will not remain in his grave much longer. His Saxon blood line is stirring again and according to the legend, those things which were hidden will be revealed by God's own hand, when that blood line re-emerges.

This story started in Crowhurst in East Sussex with a vision in 1986, but does not end in Crowhurst. The reason I dedicated 24 years of my life to this project is recorded in my first book called the Book of Life, published in 2003. It was explained to me that in order to write such a book it was necessary for the author to have proof of authority. I was told in my vision that proof of authority came in three parts. The first part of that proof is historical proof, contained in this book; the second proof is both historical and genetic proof, relying upon the authority of science. That proof will be published shortly. The third proof will also be in the next book and, like this one, reveals the roots of another compelling historical myth. Clearly it is not possible to read a book such as this without asking the question why I started to look for the site of the Battle of Hastings in the first place. All that can definitely be known is that no living soul could have known in 1986 what I and you know now.

I will at this stage leave the prophecy to the prophets and thank you for taking the time to follow my exploits. Now at the end of this work I am as certain as I can be that neither the Carmen, nor Poitiers, made up those versions of the events of Harold's burial, even though at first one appears to contradict the other. Malmesbury's version of taking Harold's body to Waltham is romantic make-believe in comparison. It is no longer taken seriously by most historians, who can see no evidence to support what was an unsubstantiated third party report designed to get his paymaster William off the hook, having disgraced his position, by failing to give Harold the honours he was due, even in death. The Carmen and Poitiers on the other hand wrote down what they knew to be true and appear to be reports of events as they happened. Both recorded the truth as they knew it from the same story, each knowing only part of the final story. Yet again those who read these events failed to understand the chronology and therefore assumed them to be wrongly recorded.

It should therefore come as no surprise to historians or archaeologists if something unexpected happens in the next few years that will blow the whole story onto our front pages. The evidence is now before you and time will be my judge. None of these great historical documents that we have studied lied, with the sole exception of the Chronicle of Battle Abbey. Only the Church had the motive to lie, and then only in support of God's work as they saw it. It never occurred to those who lived in the Victorian age that the Church was capable of such deceit – and of course that was the reason the fraud operated for so long unchallenged. It continues to this day by claiming that deceit to be a tradition. The error in understanding the documentation has been in the eyes of those who looked at them, not in those who wrote them. All those documents point you to one inevitable conclusion – that history cannot suffer lies, because the truth will always come out in time if it is God's will – even at the Battle of Hastings.

Nick Austin

1st June 2011

Come and visit – and do your bit – your support is welcome:

Support conservation - A small charge may apply for these private premises.

Wilting Manor Farm Trust, Crowhurst, East Sussex TN38 8EG Invasion Walk and Domesday Manor 01424 830613

Crowhurst Manor House Martin White for archaeology and historical research purposes

Support for archaeological investigation and preservation of Crowhurst and Wilting Manors:

English Heritage Head of Visitor Operations, Battle Abbey, TN33 OAD 01424 776783

English Heritage, Chairman Baroness Andrews, Contact phone number 0870 333 1181

Secretary of State for Culture, Jeremy Hunt 020 7211 6000

East Sussex County Archaeologist, Casper Johnson 01273 481608

East Sussex Council Trading Standards Officer 01323 463420

Chief Executive Rother District Council (Crowhurst and Battle area) Derek Stevens 01424 787878

Battlefields Trust www.battlefieldstrust.com

The Plough Inn, Crowhurst – The only pub on the battle site - book your lunch –TN33 9AW tel 01424 830310

Chapter 76: FOOTNOTES

1) English Historical Documents 1042 - 1189 edited by David C. Douglas and George W. Greenaway 1953 (Eyre and   Spottiswood) p.216.

2) 5th January 1066.

3) William was crowned Christmas 1066.

4) Published by Paladin (1970) p.264/5.

5) Other sources include The Cambridge Medieval History vol v p498 (5,000), Feudal England J. H. Round (George Allen and Unwin Ltd) 1895 p289/293 (5,000), L'Art Militaire et les Armées au Moyen Age (1946) vol 1,p.285 (probably less than 7,000).

6) In The Foundations of England Sir James Ramsay notes that at Harfleur Henry's 8-10,000 men took three days in August for the landing. This landing was completed in twelve hours in October.

7) Pevensey Castle, Sir Charles Peers CBE (English Heritage) 1953.

8) The Carmen manuscript is examined in depth in its own chapter.

9) The Carmen states 'You restored the dismantled forts that had stood there formerly. . '

10) Jumieges refers to Pevensey whilst the Carmen refers to a camp at Hastings.

11) Built by the Romans in the 4th century. Source: Pevensey Castle, Sir Charles Peers CBE, (English Heritage)1985.

12) Reported by Charles Dawson, History Of Hastings Castle Vol1 p.17 (Constable and Co) 1909.

13) Jennings and Smyth Sussex Archaeological Collections 126 (1988) 1 – 19.

14) The Norman Achievement by Richard F Cassady (Sidgwick & Jackson) 1986 p.99.

15) English Historical Documents 1042 - 1189 edited by David C. Douglas and George W. Greenaway 1953 (Eyre and Spottiswood) p.217-231.

16) Known as the Fryd.

17) Edited by Catherine Morton and Hope Muntz 1972 Oxford Medieval Texts.

18) Latin poetry and the Anglo-Norman Court 1066-1135 Journal of Medieval History 15 (1989) 39-62.

19) See R. L. Poole Medieval Reckonings of Time 1921 (London) p.11.

20) Confirmed by Wace - Master Wace, His Chronicle of the Norman Conquest, William Pickering (Oxford) 1972 p.120. and The Carmen of Hastingae Proelio, Catherine Morton and Hope Muntz (Oxford)1972 p.7.

21) Late September 1066.

22) See reference (22a) later in this chapter.

23) A claim that the ships were incapacitated in some way is supported by Wace. See Wace (23a).

24) Hastings Castle - Charles Dawson (Constable and Co) 1909 p.513.

25) Hastings Castle - Charles Dawson (Constable and Co) 1909 p.517.

26) See Plate 13 .

27) Dawson reports that the Anglo-Saxon Chronicle says: '*Hi. . . worhton castel aet Hastinga Port*'

28) See (28a), Wace's version of the same event.

29) Customary funeral rights might infer a Christian burial, however subsequent evidence in this and other texts infer a Viking funeral under a pile of stones on a headland- See The Funeral of Harold in the Carmen page xliii The Carmen of Hastingae Proelio Edited by Catherine Morton and Hope Muntz 1972 (Oxford medieval Texts).

30) See 'The Funeral of Harold' - The Carmen of Hastingae Proelio, Catherine Morton and Hope Muntz (Oxford) 1972 page xliii.

31) Wace states that Harold's body was taken to Waltham, as does William of Malmsbury, but circumstances suggest creative writing to cover the failure to adequately identify the body.

32) See Catherine Morton and Hope Muntz edition of the Carmen p.10.

33) Lt. Col. C. H. Lemmon in The Field of Hastings 1965 suggests that the logistics of William's invasion was comparable with those of the invasion of Europe in 1944.

34) The Companions of the Conqueror - The Genealogists Magazine 1X (1944) p.422.

35) The Carmen of Hastingae Proelio (Oxford Medieval Texts) Clarendon Press 1972.

36) The Chronicle of Battle Abbey edited and translated by Eleanor Searle 1980 (Oxford Medieval Texts).

37) A type of body armour.

38) Studied in detail in the next section.

39) J. H. Round's famous criticism of Freeman called Mr Freeman and the Battle of Hastings in Feudal England p.332-398 1895 demolished the basis of Freeman's work and in so doing discredited Wace.

40) Wace's manuscript is extensively quoted as the leading authority at the Centre Guillaume le Conquérant in Bayeux, which houses the Bayeux Tapestry.

41) Documented by Eleanor Searle Battle Abbey and Exemption: The Forged Charters, English Historical Review 1968

42) The Chronicle was written some time after 1155 and most probably around 1180 in two parts by different scribes. In consequence it was written in the region of 100 years after the actual events and the most removed of all those manuscripts we shall study.

43) Master Wace his Chronicles of the Norman Conquest from the Roman de Rou translated by Edgar Taylor Esq F. S. A1837 (William Pickering London).

44) Wace does not name his authority, but refers to many men he knew who saw the comet.

45) An incredible 16,547 lines of detailed text.

46) Over 100 years since the Invasion.

47) A probable reference to Jumieges manuscript.

48) The fleet sailed on the night of 28th September 1066.

49) Littleton,1. 464.

50) Compare ships oar ports (Plate 10) and with lower fort construction Plate 12(see 50a).

50a) Also see Plate 12 (50).

51) LtCol C. H. Lemmon DSO Lecture to Battle and District Historical Society 17 Feb 1956, Richard F Cassady in The Norman Achievement (Sidgwick and Jackson) 1986, Roger S.Porter Chevalier des Palmes Académiques - Puzzles of the Bayeux Tapestry (Ferndale Press) 1986, B. H. Lucas Where did William land? Sussex County Magazine vol.24 p.555-7 vol.25 p.248-9.

52) See The Domesday Chapter.

53) A ditch, also confirmed in the Bayeux Tapestry see Plate 13.

54) The same story is told in the Carmen but there the reference is to '. . . *the King*'.

55) Domesday Book text and translation by John Morris - Sussex edited from a draft translation prepared by Janet Mothersill 1976 (Phillimore).

56) A land unit in the region of 120 acres in most counties.

57) The maps on this and the following page have been sourced from the Domesday Book text and translation by John Morris – Sussex, edited from a draft translation prepared by Janet Mothersill 1976 (Phillimore).

58) Detailed in (Domesday Chapter 9) numbered paragraphs 1& 2.

59) See Annex.

60) Confirmed by E. M. Ward The Evolution of the Hastings Coastline 1920 Geographical Journal 56, 102-123, Straker and Lewis Romano British Bloomery in East Sussex 1938 (Sussex Archaeological Collection) 79, p.224-229 Millward and Robinson South-East England - The Channel Coastlands 1973 (Macmillan London). A Calendar of Patent Rolls 1494 - 1509 p.214.

61) A detailed study of shingle movement is provided by Charles Dawson The History of Hastings Castle (Constable and Co) 1909 p.1-6 and Coastline Changes and Land Management of East Sussex, Ocean and Shoreline Management (1988) Smyth and Jennings p.375 - 394.

62) J. A. Williamson Evolution of England (Clarendon Press) 1944.

63) The 5 meter line is the first available contour line from which comparisons can be drawn on the available survey maps. According to Jennings and Smyth (Halocene evolution of the gravel coastline of East Sussex 1990) auger tests show that Spring tide levels in the Combe Haven valley in 1066 and now were virtually the same p215 (app. 1 meter or less lower than present day).

64) The Carmen, edited by Catherine Morton and Hope Muntz (Oxford) 1972 supports Williamson's hypothesis concerning Battle being the head of a peninsula (pages 75,76,77 and 79) faithfully reproducing the original (page 110) without reference to the correct contours, whilst Patrick Thornhill's The Battle of Hastings (London, Methuen and co) 1966 page 38 reproduces a contour map of the head of the '*peninsula*' showing marshy valleys at 200 feet elevation without addressing the Telham/Broomham ridge crossing.

65) Shown shaded on Map5 earlier this chapter.

66) Source: The official guide to the Bayeux Tapestry at the Centre Guillaume le Conquerant Bayeux 1993.

67) The Bayeux Tapestry and the Battle of Hastings by Mogens Rud (Christian Eilers) Copenhagen 1988.

68) The Bayeux Tapestry and the Battle of Hastings 1066, Mogens Rud Christian Eilers Copenhagen 1983 p.50.

69) Sir James Ramsey The Foundations of England vol.2 p.17 - 5,000 men, J. H. Round, Feudal England (1895) 5,000 men, The Cambridge Medieval History vol.5 5,000 men, Wilhelm Spatz Die Schlacht von Hastings (1896) not more than 6-7,000 men.

70) Volume 2 p.17.

71) Ulvjot Law. Source: The Bayeux Tapestry, Mogens Rud (Christopher Eilers) 1988 p.65.

72) The fact that these properties feature so prominently suggests to the writer that they may be representations of Manor Houses. Especially bearing in mind the stylistic similarity between the property shown on the left of Plate 11 and that of Plate 14 showing a property of some importance being burnt with a roof of the same construction on both images.

73) The feast of St Michael was 29th September in 1066.

74) Hastings Castle, Charles Dawson 1909 (Constable) p.518.

75) Hastings Castle, Charles Dawson 1909 (Constable) p.519.

76) The Castles of the Conquest 23rd January 1902(Archaeologica Vol. 58) p.313 -339.

77) The Cricket Ground Archaeological Survey (Hastings Borough Council) 1991.

78) A complete list of all known works is available at Hastings Reference Library.

79) See Battle Abbey and Exemption: the forged charters, Eleanor Searle, English Historical Review lxxxiii (1968) p.449 - 480 as well as The Chronicle of Battle Abbey, Eleanor Searle (Oxford) 1980 p.2 - 28.

80) The History of the Norman Conquest of England, 6 vols 1867 - 79.

81) See J. H. Round The Battle Of Hastings Sussex Archaeological Collections vol.42 p54-63.

82) Salzman, Dawson, Mainwaring Baines, Hastings Museum and library, as well as those other sources listed at the end of this book.

83) History of Hastings Castle (Constable) 1909 p3.

84) According to Dawson Cott Liber. , BIV. Version, British Museum.

85) Page 517 - 518 Dawson, Hastings Castle.

86) Page 389 Dawson, Hastings Castle.

87) Page 499 Dawson, Hastings Castle.

88) Dawson, Hastings Castle.

89) Page 120 Dawson, Hastings Castle.

90) Interviews with land owners on the northern shore of the Combe Haven.

91) The America Ground, Barry Funnell (HAARG) 1989 p.1.

92) Geographical Journal 56, p.102 - 123.

93) Roman British Bloomeries in East Sussex (Archaeological Collections79) p.224-229.

94) South-East England - The Channel Coastlands (Macmillan) 1973.

95) Calendar of Patent Rolls 1494 - 1509, p.214.

96) Historic Hastings, J. Mainwaring Baines 1986 (Cinque Port Press) p.7 -17.

97) See Plate 14 for details.

98) Dawson, Hastings Castle p.19.

99) Pipe Rolls 28, Henry II, m7. dors'*Sudsexe*'.

100) Christopher Saxton 1589.

101) John Speede 1610.

102) Hastings Cricket Ground Archaeological Report , Mark Gardiner Institute of Archaeology 1987.

103) Huntingdonshire.

104) Over 550 pages of detailed inspection of the record.

105) Page 525.

106) Page 521.

107) Benoit de St Maur.

108) App. 1090.

109) Dawson History of Hastings Castle p.1 - 6.

110) As shown in previous chapter.

111) Charles Dawson History of Hastings Castle.

112) Dawson makes the point that there is no evidence of a main road running along the ridge between the new Hastings and Battle town at this early period, or indeed for many years after. Page 520 Hastings Castle, Dawson.

113) Wilting fell chiefly to Ingelran and partly to Reinbert, the founder of the Norman family '*de Etchingham*', prominent for three centuries in the district. '*Reinbert appears to have been the first Sheriff of the Rape and Ingelran his successor*': C. T. Chevallier p.34 Crowhurst Before the Normans, Jan 1969. Also tenancy confirmed by Chronology of Tenants Upper Wilting Farm, HAARG 1987 p.5.

114) Page 41 of 79 September 1994 ref 10059/RC/0478/8/A (Highways Agency document reference).

115) Ditto 114.

116) Page 42 of 79 September 1994 ref 10059/RC/0478/8/A (Highways Agency document reference).

117) Page 44 of 79 September 1994 ref 10059/RC/0478/8/A (Highways Agency document reference).

118) Page 44 of 79 September 1994 ref 10059/RC/0478/8/A (Highways Agency document reference).

119) Page 14 of 79 September 1994 ref 10059/RC/0478/8/A (Highways Agency document reference).

122) See Aerial photography chapter.

123) Roman Ways in the Weald, I. D. Margery (Phoenix House) 1948.

124) A bloomery is where the Romans used to smelt iron.

125) Confirmed by Jennings and Smyth, work still to be published.

126) The Iron Industry of the Weald, Henry Cleere and David Crossley (Leicester University Press) 1985 p.80.

127) This contradicts evidence provided by the Department of Transport in their archaeological survey, where they incorrectly state that the valley was '*subject to periodic inundation's*' p.4 of 17 September 1994. They also make the claim that coastal drift and salt marsh '*commenced in the 8th century,*' although no other authority agrees with this until the 13th century. Jennings and Smyth letter responding to periodic inundations in Combe Haven Valley is currently being transcribed to HTML. Jennings and Smyth deny inundations and also subscribe to navigability up to the landing site in direct contradiction of Highways Agency '*expert*' evidence.

128) When iron has been left in an acid soil such as that at Wilting the iron molecules migrate leaving an image in the soil. This image is not detectable from magnetic equipment, but requires sophisticated technology to conserve the phosphate remains.

129) Stock and trade for investigations involving ancient sites.

130) Confirmed by Jennings and Smyth Mid to Late Holocene Forest Composition and the Effects of Clearance in the Combe Haven Valley, East Sussex, Sussex Archaeological Collections 126 (1988) 1 - 20.

131) Dawson History of Hastings Castle 1909 (Constable) p.13.

132) Place Names of Sussex, A. Mawer and F. M. Stenton with J. E. B. Gover 1969 (Cambridge) xiv.

133) The Queensway is the road which links north Hastings with west Hastings and is due to be upgraded to a trunk road when the bypass scheme is introduced.

134) Hastings Area Archaeological Research Group (HAARG) produced a report in 1987 where the record of the farm was studied, called '*the Domesday Project*'. However the Wilting manor records are currently in the East Sussex Records office and have not been catalogued.

135) see Conclusion of Site Requirements.

137) Field number 373 on the copy deposited in the Hastings library.

140) The Chronicle states '*Most of the boats had already been burnt at his order. . .*'

141) The HAARG report on Wilting in 1987 reported 7 species on one side of the lane and 8 on the other indicating an age of at least 100 years per species.

141a) Subsequent investigation of this part of the thesis shows that the route through the centre of the field is the oldest and the one in use at the time of the Norman Invasion is the one marked on this plan as the '*later road route*' which runs next to the boundary with the ancient hedgerow.

142) At the rate of 1 species per hundred years as a yardstick.

143) HAARG Report Page 22.

144) HAARG Report Page 49.

145) Wace says '. . *and prayed to him in their chapels which were fitted up throughout the host*' p159 Master Wace and his Chronicle of the Norman Conquest.

146) Archbishop Anselm's secretary Eadmer, refers to '*the church of St Mary, the Holy Mother of God, which is in the Castle itself*' Dawson p.535.

147) In Crowhurst Parish.

148) English Place Name Society Volume VII 1969 p.535.

149) English Place Name Society Volume VII 1969 p.504.

150) English Historical Documents, David C. Douglas and George Greenaway 1953 (Eyre and Spottiswoode).

151) see Site Conclusions.

152) Taking into account the Wace and Carmen evidence and new understanding of what is actually meant.

153) As detailed in the Wace chapter earlier.

154) Points 17, 18, 19, 31, 33 and 38.

157) The right of a member of a chapter to his share in revenues of a cathedral Catholic Encyclopaedia

158) An object with magical or supernatural power – in this case presumably a cloth of some sort.

159) Wace uses this expression to describe English arrows. I can find no other.

160) A traditional subdivision of the county of Sussex England, origin unknown, predates Norman Conquest.

161) Figure A3/4 Fields 841/2 on page 88 of Chris Blandford document

Books by Nick Austin:

THE BOOK OF LIFE

www.ogmium.com

Paperback ISBN 978-0-9544801-0-3

Ebook ISBN 978-0-9544801-2-7

SECRETS OF THE NORMAN INVASION

www.secretsofthenormaninvasion.com

Paperback ISBN 978-0-9544801-3-4

Ebook ISBN 978-0-9544801-4-1

UNLOCK YOUR PAST

www.ancestralpattern.com

A guide to Ancestral Pattern

Ebook ISBN 978-0-9544801-8-9

Comment and become a friend of Secrets
on Facebook to get the latest news at the
Secrets of the Norman Invasion page
www.facebook.com/#!/groups/secretsofthenormaninvasion/

v.1.040